NAPOLEON'S
CONQUEST OF
PRUSSIA—1806

NAPOLEON IN 1807

NAPOLEON'S
CONQUEST OF PRUSSIA—1806
BY F. LORAINE PETRE
WITH AN INTRODUCTION BY
FIELD MARSHAL EARL
ROBERTS, V.C., K.G., Etc.
WITH SEVEN MAPS AND BATTLE PLANS AND
NUMEROUS PORTRAITS & OTHER ILLUSTRATIONS

The Naval & Military Press Ltd

Reproduced by kind permission of the Central Library,
Royal Military Academy, Sandhurst

Published by
The Naval & Military Press Ltd
Unit 10, Ridgewood Industrial Park,
Uckfield, East Sussex,
TN22 5QE England
Tel: +44 (0) 1825 749494
Fax: +44 (0) 1825 765701
www.naval-military-press.com
www.military-genealogy.com

© The Naval & Military Press Ltd 2007

The Naval & Military Press ...

...offer specialist books for the serious student of conflict. The range of titles stocked covers the whole spectrum of military history with titles on uniforms, battles, official histories, specialist works containing Medal Rolls and Casualties Lists, and numismatic titles for medal collectors and researchers.

The innovative approach they have to military bookselling and their commitment to publishing have made them Britain's leading independent military bookseller.

In reprinting in facsimile from the original, any imperfections are inevitably reproduced and the quality may fall short of modern type and cartographic standards.

AUTHOR'S PREFACE

THE first object of this Preface is a grateful acknowledgment of the great kindness of Lord Roberts in consenting to write his valuable introduction to this volume, and in sparing the time necessary for doing so. What he has been good enough to write obviates any necessity for further allusion, on the author's part, to the scope and objects of the book.

As some excuse for the appearance of the history of a campaign generally supposed to be so well known as that of Jena, it may be pointed out that there has been no detailed account of it written in English since the publication of the full information now available. Hoepfner's *Krieg von* 1806–1807 long ago provided much official information on the Prussian side, but it was not till some sixteen or eighteen years ago that Captain Foucart's *Guerre de Prusse* gave to the world the many valuable documents bearing on the subject in the French War Office, other than those which had already appeared in the *Correspondance de Napoleon Ier*. The work of Colonel Montbé gives the official information on the Saxon side, and Lettow-Vorbeck's

Author's Preface

Krieg von 1806–1807 is based on the books of Hoepfner, Foucart, and Montbé, as well as on further researches in the Prussian offices. I have not overburdened the volume with notes and references, as I believe that the former are apt to be overlooked, or to be an object of annoyance to most readers, and that it is better to incorporate them in the text. As for references to official documents, the reader may assume that they are all, unless otherwise stated, to be found in the three German and one French work above-named.

The majority of the illustrations are reproduced from works in the unique Napoleon collection of Mr. A. M. Broadley of The Knapp, Bridport, from whom Mr. John Lane obtained courteous permission to utilise them.

The remaining six views, of scenes in the earlier part of the campaign, were taken by the author in September 1906, almost exactly a century after the events which occurred during Napoleon's invasion of Saxony. Across the lower part of the Saalfeld battlefield now runs a railway; but the fields on which were fought the decisive battles of Jena and Auerstädt are almost precisely as they were one hundred years ago. As the camera was rested on the Napoleonstein, marking the spot where Napoleon stood with Lannes on the afternoon of the 13th October 1806, it required but a slight effort of the imagi-

Author's Preface

nation to conjure up a vision of the two, and of what they saw. All around them was the vanguard of Lannes' corps, whilst, from the steep descent towards Jena behind them, the rest of the corps hurried up to hold the dangerous position on the angle of the plateau. Half a mile in front were Tauenzien's Prussians, taking up their positions on the Dornberg, and at Lutzeroda and Closewitz. Far away white specks showed where Hohenlohe's camp stood in fancied security. So, too, as the photograph of the Isserstadt-Vierzehnheiligen position was taken, from close to the spot whence Napoleon watched the battle after 11 A.M. on the 14th October, it was easy to picture the desperate struggle at the villages, and the mighty avalanche of cavalry, with Murat at its head, which descended on the broken army of Hohenlohe. At Hassenhausen there rose before the imagination the desperate struggle of Gudin's infantry, the ruin of the Prussian cavalry, and, finally, the defeat, by a force scarcely more than half their strength, of the flower of the Prussian army.

F. L. P.

20th January 1907.

INTRODUCTION

GENERAL HAMLEY says in his Introduction to the "Operations of War," a book which thirty years ago gave a much-needed stimulus to the study of Military History in this country, "No kind of history so fascinates mankind as the history of wars." But he deplores the fact that it was the romantic aspect of military history by which the many were attracted rather than the knowledge such history should teach. "Reading," he adds, "can be profitable only in proportion to the means the student may possess of judging of the events of the past, and deducing from them lessons for the future."

Since the time at which Hamley wrote, a change has taken place in the study of Military History (at least so far as soldiers are concerned), which would have rejoiced his heart; for the rising generation of soldiers read it now with a keen desire to profit by its practical teaching as well as with intense interest in the romance of war.

But, I think, what is even more satisfactory to the lover of national prosperity is the knowledge that the study of Military History is not confined to military men, but is also engaging the attention of literary civilians, as instanced by the many instructive accounts of campaigns that have been published by them of late years. Satisfactory because it shows that men of thoughtful minds recognise that the lessons to be learnt from the histories of wars, if properly understood, are as valuable to the civilian as to the soldier, and that the history of wars is practically the history of nations; for is not war still the final Court of Appeal when nations are not in agreement, when national interests violently clash, and when national honour is at stake? It has been so from time most remote, and will be so to the end of time. Arbitration on issues of a secondary importance has been useful in the past, and no doubt will often render good service to the cause of humanity and

Introduction

civilisation in the future. But where vital principles are involved, and it may be the existence of a nation is imperilled, the appeal assuredly will always be to arms, and woe to that nation that does not recognise and appreciate this, and does not hold itself prepared to fight, when the need arises, in defence of its honour, its rights, and its liberty.

One cannot read the story of the Jena Campaign, as told by Mr. Petre, without realising from the tragedy of Prussia in 1806, as depicted therein, a tragedy without a parallel in modern times—the fate, amazing in its swiftness and appalling in its severity, which may at any moment overtake a state which exists in fancied security, based on traditions of a heroic past, and wrapped in a selfish indifference, hoping, ostrich-like, to escape the danger it refuses to see.

It is just one hundred years ago since the stirring events recorded in this book took place. A united Empire of Germany did not then exist, but there was a strong compact kingdom of Prussia, which had been established by the military genius of

Frederick the Great. That grand commander had been dead only just twenty years, but in that time events had happened which had altogether changed the political and military situation in Europe. As the result of the French Revolution France had been engaged in incessant wars for fifteen years, and Napoleon, who had risen to power by his masterful treatment of several campaigns, had reorganised the French army, revolutionised the art of war, and, striking down one adversary after another, had more or less rearranged the map of Europe.

Meanwhile Prussia had stood still. While ready enough to acquire territory by any means other than war, she was averse to fighting, and in her desire for peace had neglected to take the only means by which peace and the safety of her possessions could be secured. Her rôle had been to keep out of quarrels as far as possible, and to preserve an attitude of strict neutrality regardless of the growing menace of France. It was a selfish and suicidal policy. Her army at that period was a purely professional army, officered almost entirely by the aristocracy, and regarded rather as the private property of the king than as having any connection with the nation. There was, indeed, in addition to the Regular Army, a Militia 120,000 strong, but, like our own Militia at the present day, it had little training and less organisation, and was entirely without value for purposes of expansion or as a Reserve. A few far-seeing men in Prussia had recognised the danger that was impending, and had urged that the whole military system required reconstruction and revitalising. Many schemes of reform had been proposed during the years that immediately preceded the catastrophe of Jena, but no agreement had been arrived at and nothing had been done; there was no one man strong enough to insist on vigorous action, or indeed any action at all. And so, while divided counsels prevailed, while the nation, considering the Army as altogether apart from itself, remained indifferent, the blow fell.

In 1805, in the prosecution of his designs against Austria which culminated in the capitulation of Mack at Ulm, Napoleon, with splendid insolence, violated the neutrality of Prussia by marching Bernadotte's corps d'armée through the Prussian territory of Anspach. It required this outrage to convince the Cabinet at Berlin that the time had come to act. Mobilisation was at once ordered, and an ambassador was sent to Napoleon to demand satisfaction on pain of Prussia, with 200,000 men, joining Austria and Russia against France. But before the ambassador could deliver the ultimatum, the news of Napoleon's crushing defeat of the Austrian army at Austerlitz was received at Berlin. This changed, as Napoleon foresaw it would, the whole aspect of affairs, and, in place of the ultimatum, congratulations were offered to the Emperor on his splendid victory. Prussia was then indeed in a sorry plight. Totally unprepared for war, she had to submit to being treated by Napoleon as a vanquished enemy, and, in accordance with his decree, to separate herself from her allies, England and Russia.

Better would it have been for Prussia had she then and there flung down the gauntlet, for Napoleon was determined to compass her humiliation, and ere many months had passed he compelled her to draw the sword, rather as an act of desperation than as the result of sober conviction founded on a reasoned policy and justified by adequate preparation.

The result may be told in a few words.

A Prussian ultimatum was despatched to Paris on the 25th September 1806. It was not, however, until the 7th October that it reached Napoleon, who was then with his army south of the Main. The Emperor's answer was the entry of his troops on the following day into Prussian territory. On the 14th October the Prussians were defeated in the battles of Jena and Auerstädt, fought on the same day, with losses amounting to upwards of 20,000 killed and wounded, an almost equal number of prisoners, 60 colours and 200 guns. In the pursuit the Prussian army was annihilated, and the panic and demoralisation were so great that fortified places surrendered without a struggle one after the other.

Napoleon entered Berlin on the 25th October. Never was a blow more terrible;

never was ruin more complete. Expelled from his country, accompanied by a mere handful of his men, the King of Prussia threw in his lot with Russia, but on the bloody fields of Eylau and Friedland in the following year the Russians were also struck down by Napoleon, and in the Treaty of Tilsit (7th July 1807) both Russians and Prussians had to submit to the terms dictated by the Emperor.

So far as Prussia was concerned those terms were of the most ruinous and humiliating nature. Whole provinces were wrested from her, her fortresses were filled with French troops, requisitions of the most grinding nature were imposed upon her, and the armed strength, that she was thenceforth permitted to maintain, was restricted within the narrowest limits. During the six years that followed, it was at times doubtful whether Napoleon would allow Prussia to exist at all, even as a merely nominal independent state.

Such was the punishment Prussia met with for her selfishness and her unpreparedness. Such must ever be the fate of a nation that is indifferent to its obligations, regardless of its responsibilities, and that refuses to adapt itself to the ever-changing conditions of war. In the *débâcle* of 1806 is to be seen the "writing on the wall" in the boldest type, and all who run may read.

I earnestly recommend this volume to all classes of British subjects, and more particularly to statesmen, on whose shoulders rests the responsibility of power. Mr. Petre has done his work well. He has consulted the best authorities for his facts, and he has visited and explored the theatre of war and the battlefields which he so graphically describes. His book, which is lucid in style and admirable in arrangement, gives a more complete and concise account of this epoch-making struggle than has yet appeared in the English language. Its value is greatly enhanced by the admirable maps and plans which accompany and illumine the text.

ROBERTS, *F.M.*

20th December 1906.

CONTENTS

	PAGE
AUTHOR'S PREFACE	v
INTRODUCTION	ix

CHAPTER I
THE ORIGIN OF THE WAR 1

CHAPTER II
THE ARMIES OF THE CONTENDING POWERS . . . 18

CHAPTER III
THE PLANS OF CAMPAIGN 48

CHAPTER IV
MOVEMENTS OF BOTH SIDES UP TO THE 10TH OCTOBER 72

CHAPTER V
THE ACTION OF SAALFELD (OCT. 10) 91

CHAPTER VI
OPERATIONS FROM THE 10TH TO THE 13TH OCTOBER . 103

CHAPTER VII
THE BATTLE OF JENA 121

xx   Contents

CHAPTER VIII
                                                        PAGE
THE BATTLE OF AUERSTÄDT 149

CHAPTER IX
STRATEGY AND TACTICS OF THE FIRST PERIOD OF THE WAR 165

CHAPTER X
EVENTS OF THE 15TH TO 17TH OCTOBER . . . 181

CHAPTER XI
FROM THE ACTION OF HALLE TO THE OCCUPATION OF BERLIN 212

CHAPTER XII
THE PURSUIT OF HOHENLOHE AND HIS CAPITULATION AT PRENZLAU 236

CHAPTER XIII
BLUCHER'S MARCH TO LÜBECK AND SURRENDER AT RATKAU 256

CHAPTER XIV
THE FATE OF MAGDEBURG, HESSE-CASSEL, AND HAMELN 288

CHAPTER XV
CONCLUDING REMARKS ON THE SECOND PERIOD OF THE WAR 300

INDEX 313

ILLUSTRATIONS

Napoleon in 1807		*Frontispiece*
*Frederick William III., King of Prussia	*Facing p.*	16
*Luise, Queen of Prussia	,,	30
*The Duke of Brunswick	,,	46
Prince Louis Ferdinand	,,	62
†Battlefield of Saalfeld	,,	92
†The Saale near Kahla	,,	92
*Marshal Lannes	,,	112
†Battlefield of Jena (from the Napoleonsberg)	,,	128
†Battlefield of Jena (Prussian Main Position)	,,	128
†Battlefield of Auerstädt (from Hassenhausen)	,,	150
†Battlefield of Auerstädt (from Brunswick's Monument)	,,	150
*Marshal Davout	,,	164
*Marshal Bernadotte	,,	184
*Marshal Augereau	,,	218
*The Capitulation of Prenzlau	,,	250
*General Blucher	,,	266
*Marshal Soult	,,	282
*Marshal Ney	,,	298

* *Reproduced by permission from the Collection of A. M. Broadley, Esq.*
† *From Photographs taken by the Author in 1906.*

MAPS AND PLANS

PLAN FOR THE ACTION OF SAALFELD . . *Facing p.* 102
PLAN FOR THE BATTLES OF JENA AND AUER-
    STÄDT . . . . ,, 180
PLAN FOR THE ACTION OF HALLE . . . ,, 210
PLAN FOR THE ACTION OF PRENZLAU . . ,, 254
PLAN FOR THE STORMING OF LÜBECK . . ,, 286
MAP FOR OPERATIONS, 9TH TO 20TH OCTOBER
    1806 . . . . *At end of volume*
MAP FOR PURSUIT OF HOHENLOHE TO PRENZ-
    LAU, AND BLUCHER TO LÜBECK . . *At end of volume*

NAPOLEON'S CONQUEST OF PRUSSIA, 1806

CHAPTER I

THE ORIGIN OF THE WAR

IN 1795 Prussia, by the Treaty of Basel, cut herself adrift from the Austrian alliance against the French Republic, and, henceforth, until 1805, maintained a strict neutrality in the continental quarrels of the latter state. Yet her policy from this time up to 1813 was characterised by a gross dishonesty and a selfishness which serve to alienate from the Government much of the sympathy which would otherwise be felt for it in its misfortunes. This policy of neutrality was chiefly devised and carried out by Count von Haugwitz, the Prussian Minister, who greatly prided himself on his achievement. There is a little book entitled *Fragment des Mémoires inédits du Comte de Haugwitz*, in which it is stated that "la neutralité fût l'ouvrage de Haugwitz, sa gloire, son enfant chéri." It was, therefore, by a curious turn of fortune that, in November 1805, this statesman was compelled to be the bearer of proposals of mediation, which were in reality but a thinly veiled

2 Napoleon's Conquest of Prussia

ultimatum, addressed by Prussia to Napoleon, and which sounded the death-knell of the policy of neutrality. Prussia had, at last, taken mortal offence at the overbearing methods of Napoleon, the latest example of which had been furnished by his violation of Prussian territory in marching Bernadotte's corps through Ansbach during the advance which ended in the capitulation of the Austrian Mack at Ulm. After that had come the visit of the Tsar to Berlin and the solemn compact between him, Frederick William of Prussia, and the Emperor of Austria, under which the North German kingdom was to intervene in favour of the other two powers, then at war with Napoleon. As between the Tsar and Frederick William of Prussia, the compact was somewhat theatrically ratified during a midnight visit to the tomb of Frederick the Great organised by Queen Luise.

In pursuance of this secret agreement, Haugwitz was despatched to the French headquarters, towards the end of November 1805, with Prussia's proposals. He reached Napoleon's camp at Brunn on November 28, at a moment when the advance of the Austro-Russian army indicated the approach of a decisive battle. Had Prussia decided two months earlier to throw in her lot with the allies, she would effectually have prevented Napoleon's march from Boulogne to the Upper Danube and the great disaster of Ulm. Even at this late date, her intervention, menacing as she did his communications with France, would have been a cause of grave anxiety to the Emperor. As it was she was still bound to gain time, for her military advisers expressed their

The Origin of the War 3

inability to complete their preparations for war before December 15.

The memoir just quoted describes the first interview of the Prussian envoy with the French Emperor. Haugwitz was received by Napoleon in an audience which lasted four hours, and was characterised by a fierce outburst on the part of the Emperor. He roundly taxed Haugwitz with the convention of Potsdam, which had not escaped his notice, though at this moment he had no very accurate knowledge of its details. Haugwitz admitted the purport of the tripartite agreement, and defended it as being in the interests of peace. The Emperor, anxious to avoid the precipitation of war with Prussia, and foreseeing that a great victory within the next few days would radically alter her views, succeeded in closing the interview before Haugwitz could formally deliver his message. The Minister was sent off to Vienna to be amused by Talleyrand until the decision of the impending battle. From Talleyrand he could draw nothing but polite though meaningless speeches. On December 3 he received news of the great defeat of the Austrians and Russians at Austerlitz on the previous day. On the 4th, Count Stadion intimated to Haugwitz the readiness of Austria to accept Prussian mediation; but, on the following day, Haugwitz's hopes of being able to play a leading part were dashed by the joint announcement of Stadion and Talleyrand that the French and Austrian emperors had already concluded an armistice, preparatory to peace, on the basis of the withdrawal of the Russian troops. Neither Napoleon nor the Emperor of Austria, he was

4 Napoleon's Conquest of Prussia

informed, any longer desired the good offices of a third power. Henceforward, he found himself treated with scant courtesy. He was kept idling about Vienna, without excuse or apology, and it was not till December 15, two days after Napoleon's return to Schönbrunn, that he was accorded an interview with the conqueror.

The news of the disaster of Austerlitz reached Berlin only on December 11, and resulted in an immediate stoppage of Prussia's preparations. The troops which she was already marching towards Franconia were stopped and withdrawn. However willing Frederick William might be to hazard war with Napoleon when Austria and Russia were still to be relied on, he thought otherwise when Austria was already negotiating for a separate peace, and the Russians were retiring to their own country.

Meanwhile, Haugwitz had assumed the responsibility of neglecting to send to his master any report of his doings. The Prussian Court, urged on the one hand by Russia and England to intervene in accordance with its promise, having, on the other hand, the knowledge that the Prussian army was not yet ready for war, was in a condition of the greatest perplexity. Unable to hear anything of the doings of his plenipotentiary, Frederick William despatched Colonel Phull to Vienna. On his way that officer met Haugwitz returning with the Convention of Vienna, which he had concluded with Napoleon. Austerlitz had completely cowed him, and the virtual ultimatum now gave place to congratulations to the Emperor on his splendid victory. As Napoleon sarcastically remarked,

The Origin of the War 5

the address of these congratulations had been changed by the result of the battle.

Haugwitz now found his position entirely reversed. He could no longer pose as the representative of a power ready, or nearly ready, to turn the balance of events by the threat of war. The Austrian cause was for the moment lost, and the whole weight of Prussia thrown into that scale could not restore equilibrium. The issue of peace or war was in the hands of Napoleon, who for the moment desired peace. Haugwitz, no doubt, would have wished to return to his old position of neutrality, but it was too late. When, therefore, the Emperor offered him peace he had no hesitation in accepting the proposal, gilded as it was with the offer of the province of Hanover.

Napoleon desired to give to his brother-in-law, Murat, a Grand Duchy, composed of the Duchies of Berg and Cleve. To provide for Berthier he required the outlying principality of Neufchatel. For his ally, the new King of Bavaria, he wanted that very territory of Ansbach, the violation of which had been the latest insult to Prussia. In exchange for these he was prepared to obtain from Bavaria for Prussia a small area, containing 20,000 inhabitants, to round off her province of Baireuth, and to cede the electorate of Hanover, which Prussia had long coveted. Napoleon had occupied Hanover in pursuance of his war with England; but he had since greatly relaxed his hold on it, and his troops held little more of it than the fortress of Hameln. It belonged to the reigning family of England, and the state which should occupy it was bound to be at war

6 Napoleon's Conquest of Prussia

with the great maritime power. If Prussia accepted it her alliance with England would be immediately dissolved—an object which Napoleon earnestly desired. With him no half measures were possible—there must either be hostility or alliance, offensive and defensive. He, therefore, required Prussia, casting off her alliance with England and Russia, to transfer it to himself. Such were the chief conditions of the agreement arrived at between Haugwitz and the Emperor at Vienna.

The Prussian Court, which had meanwhile been busily cementing that alliance with England and Russia, the dissolution of which Haugwitz was simultaneously arranging, received the Convention of Vienna with consternation. The aristocratic and military party, headed by Queen Luise of Prussia and Prince Louis Ferdinand, had lately been gaining much ground in the State councils. It now saw the whole of its policy of alliance with England and Russia about to be overturned by the inevitable embroilment with the former power which must follow the annexation by Prussia of Hanover. It was proposed, therefore, that the King should ratify the treaty on the distinct understanding that its provisions should only be fully carried into effect on the conclusion of a general peace, and then only with the consent of England to the transfer of Hanover. To the latter power assurances were at the same time to be given that, if Prussia consented meanwhile to occupy Hanover, she would do so solely for the purpose of ridding Northern Germany of French troops, and providing a base of operations for a fresh coalition.

The Origin of the War

On the 14th January 1806 Haugwitz was despatched to Paris to re-open negotiations. At the same time the Duke of Brunswick was sent on a mission of conciliation to Russia. Haugwitz had not been long in Paris before he was undeceived as to the possibility of imposing on the Emperor by the course taken. The assurances conveyed to England by Prussia were known in Paris, and the only result of Haugwitz's mission was the substitution of a more stringent and plain-spoken treaty for the Convention of Vienna. The French Emperor insisted that the treaty should be carried out at once, that Prussia should absolutely, unconditionally, and completely occupy Hanover; that she should finally separate herself from England and Russia, and that the ports of the North German coast should be closed against the British flag. It was made abundantly clear that Prussia had only two alternatives to choose from—ratification of the new treaty, or war with France. For the latter she was still not ready. This treaty, which had been signed by Haugwitz on the 15th February, was ratified on the 24th, on which date its execution was commenced, by Bernadotte's occupation of Ansbach on behalf of Bavaria. On the 18th March Hameln was surrendered by the French garrison to Prussian troops, Wesel received a French garrison, Murat entered into possession of his new Grand Duchy of Berg, and Berthier into that of his principality of Neufchatel.

The King of Prussia, eager to give assurances of his sincerity, recalled to power Haugwitz, who had recently given place, as Minister, to the anti-

8 Napoleon's Conquest of Prussia

French Hardenberg. The exclusion of British commerce from the northern ports was notified, and the arrival of Prussian troops in Hanover compelled the Regency to retire thence and place themselves under the protection of the King of Sweden, who still made a show of holding, on behalf of England, the Hanoverian territory on the right bank of the Elbe. Thence, however, he was soon compelled to withdraw his troops before the superior forces of Prussia. Nothing could have been more pusillanimous than the conduct of Prussia in this affair. As Fox, then Foreign Minister of England, remarked, other nations had been forced to make concessions to France, but none had, like Prussia, been degraded to the point of becoming the ministers of the injustice and the rapacity of a master. The whole policy of Prussia at this period was characterised by a duplicity which was manifest to the rest of Europe. Without going so far as to regard Napoleon's methods of diplomacy with approval, it seems at least doubtful if he was ever more dishonest than Prussia was in 1805–1806. War was, of course, declared by England against Prussia, though it cannot be said to have been prosecuted with any show of vigour.

Napoleon had completely succeeded in outwitting Prussia, and rendering her an object of contempt to her late allies. He now set to work to separate England from Russia, by treating with each separately. The former was loyal enough to refuse any such overtures, the latter was less firm, and opened negotiations through Count d'Oubril, first at Vienna, later at Paris. A treaty was executed by d'Oubril, but, on his

The Origin of the War

return to Russia, his action was disavowed by the Tsar, who, by refusing to ratify the treaty, disappointed Napoleon's hopes of isolating England. Though the latter had persistently refused to conclude a separate peace, she had entered into informal negotiations with the Emperor, through Lord Yarmouth, who was succeeded later by Lord Lauderdale. At no time was there much hope of their success in the face of Napoleon's excessive demands, and they had practically reached a hopeless stage before the death of Fox, on the 13th September 1806, removed the last chance of their coming to anything. We have to some extent anticipated events as regards England, and it is desirable to cast a brief glance at what Napoleon had been doing to consolidate and extend his conquests, since the submission of Austria by the Peace of Presburg. He had subjugated Naples, driving out its Bourbon sovereigns and substituting the rule of his brother Joseph. The Dutch he cajoled into constituting a kingdom, in place of the republic; this state fell to the lot of another brother, Louis. Napoleon annexed, or exchanged, territories without any regard to the feelings of their inhabitants, and the latter, as in the case of the Tyrolese, transferred from Austrian to Bavarian rule, were not always inclined meekly to accept the change. Much of the Emperor's attention during 1806 was devoted to endeavours, by no means invariably successful, to harmonise the relations between subjects whose allegiance had been thus forcibly transferred and their new rulers. A still greater work on which he was engaged was the construction of the Confederation of the Rhine, by which he hoped to create an effective counterpoise, under his own protection and control, to the rival pretensions of Austria and Prussia. By a treaty, signed at Paris on the 12th July 1806, Bavaria, Würtemberg, Baden, Hesse-Darmstadt, and several smaller states, agreed to separate themselves from the German Empire, and to pass under the protection of that of France, with which the new Confederation entered into an offensive and defensive alliance. France, in case of war, was to provide 200,000 men, the Confederation was responsible for a contingent of 63,000.[1] Bavaria agreed to fortify Augsburg and Lindau, making of them great depôts for the support of an armed advance against either Austria or Prussia. The Confederation was bound to arm in response to any armament of the two great German powers; but the word to do so was to be given by the Emperor only. The former Arch-Chancellor of the Roman Empire (Dalberg) became, under the title of "Prince Primate," President of the new diet.

It was clear that, with the constitution of the Rhenish Confederation, the Roman Empire had practically ceased to exist. The Emperor, seeing himself a Roman emperor without an empire, anxious, moreover, to expedite the withdrawal of the large French army still quartered in Southern Germany, had little hesitation in divesting himself of his shadowy title, and declaring himself the first Emperor of Austria only, on the 6th August 1806.

[1] Divided as follows: Bavaria, 30,000; Würtemberg, 12,000; Baden, 8000; Berg, 5000; Hesse-Darmstadt, 4000; other smaller states, 4000. Total, 63,000.

The Origin of the War

In Prussia the constitution of the Confederation of the Rhine was received with dismay. To counteract this evil impression, Napoleon suggested that Prussia would be allowed to construct a confederation of the northern states, looking to her for protection as that of the south looked to France. It soon, however, became clear that the hopes thus raised were illusory. The Emperor positively refused to allow the inclusion in the Confederation of the Hanseatic towns. The two most important constituents remaining available for it were Saxony and Hesse-Cassel. As regards the latter, Napoleon urgently pressed the Elector to join the Southern Confederation, to which his territory was contiguous. That potentate, strongly favouring Prussia, declined the French overtures, and, later on, attempted to run with the hare and hunt with the hounds in a way which resulted in his own ruin.

The position of Saxony was peculiar, and in her case the Emperor made it clear that he would allow no pressure to be put on her by Prussia, whilst he himself urged the Elector to join the Rhenish Confederation, dangling before his eyes at the same time the bait of a royal crown, on an equality with his brother sovereigns of Bavaria and Würtemberg, recently raised by Napoleon to the dignity of kingship. The Elector would willingly have held aloof from the impending struggle, but the dissolution of the Roman Empire, and the progress of Napoleon's efforts to reconstruct a Germany under French influence and protection, from which both Austria and Prussia should be excluded, warned him that the time was fast approaching when it would be impossible for him any longer to avoid taking part in the contest which was closing in upon his frontiers. Austria being for the moment out of the field, Saxony's choice lay between following Bavaria into the French alliance, or cleaving to Prussia in a last struggle to maintain a German, as opposed to a French Germany. She might have elected to consolidate her power by a closer union with the Thuringian states, ruled by princes allied to her own governing house, but such a course, certain to be opposed by both Prussia and Russia, could only have been followed with the support of France. Saxony was already largely under the influence of Prussia, but she still regarded with suspicion the possible designs on her independence which that state might entertain in endeavouring to draw her into the proposed Northern Confederation. Still more suspicious were the endeavours of Napoleon to obtain her adherence to the Confederation of the Rhine, though he was careful to make a pretence of leaving her absolute liberty of choice. The one lure he did use was the suggestion of a possible crown. Prussia was far more insistent in her demands for the adhesion of the Elector to her cause, and, as time went on, it became clear that she would not hesitate to employ force to obtain her end. Prussia had resolved on war before the breakdown of the Franco-Russian negotiations, which assured her the eventual support of Russia; but she required allies for her first struggle, of whom Saxony was the most important. Yet, by attempting to force Saxony, she was playing into Napoleon's hands; for she was gaining only an unwilling ally, whilst

The Origin of the War

offering to the Emperor an excellent opportunity for posing as the protector of Saxony against Prussian violence, thus throwing on his enemy much of the odium of precipitating hostilities. Nevertheless, it was he himself who, by his constant insults and annoyances, really forced Prussia into war. The last insult which that power had to endure was the discovery that Napoleon, in order to render possible a peace with England, was prepared to take again from Prussia the province, Hanover, the annexation of which had embroiled her with England. It is hardly surprising that in these circumstances the opinions of the aristocratic party, which saw no salvation but in war, should prevail, or that war was resolved upon at Berlin on the 7th August.

Prince Kraft thinks that Napoleon "himself believed that he could offer her (Prussia) almost any insult, and yet she would not take up arms." It seems scarcely credible that he should not have felt, whatever he may have said, that a point must come when even the probability of defeat would be a lesser evil to contemplate than the continued accumulation of insult. Even so late as the 10th September, he wrote to Berthier that he did not believe in a rupture; but who can tell what were the inner thoughts of the man who wrote thus?[1]

It was the news, brought by the Prussian ambassador Luchesini, regarding the proposed retrocession of Hanover, added to a rumour that Napoleon was prepared to conciliate Russia

[1] De Ségur states that in the beginning of September Napoleon said to him: "Take a holiday and get married; there is time for everything, and there is no question of war just now" (p. 273). Savary also (ii. 268) says the Emperor really believed in peace.

by the cession of Prussian Poland, which finally convinced the Prussian Court that war was inevitable.

Yet at this very time Napoleon was apparently endeavouring to maintain peace for the present. On the 2nd August he wrote to Talleyrand to instruct Laforest, the French ambassador at Berlin, as to his conduct. He was to represent that negotiations for peace with England were on the point of breaking down, because the Emperor would not again take Hanover from Prussia, with whom, above all things, he desired to stand well. The Emperor made little pretence that this was anything but a deliberate falsehood. When he had written so far, it seems to have struck him that perhaps it was not safe to trust Laforest with the truth when he was required to tell a lie; for he says, "laissez le (Laforest) s'il le faut, dans la conviction que je ne fais pas la paix avec l'Angleterre à cause du Hanovre." Murat he was quite sure he could not trust with the truth; therefore, on the same date, he writes to his brother-in-law, "je cesse de faire la paix avec l'Angleterre pour lui (à la Prusse) conserver le Hanovre." Of course, Napoleon, in writing to Talleyrand, does not say, in so many words, that his story about Hanover is false; but, from the context, it is perfectly clear that it was so, and that Talleyrand was meant to infer that it was.

Laforest was to say nothing, unless Prussia suddenly took, and showed, alarm. Such was not her intention; recognising that war was inevitable, she required to gain time to complete her military preparations. In making up her

The Origin of the War 15

mind on the 7th August for war, she gained a political initiative of six weeks; for it was not till the 18th September that Napoleon positively decided on war. Prussia's military preparations had to commence at a much earlier stage than Napoleon's. The latter had commenced his arrangements for a possible campaign against Prussia immediately after the defeat of Austria. He had been steadily engaged in repairing the losses of Ulm and Austerlitz by constant reinforcements sent from France, to which country he had not withdrawn a single corps, except the Guard. All this was a general preparation; it was on the 5th September that he began his special preparations, though it was not till the 19th that he issued orders for the concentration of his corps in Southern Germany. Early in September, the Tsar's refusal to ratify d'Oubril's treaty had convinced Napoleon that the next step must be the drawing together of Prussia and Russia, in a sense hostile to himself.

On the 12th September we find him instructing his ambassador at Berlin to warn Haugwitz that Prussian armaments, which before the Tsar's refusal to ratify could be looked upon as mere folly, must now be regarded seriously. Disarmament was to be urged on Prussia in moderate and discreet language; but the ambassador, speaking more plainly, was to make it clear that any attempt to compel Saxony to arm against France would entail the immediate rupture of diplomatic relations. The Emperor had seized upon the question of the independence of Saxony as a convenient one for throwing the blame of war on Prussia. "Vouz ferez tout rouler sur l'indépendance de la Saxe," writes Napoleon to Talleyrand on the 12th September. It was at this time that the conciliatory language already referred to was used to the Saxon Elector. To Hesse-Cassel threats only were held out should she arm, though the Emperor professed his willingness to allow her to be neutral, provided her neutrality was genuine.[1]

All this time Prussia, with a Napoleonic disregard of truth, had been, through her ambassador at Paris, assuring the Emperor of her peaceful intentions, and he seems to have to some extent believed in them. On the 10th September even, he writes to Berthier, that he does not believe in a rupture. We may perhaps hesitate to believe him. Anyhow, by the evening of the 18th of September he was convinced that war was inevitable, and the 19th witnessed the issue of his orders for movements preparatory to early hostilities.

The Prussian ultimatum was at last resolved upon and despatched to Paris on the 25th September, the very day on which Napoleon started to join his army south of the Main. General von Knobelsdorf, the bearer of it, found the Emperor gone when he himself reached Paris on the 1st October. It was not till the 7th October that the delayed despatch reached the Emperor's headquarters at Bamberg, though it is permissible to surmise that Napoleon was not ignorant of its existence and purport. He had, what no other power then had, the means of rapid communication, by semaphore telegraph,

[1] Napoleon to the Prince Primate (Dalberg), 1st October 1806 (Foucart, i. 238).

FREDERICK WILLIAM III, KING OF PRUSSIA
(From an engraving in Mr. Broadley's collection)

The Origin of the War 17

between his capital and his own headquarters. The terms of the ultimatum were: (1) The immediate withdrawal of all French troops beyond the Rhine. (2) France to engage not to put any hindrance in the way of the construction of a North German Confederation embracing all states not already included in the Confederation of the Rhine. (3) The immediate opening of negotiations for the permanent settlement of all remaining points of dispute, and, as a preliminary condition, the separation of Wesel from the French Empire, and the evacuation by Murat of the three abbacies which he had seized.

An immediate answer, to reach Prussian headquarters by the 8th October, was demanded. Such an ultimatum, addressed to the conqueror of Austerlitz, could lead to nothing but war, and there is not the slightest reason for supposing that Prussia expected, or desired, any other issue. The Emperor's answer was the passage, on the 8th October, of his troops into Prussian territory. It was not till the 12th, after the actions of Schleiz and Saalfeld, that he deigned to send a written reply.

CHAPTER II

THE ARMIES OF THE CONTENDING POWERS

THE army of Ulm and Austerlitz was probably the finest that Napoleon ever commanded, and it was with this army, reinforced, and its losses repaired by drafts of trained men, not the immature conscripts of later years, that he was about to attack Prussia. In it was no conscript prematurely called up; there were no Spanish or Italian troops; the contingents of the German states took but an infinitesimal share in the operations before the complete destruction of the Prussian army; the Dutch were only employed in an army of observation, on which no share of fighting fell, during the same period. Many of the French soldiers were veterans of Italy and Egypt; the great majority had just emerged triumphant from the struggle of 1805.

The fighting spirit of men and officers was at its highest point, though the motives on which it was based were now beginning to degenerate. The French armies of the Italian wars had been armies fighting for the existence of their nationality, under a leader who was nominally only a general carrying out the projects of others. The General Bonaparte of the Republic had now become the Emperor, whose boundless ambition sought not merely the preservation of his country, but the furtherance of his own projects of universal empire. To ensure the willing co-operation of his soldiers in his own plans, the Emperor saw that he must provide other motives than mere patriotism, or even the prospect of escape from immediate misery which he had used as an incentive in 1796. Those motives he found in the promised plunder of Europe, certain though it was, in the end, to ruin the discipline of his armies.[1]

The French army was now entering on that long career of rapine and pillage which was to render both officers and men infamous throughout Europe, and to set an example to their allies, as well as their enemies, which was readily followed, and resulted in the devastation of France when the tide of war at last set against her.

Of the campaign which we are now about to describe De Fezensac says, " Never was pillage carried further than in this campaign, and disorder extended even to insubordination." After Jena, Soult was compelled to issue the most stringent orders for the prevention of the disorder consequent upon unbridled pillage. Not that Soult himself in later years set anything but the worst example in this respect, as may be judged from the catalogue of pictures sold at his death, all looted by him in Spain. The majority of the superior officers set a similar example, which was only too eagerly followed by the

---

[1] Count Yorck thinks Napoleon was only logical in his treatment of his army. "He could only conquer the world by abandoning its constituent parts to his instruments as their booty" ("Napoleon as a General," i. 309).

soldiery. Massena was notorious; Bernadotte's baggage, captured by the Russians at Mohrungen, was full of plundered money and plate extorted from the minor German states; many of the disasters of the retreat from Russia were the direct result of the delay caused by reluctance to abandon the plunder of Moscow. The Prussian army, on the other hand, was at present free from this vice. In the commissariat of the two armies the system emphasised this difference. Frederick the Great had waged war more often in his own than in his neighbours' territory, and, consequently, he was chary of ruining the country by ransacking it for supplies for his armies. He supported them by a system of magazines, instead of by requisitions, and the Prussian soldier, accustomed to look to these for his food, was, when occasionally required to find his own supplies, unable to do so. Napoleon openly preached that war must be made to support war, and, though he was careful to collect great depôts of stores as a reserve at central points, his armies, as a rule, lived by requisitions. When they had to pass through a poor tract, deficient in population and supplies, the Emperor insisted on their bearing on their backs a sufficient store of food to carry them beyond it. Thus the French soldier was an adept at systematically extracting from the country every atom of available food, without regard to the sufferings of the inhabitants. A village, which had failed to yield much to the perfunctory requisitions of a Prussian force, would often, in the hands of a French regiment a few hours later, be found able to provide ample stores. The Prussian, burdened with two or three days'

The Contending Armies 21

supply of food, would, relying on his commissariat, throw it away to lighten his load; the Frenchman, on the other hand, would carefully preserve it for an emergency.

In the infantry of the two armies there was the most complete contrast: that of Prussia was an admirable, but rigid and slow-moving machine; that of Napoleon was flexible, quick, intelligent. "The Prussian army," says De Fezensac, "the heir of the traditions of the Seven Years' War, manœuvred well, but slowly and methodically, with an infinite quantity of baggage; 5 or 6 leagues ($12\frac{1}{2}$ to 15 miles) seemed to it a long day's march." To the commanders of this slow-moving army the marches of the French seemed incredible, and they were, indeed, impossible for an army tied by the exact formations and elaborate manœuvres of the Prussian system. For six days on end, in the second week of October, the French Guard averaged over 18 miles a day, Davout's corps 16, and Lannes' 14, besides two days of fighting; yet, after these marches, all were able to go through a long day of fighting.

Later on, Lannes' advanced guard covered 65 miles in 50 hours, the rest of his corps the same time in 60 hours, and that in a poor country over which 6000 French cavalry had just passed, leaving no possibility of giving the men an extra ration, hardly any of them getting even an ordinary full meal. Between the 26th and 28th October Bernadotte's men marched, in a similar country, 75 miles in 69 hours.

On the battlefield the difference in tactics was equally marked. The army of Frederick (and the Prussian tactics in 1806 had undergone little or no change since his time) generally found it possible to move in the closest formations, to deploy slowly into line, and correct distances and dressings before opening fire. The enemy, like themselves, was in line, and the zone of effective fire was entered by both only when completely prepared. Yet it will be remembered how, when the Austrians, at Kolin, harassed the Prussians by light troops thrown out against their flank, the result was a premature attack and a disaster.

In Frederick's time the Prussian musket was superior to that of the enemy. In 1806 Hoepfner considers that it was the worst infantry arm in Europe. When, in 1806, the precise linear tactics of Frederick came into contact with the more mobile system of the French, they failed absolutely. The Prussians to some extent employed light troops as skirmishers, but they were rarely strong enough to hold back the clouds of skirmishers, constantly relieved and supported by small handy columns, which formed Napoleon's fighting line. Again and again it was proved how impossible it was to carry out, under the fire of skirmishers adept in the art of utilising cover, the solemn deployment and preparation of Frederick's days. The men, incessantly harassed by fire which they could not return with effect during their deployment, were already half defeated before they were ready to fight. The Prussian leaders, completely failing to grasp the true significance of the loose French formations, had persisted in seeing in them nothing but the natural evil outcome of the dissolving force of French revolutionary ideas.

The Contending Armies 23

In artillery, again, the French were vastly superior. The Prussian leaders had stood still at the stage of artillery tactics reached by Frederick, whose battles were rarely decided by the fire of guns. The idea of massing batteries was entirely beyond them.

Napoleon, on the other hand, himself originally an artillery officer, was devoting more and more attention to that arm. He already realised that great campaigns were not to be won with a few guns, and was meditating that system of concentration of great masses of artillery which formed so marked a feature in his later tactics, especially when, as the quality of his infantry began to deteriorate, they required more and more the moral support of guns: "The more inferior the quality of a body of troops," wrote the Emperor in 1809, "the more artillery it requires. There are some army corps with which I should require only one-third of the artillery which I need for others."[1] In the same year he had written: "The artillery, like the other arms, must be collected in mass if one wishes to attain a decisive result."[2] It has been said that the first instance of his employment of a great line of guns was the use of Sénarmont's battery against the Russian left at Friedland; but it will be found that at Jena he massed twenty-five guns, drawn from various corps, in order to fill a gap in his line.

In 1806 the proportion of artillery to infantry was greater in the Prussian than in the French army, and the former, in addition to the regular

[1] Correspondence, 18th August 1809.
[2] Napoleon to Eugène, 16th June 1809.

artillery, had two light guns attached to each of its Fusilier and Grenadier battalions. This latter system of regimental guns Napoleon, in 1809, himself decreed in a modified form, though the order seems never to have been completely carried out. The history of the campaign will show instances where superior artillery tactics and fire enabled the French to overcome a vastly superior number of guns. At Halle, for example, Bernadotte had but twelve guns against fifty-eight, and the deficiency was not made up for by any marked superiority of the other arms.

In cavalry alone could the Prussians stand fairly against Napoleon. Under Seidlitz and the other great cavalry leaders of the Seven Years' War, Frederick's horsemen had acquired a reputation which they still enjoyed. They were better mounted than the French, a fact of which Napoleon showed his appreciation, after the fall of Prussia, by remounting his men largely on German horses. Man for man the Prussian and the Saxon cavalry were more than a match for the French on the battlefield. As the "eyes of the army," the cavalry of both sides was perhaps equally indifferent. "Our cavalry," says Savary, "so ardent on the battlefield, was directed without intelligence when it was a question of getting news of the enemy." Time after time Murat's intelligence was deficient or incorrect. The reports of spies, with whom Napoleon flooded the enemy's country and camp, is a very poor substitute for news obtained by good cavalry. It has the great disadvantage of often taking days in transmission, whilst reports of cavalry should reach headquarters within a few hours.

The Contending Armies

That Napoleon saw good reason to fear the result of cavalry conflict on the battlefield is clear from his advice to Soult, to avoid pitting his own cavalry against that of the enemy until the latter had broken itself against the French infantry squares. At the same time, he evidently realised that the enemy's leaders would play into his hands by injudicious attacks on his own unbroken infantry. In the shock tactics of cavalry against cavalry there had not been much need for change since Frederick's days; even in our own time cavalry meets cavalry in much the same way as it did a hundred and fifty years ago, for the cavalry weapon has changed but little. In the combat of cavalry against infantry the case is different; the improvement in firearms has been continuous, and the difficulties of the attack by horsemen with the *arme blanche* on unbroken infantry have proportionately increased, until at the present time its impossibility is generally recognised. The Prussian and Saxon cavalry officers had failed to appreciate the change wrought in their rôle by the improvement in the infantry arm. Napoleon perhaps overestimated the superiority of the German cavalry to his own, but the complete failure of the Prussian squadrons against Davout's squares at Auerstädt demonstrated clearly the correctness of his assumptions as to their uselessness against his own infantry.

In the general organisation of his army and in that of his staff Napoleon enjoyed another great advantage over his enemy.

Up to Frederick's time comparatively small armies were closely united under the eyes of the commander; they deployed for battle in close, contiguous formations, so that it was possible for a single general to command the whole, and to rely upon his orders reaching its different parts with promptitude. By the close of the eighteenth century armies had vastly increased in size. With this increase in numbers had come a corresponding enlargement of the theatre of war, as well as of the field of battle. In an army like the French, which subsisted largely on the local resources of an enemy's country, it was no longer possible to keep it constantly in a state of close concentration; that condition was only possible for short periods, just before and during great tactical events. In 1806 Napoleon's armies numbered 600,000 men, spread over a vast area, extending from the south of Italy to Holland and from the Pyrenees to Bohemia. The army with which he moved to the conquest of Prussia was thrice as numerous as any Frederick ever commanded. Even in the Revolutionary armies it had been recognised that no one man could personally command the details of an army spread over a large tract without the intervention of an intermediate organisation, to assist in distributing the details of his general orders.

The first step had been the organisation of mixed divisions, comprising infantry, cavalry, and artillery. It was with divisions that Bonaparte conducted the campaigns of 1796 and 1800.

As his armies increased with the conscription he had found it necessary, in 1804, to make another step, by the creation of *corps-d'armée* consisting of two or three divisions. Each corps he designed to be a complete small army in itself,

The Contending Armies 27

capable of acting independently, and of avoiding risk of serious disaster till it could be supported. The corps grew in size until, in 1812, some of them almost equalled the modern army composed of several corps.

The marshals whom Napoleon appointed to command his corps were men thoroughly capable of dealing in detail with them, under his own general direction, though, it may be observed, the Emperor generally proportioned the strength of a corps to his estimate of each marshal's capacity. Thus Massena, Davout, Soult, and Bernadotte usually commanded large corps, whilst Ney, Lannes, Lefebvre, and Augereau were entrusted only with smaller ones of two divisions each.

With his army thus organised, Napoleon ordinarily required only to issue instructions as to the movements of each corps as a whole. The corps commander could be trusted to direct his divisions, whilst the divisional generals dealt with brigades, the brigadiers with regiments, and so on.

In the Prussian army it was altogether different. Having no corps, nor even a complete organisation by divisions, the commander-in-chief often found himself compelled to issue lengthy orders, going into details of regiments, even of battalions, squadrons, batteries, outposts and other matters, which should clearly be disposed of by a subordinate commander. These orders took long to write, long to distribute from headquarters to all the separate units concerned, long even to read. Consequently, they often reached their destination when the rapid movement of events had already rendered them inapplicable. Worse still, they were rarely final. Napoleon, having once decided on what he considered to be the most suitable general plan of operations, kept his mind steadily fixed on the goal, never allowing himself to be turned aside from it by secondary objects, never altering a good scheme in the hope of arriving at a possibly better one.

Not so the Prussians. Their headquarters were perpetually dropping the substance of a good scheme to grasp at the shadow of a better. All this ended in everlasting marches and countermarches, which exhausted and disheartened the troops before they ever saw the enemy.

Napoleon's troops were not thus harassed. Not only did the Emperor adhere to his general plan of operations, until tactical contact with the enemy brought to an end the period of long forecasts, but he would even then wait to issue orders till the latest safe moment. He never spared his troops where great efforts were necessary, but he never inflicted unnecessary hardships on them. Therefore, when he had met the enemy, he did not issue his orders for next day in the afternoon or evening, when later reports might compel him to make a change. He would rise about midnight, when all his reports had come in. He could still issue his orders in time for the troops to move by daybreak, thus saving them from being exhausted by unnecessary marches, or even by premature preparations. Napoleon was responsible as commander-in-chief to no one, he called no councils of war, he sought no advice. Thus his orders had the qualities of decision, clearness, and finality which those of the Prussians rarely possessed.

The Contending Armies   29

It seems almost impossible to say who was the Prussian commander-in-chief. The Duke of Brunswick nominally held the position, but he was also commander of a separate body, the so-called main army, which, with Napoleon, would have been divided into two or three corps, each with its own special chief dealing with details. From above Brunswick was hampered by the presence of the king, whose confirmation was required for all important orders. From below also he was hindered. Ruchel, and to a still greater extent Prince Hohenlohe, enjoyed a semi-independent position, as coadjutors rather than subordinates. Hohenlohe was under the influence of Colonel Massenbach, his Chief of the Staff, who frequently led him to act in a manner little short of insubordinate.

Then there were constant councils of war, a whole series at Charlottenburg in August, at Naumburg in the end of September, and another series of several days' duration at Erfurt in October, when the Prussian schemes were already breaking down. At these councils every officer of repute was allowed to have his say. Phull, Massenbach, Kalkreuth, and many others, were at liberty to submit memoranda and plans of campaign, which, however wild or impracticable, had to be discussed at length before rejection. It is scarcely to be wondered at that Brunswick seemed to abandon the struggle in despair, leaving matters to be settled by the *entourage* of the king. Frederick William himself often saw more clearly than his generals, but, being young and new to war, he was naturally unwilling to overrule men of much greater age and experience. Besides, he was never able to make up his mind definitely to any course of action until he was forced into it by some one else. Thus, in the Prussian army, there was no absolute commander who could say, as Berthier wrote of Napoleon to Ney in 1807, that he "in his general projects requires neither advice nor plans of campaign; no one else knows his designs, and it is our duty to obey."

Unlike the Emperor, the Prussian commanders were ever ready to listen to plans of campaign, never prepared to reject them in terms so clear as to preclude the possibility of doubt. It was this vagueness and uncertainty which gave some shadow of an excuse to Massenbach for believing that his scheme for concentration on the right bank of the Saale might still be entertained on the 12th October.

But, in addition to the enormous difference in the nature of the orders given to the two armies, there was at least as great a difference in the machinery for their issue. By 1805 Napoleon, with ten years' experience of war or preparation for war, had completed the organisation of his staff. Its constitution was now, in 1806, codified in a few decrees, the most important of which is that appearing, over Berthier's signature, on the 2nd October.

The brain, the soul of the whole organisation, it cannot be too clearly remembered, was Napoleon himself. He alone commanded in chief, combining in his own person the functions, not only of Chief of the State, and Generalissimo of the Army, but also of Chief of the Staff in fact, if not in name. Herein lay the great defect of this staff as an instrument of national utility. Napoleon,

LUISE, QUEEN OF PRUSSIA
(From an engraving in Mr. Broadley's collection)

The Contending Armies 31

endowed with a constitution which never during his long military career broke down for any considerable period, required, as it happened, no one to take his place for a time with the armies which he commanded in person. He was fortunate enough never to be seriously wounded. Berthier, his nominal chief of the staff, wrote thus of himself to Soult in 1807: " I am nothing in the army; I receive, in the name of the Emperor, the reports of the marshals, and I sign his orders for him; thus, as far as I am personally concerned, I am nothing." The Emperor had forged for himself an instrument which he alone could wield; as long as it was animated by him, it served its purpose thoroughly, but there was no understudy capable of filling, even for a short space, the rôle of the leading actor. Berthier was once, like Phaeton, left too long to drive the chariot of Helios. He was already allowing it to descend into the ocean of disaster, when the reins were gathered up by the master; ruin, which stared the army of 1809 in the face, was averted, and turned to success by a series of combinations which Napoleon himself always considered to be his finest effort.

The staff, unlike the modern Prussian staff, was not an educational institution. Had Moltke been wounded or fallen sick, there were other highly trained officers who could have filled his place with credit; had Napoleon's sentry, who fired on him on the eve of Jena, aimed better, the subsequent history of the campaign would have been very different from what it was. It almost seems as if Napoleon, his whole mind concentrated on self alone, acted on the principle of *après moi le deluge;* as if he knew, and recked not, that with his own disappearance the whole military machine which he had constructed must infallibly collapse from want of a guiding spirit.

Even *his* gigantic energy, however, could not do everything, so he surrounded himself with a personal secretariat and staff, for the more or less mechanical issue of orders, the framework of which emanated from his own brain.

As he moved from place to place on a campaign, he was accompanied by Berthier, by the Marshal of the Palace, the Master of the Horse, several secretaries, and a crowd of aides-de-camp and orderly officers pressing close behind him, ready, on the instant, to issue or carry his orders.

On arrival at a halting place he required, besides his own apartment, an office, in the centre of which was a table with his map spread out and the positions of the troops marked by pins on it. In the corners of the office were tables for the secretaries and the archivist.

Work commenced without delay; the Emperor, walking about the room, dictated orders with such rapidity that only the person who hurriedly took them down could decipher and fair out his own notes. The dictation was generally made to a secretary, but sometimes the recipient was Berthier, or Duroc, or Daru the Intendant-General, or an aide-de-camp. As soon as the orders were faired out, they were presented by the Secretary of the Portfolio for the Emperor's initial. An abstract record (*Feuille de travail*) of each day's orders was maintained by the archivist. It was

The Contending Armies 33

thus that Berthier received his general orders, sometimes in the form of a letter addressed to him, sometimes in that of a note dictated to himself.

His title, as Chief of the General Staff, was "Major-General de l'armée." With that post, in 1806, he combined the office of Minister of War; a year later a separate Ministry of War was created, for the labour of the double office was beyond the capacity of a single individual. This relieved Berthier of much work, especially in connection with promotions, retirements, and similar matters. In future he only dealt, as agent of the War Minister, with special promotions in the field.

As Chief of the Staff he was merely the channel of official communication between the Emperor and the army. He had an unrivalled knowledge of detail and a most intimate acquaintance with Napoleon's methods of work and command, which makes it all the more remarkable that he should have shown himself so incompetent to play, even temporarily, the master's part. He was an illustration of the evil of Napoleon's system of suppression of all independence on the part of his subordinates. Later, the Emperor complained that his marshals had failed, in Spain, or at a distance from him, because they did not understand his system. His methods of command excluded them from the sphere of higher strategy. It is true that, in addition to the formal orders sent through Berthier, Napoleon frequently wrote what may be called demi-official letters to some of his marshals. In these he would explain fully his

C

motives and objects; many of them were almost treatises on strategy or tactics. Read, for instance, his letters to Soult in September 1806, and those to Cambacérès and Louis Bonaparte on the defence of the coasts against a possible British raid, or the rôle of the army of Holland. But these letters were not written to all; it seems as if the Emperor considered men of the stamp of Ney, Augereau, or Lefebvre unworthy to receive, or unable to understand them. To a later generation they are of immense value, for they disclose Napoleon's real designs and hopes at the time they were written, serving to correct what he afterwards saw fit to put forward at St. Helena.

To return to Berthier: he had, in the first place, a large personal staff of aides-de-camp and orderly officers of all ranks. Like his master, he also had his private secretary and cashier as well as a small accounts department. Another secretary was concerned with the movement of troops, another with the secret department; each had a small establishment. This constituted Berthier's personal staff.

At the head of the departments of the general staff office was the "Assistant to the Major-General, Chief of the General Staff." By the decree of the 2nd October 1806 the office was divided into three departments, but this division seems not to have been used in practice. Instead of it the Assistant to the Major-General distributed the work amongst his subordinates, assigning to each, or to small groups, a separate branch.

When Berthier received a written order from

The Contending Armies

the Emperor, he, after reading it himself, handed it to the secretary whose department it concerned. If it concerned more than one, each in turn, after noting the part concerning himself, passed it to his neighbour. When the detailed orders required had been prepared, they were handed to the Assistant Major-General for issue through the department concerned. In addition to Berthier, there were at headquarters the officers commanding the artillery and the engineers, each with a staff of about twenty officers, whilst the Intendant-General had over forty. It is remarkable that Napoleon made large use of civilians, or retired officers, for the secretariat of his staffs. His own and Berthier's private secretaries and their assistants were civilians. Berthier's secretary for the department of movement of troops was a retired captain. The Intendant-General and his staff were civilians. This last department dealt with the commissariat, transport, clothing, and army administration generally. Officers on active service could not be spared for sedentary work, for which they were often ill-fitted.

The weak point in the executive staff seems to have been in the carrying of orders. Where the losses of a campaign had been heavy, aides-de-camp and orderly officers had to be sent to regimental duties, their place being taken by cadets from St. Cyr on their way to join their regiments. It was one of these unfortunate youths who was captured, in 1807, when carrying to Bernadotte a despatch on which depended the success of the Eylau campaign. The copy which he carried was the only one sent, and it was not in cypher; therefore, not only did it disclose to the Russians

Napoleon's plan, but, worse still, Bernadotte never received any orders till it was too late for him to play his part. Perhaps he would have realised, without orders, what that part should be, had it not been for Napoleon's habitual suppression of initiative in his marshals. Ney, as Bernadotte knew, had just had an unpleasant experience of Napoleon's wrath when he moved, without orders, towards Königsberg. In his case, too, a despatch had taken ten days to cover a distance which should, at the outside, have required thirty-six hours.

Notwithstanding its faults, Napoleon's staff system worked admirably in his own hands. It was all that was required by a general who seems to have believed himself above the risk of illness or wounds, who had no thought really for the nation, which in his youth he had hated, and whose one object was self-aggrandisement.

In addition to the general staff, each corps commander had his chief of the staff, with aides-de-camp for the distribution, to divisions and smaller units, of the details of general orders received through Berthier.

What had Prussia to oppose to this elaborate organisation?

In 1806, Geusau, who was nominally Quartermaster-General, corresponding to Chief of the General Staff, was a mere cypher. He was worn out by age and overburdened by other duties unconnected with his proper work. The real Chiefs of the Staff were his three Lieutenant Quartermasters-General, of whom the most prominent were Phull and Massenbach. Each Lieutenant Quartermaster-General had under him two Quartermasters, two Lieutenant Quartermasters, and a small survey establishment.

The three divisions, thus constituted, were in time of peace assigned respectively to three geographical areas of Prussia. In the war they were distributed to the three armies, Brunswick's, Ruchel's, and Hohenlohe's. There was nothing corresponding to Napoleon's staffs of corps, for corps did not exist. The duties of the staff were, under the system devised by Massenbach :—

1. Permanent, namely, the development of the general principles on which military operations are conducted.

2. Casual, viz., ordinary military subjects and literature, as well as the consideration and solution of all probable cases of war.

Napoleon's staff was thoroughly practical, designed—by the man who was before all things practical—for dealing with war as it existed; theory engaged but little of its attention. The Prussian staff, on the contrary, was stuffed to repletion with unpractical theory; theory which dealt entirely with geometrical systems of strategy and tactics, which laid all stress upon terrain and manœuvres, whilst leaving almost out of account moral qualifications and the strength of an enemy.

The leading spirits were Phull and Massenbach, both men of narrow, unpractical military ideas. Massenbach, in particular, seems to have thought that he could draw up a sort of military receipt-book, in which a commander would find instructions for his guidance in every possible situation. In peace time the duties of the three staff divisions consisted mainly in surveying, during the summer months, the various possible theatres of war and battlefields in Prussian territory. During the winter the results of their surveys were utilised for the construction of hypothetical plans of operations or battles.

Yet, with all his schemes, Massenbach made no provision for a war with France! There was no organisation, such as Napoleon had, for drafting and rapidly issuing orders, no trained staff of secretaries or aides-de-camp.

To make up for this deficiency, a pernicious practice was followed of summoning the commanders, or chief staff officers, of separate bodies of troops to headquarters to receive verbal instructions. The consequence of this was that much valuable time was lost, and orders often reached their destination at a time when the ever-changing course of events had rendered them no longer applicable to existing circumstances. When, on the morning of the 13th October 1806, it had been resolved to retreat by a flank to the Elbe, Massenbach was sent for to receive orders for Hohenlohe. Prince Kraft, probably rightly, infers that he, at last, received a severe reprimand for his persistent endeavours to drag the whole army across the Saale. He returned to Hohenlohe about noon with orders to act on the defensive, covering the flank of the main army as it marched, north-eastwards, behind the Ilm. Circumstances meanwhile had changed. Lannes, with only part of his corps, without artillery, was clinging to the Landgrafenberg, with no support at hand. Hohenlohe, with quadruple forces, was rightly preparing to hurl him from his perilous position. But Massenbach had

The Contending Armies 39

been so impressed with the idea of the defensive that he now believed that the strategical rôle prescribed precluded, equally, the tactical offensive. Therefore, he dissuaded Hohenlohe from his intention; the great opportunity of inflicting a severe check on the French was lost for ever.

Napoleon, at this period at any rate, never sent for his marshals to headquarters. When, on the 13th October, he found himself facing, above Jena, what he believed to be the whole Prussian army, and recognised that the great battle must come two days earlier than he had expected, with his army not yet concentrated for battle, he acted very differently from the Prussian leaders. Brunswick, in his place, would have sent for Bernadotte and Davout, perhaps for Augereau, all of them a day's march distant. Their corps would not have been able to move till their leaders had, like Massenbach, ridden the double journey. Napoleon at once despatched brief orders to Augereau, and to the corps in rear, merely directing them to hurry to the battlefield. To Bernadotte and Davout he sent orders, almost as brief, requiring them, if they should hear a serious attack on Lannes' exposed corps that afternoon, to march against the enemy's left flank. When the attack did not come off, further orders were sent for the next day. Those further orders were sent through Davout; Bernadotte chose to misinterpret them; but the more they are studied the more difficult it is to lay the blame for Bernadotte's failure to appear on any other shoulders but his own.

As for Brunswick, Prince Kraft had drafted a short order which, if sent to Hohenlohe on the morning of the 13th, would have saved the delay caused by Massenbach's visit to headquarters, and would have left no room for doubt.

This is but one example, out of many which could be cited, to show how far Napoleon's system of command and staff organisation was at this period ahead of that of the rest of Europe. Previous to Napoleon's time, these subjects had not, in comparatively small, closely concentrated armies, acquired the supreme importance which they had in the great armies of the early nineteenth century. The victories of earlier commanders had depended more on the unaided genius of one man, personally controlling a compact force. Napoleon, waging war with an army recruited by conscription, ever increasing in size, and designed for the conquest of the world, was the first to perceive that the highest genius, the greatest energy, were insufficient to enable one man to command, in the new conditions, without well-organised assistance.

The staff which he elaborated, it is true, was not educated, in the sense of the modern German staff, but it was thoroughly practical, as was everything he did, and even in education it was far ahead of those of other European armies. That of Prussia has already been described; Russia was hopelessly behind the times. As for Austria, she still had her evil system of a command centralised, not at the front, but at the capital; that was even worse than the Prussian system.

Possibly Napoleon himself realised the necessity for a nation of a highly educated staff, even of an educated army, but if he did, it did not suit his selfish policy to create a school for the upbringing of possible rivals, or successors, to himself. Therefore, he was content to educate his staff sufficiently only to render it an admirable instrument in his own hands. He failed to foresee the day when he must stand, with his back to the wall, facing all Europe, which had not been altogether idle in learning the lessons which he had taught it. He made no provision for the time when his armies were actively engaged from Spain to Russia, far beyond the control of his own voice. Then, no doubt, he regretted his own persistent crushing of independence in his subordinates, who succumbed largely from want of the guiding control to which they had been accustomed.

Of the French commanders it is unnecessary to add to what has already been said in another volume.[1] Of the Prussian generals Count Yorck von Wartenburg[2] says: "In the presence of the young and reckless French leaders, the old, weak, and irresolute Prussian commandants showed themselves simply incapable of resistance. When the framework of the military system, which alone lent them some stability, had been once broken, they had no longer strength to stand. The Emperor was more careful in dismissing his officers as soon as they became old. 'The third battalions are full of officers who have a right to be pensioned off, and who, on account of physical incapacity, can no longer serve. The corps of officers must be rejuvenated' (Napoleon to Lacuée, September 29, 1806)." Hoepfner de-

[1] The author's "Napoleon's Campaign in Poland," chap. ii.
[2] "Napoleon as a General," i. 314.

scribes how one of the infirm Prussian generals pleaded inability to attend a council of war at the hour named, on the ground that he had not yet completed his usual morning sweat—a part of his "kur."

The Duke of Brunswick and Marshal Mollendorf, veterans of the wars of Frederick, were borne down by the burden of 71 and 82 years respectively. Kalkreuth was 69; Kleist, the Governor of Magdeburg, was 73; Blucher, 63; Winning, 70; Hohenlohe, 60. The younger generals were Tauenzien, 45; Weimar, 49; Eugene of Würtemberg, 48; and Prince Louis, 33. Lettow-Vorbeck states that in the infantry of the line 28 colonels, out of a total of 66, were over 60 years of age. Of 281 majors, 86 were over 55, and 190 over 50 years old.

Baron von der Goltz, as well as Prince Kraft, has taken up the cudgels in defence of the Prussian generals of 1806, and of the propriety of their selection. As usual in such cases, hasty critics, judging after the disastrous result of the campaign, have condemned wholesale the Prussian leaders as incompetent. Baron von der Goltz shows that before the campaign these men enjoyed and deserved the highest military reputation. No one then could have been found to condemn their selection. Their misfortune was that they were to be pitted against a general whose abilities as far transcended those of all his contemporaries as the genius of Frederick overshadowed the mediocrity or incompetence of Soubise or Daun. Many of them were amongst those who, a few years later, bore a distinguished part in the operations which ended

The Contending Armies 43

in the downfall of Napoleon's power. It is absurd to characterise as imbeciles men like Blucher, Scharnhorst, Müffling, or the younger Kleist. Hohenlohe, who was in command on some of the most disastrous occasions in 1806, had been highly valued by Frederick, and had greatly distinguished himself in the wars against the French Republic. Brunswick, if old, was still full of vigour. Kalkreuth had distinguished himself at the siege of Mayence in 1793, and was again to show himself full of vigour and resource in his defence of Dantzig in 1807.

Two selections were admittedly bad, Phull and Massenbach. The unfortunate influence which the latter, who "has clearly shown by his own writings that he was a fantastic man and an uncertain character,"[1] had acquired over Hohenlohe did much to ruin the Prussian cause, as will be seen in the course of this history. Of Hohenlohe himself, Baron von der Goltz says: "Two special circumstances influenced unfavourably the actions of Hohenlohe; he was in bad health, and his nerves were not in a condition to bear the shock of a great catastrophe; he was wanting in breadth of view, which placed him too much in dependence on Massenbach, and compelled him at Prenzlau to suffer the consequences of the latter's narrowness."[2] The faults of the generals were not theirs individually so much as the failings of their time, and the fact that their army was not, as had been Frederick's at Rossbach, the tactical superior of the French.

The Prussian army of 1806, according to the

[1] Von der Goltz, *Rossbach et Jena*, p. 61.
[2] *Ibid.*, p. 67.

author just quoted, was still the army of Frederick, and would still have beaten the Austrians of Leuthen; but it had to contend not with the Austrians of Leuthen, but with a very different foe, the French of Austerlitz. Undoubtedly the spirit of the times was the principal cause of the interior weakness of the army. Good discipline, as then understood in Prussia, meant the abandonment of all initiative. Radical reform was required, but the necessity was overlooked, largely through a false respect for Frederick the Great and the past. Instead of slavishly adhering to the methods of the Seven Years' War, Prussia should have considered what Frederick himself would have done in the altered circumstances of half a century later. To the French conscription he would have opposed a Prussian national army; to the French skirmishers followed by small columns he would have opposed Prussian skirmishers followed by lines. To sum up the causes of the great collapse: "It was not the pride of the younger men nor the infatuation of the aristocracy which led Prussia from Rossbach to Jena, but a policy which chose to employ cunning without force; a false conception of the conduct of war; the influence which the spirit of the epoch, hardened in a frivolous civilisation, in a false honesty, in the taste for pleasures and in egoism, exercised on the army which, on account of its perilous situation and its consequent timidity, was unable to utilise, without hesitation, the opportunities offered to it during the war; the voluntary self-effacement of the king, who, though more clear-sighted than his councillors, submitted himself, from diffidence, to their judg-

The Contending Armies 45

ment; the fear of offending the country and imposing excessive charges on it; a false economy, the result of an exaggerated scrupulosity; lastly, a respect for the past, which concerned itself with trivial things, instead of holding to serious matters, little by little obscured judgment."[1]

The English reader will perhaps turn back and re-peruse these words of one of the ablest and most enlightened German critics; better still, he will perhaps be tempted to read the whole of the volume from which they are extracted, and which has been admirably translated into French under the title quoted in the footnote. The extract is only a very general summary of the conclusions carefully thought out by Baron von der Goltz. Is there nothing in it which England can lay to heart as a lesson in the necessity for preparation and national self-sacrifice? Is there not in England of the twentieth century "a fear of offending the country and imposing excessive charges on it"? Is there no "false economy, the result of an exaggerated scrupulosity"? Is there no cause for such fears of offending and for such false economy in the unwillingness or the neglect of a great part of the manhood of the nation to make the sacrifices of its time and convenience which alone can enable it to place itself in a position of effective defence? Are we quite free from a "spirit of the epoch, hardened in a frivolous civilisation, in a false honesty, in the taste for pleasures, and in egoism"? Lastly, can we plead "not guilty" to charges of undue satisfaction with the past, of neglect of the future,

---

[1] *Rossbach et Jena*, pp. 409–410.

of concerning ourselves with trivialities instead of holding to serious matters?

Turning now to the question of numbers on either side, we find the Prussians, even when they saw that war was inevitable, neglecting to mobilise their army completely, and leaving a portion of it in Silesia and the Polish provinces, where it was absolutely useless. With the approach of the Russians in view there was no fear of a Polish insurrection, so long as the armies in the field were undefeated. Every available man should have been assembled on the theatre which it had been determined to utilise. Thus, though Hoepfner calculates the whole Prussian army at nearly 250,000 men, and that of Saxony at 50,000, there stood ready to meet Napoleon's advance, or to take the offensive against him, but 130,000 Prussians and 20,000 Saxons, scarcely over one-half of the total available. Of these about 35,000 were cavalry and 5000 artillerymen. The regular artillery guns numbered 300, those attached to the infantry about 250. Against these Napoleon had assembling on the Upper Main about 180,000 men, of whom about 32,000 were cavalry, the rest infantry, artillery, engineers, &c. The guns about equalled in number those of the Prussian regular artillery.

Of this army not more than 10,000 were Bavarians and Hesse-Darmstadt troops. Behind these, in Southern Germany, there were some 26,000 troops of the Rhenish Confederation, besides the Bavarian troops left in the Tyrol, or to watch the Austrian frontier on the Inn. On his left, about Mainz and Frankfort, Napoleon had Mortier's corps, which was expected to reach a strength of 20,000.

THE DUKE OF BRUNSWICK
(From an engraving in Mr. Broadley's collection)

The Contending Armies

In the north, at Wesel and in Holland, he had some 20,000 French and Dutch troops, under King Louis, threatening Hanover and the Prussian communications in that direction. The total forces available for offence, and for the defence of the Empire in France and Italy, amounted to over 600,000 men, including Dutch, German, and Italian auxiliaries.

CHAPTER III

THE PLANS OF CAMPAIGN

HOLDING, as he did in 1806, the lines of the Rhine and the Main with all their passages, Napoleon had the choice of several lines of advance to the invasion of Prussia and Saxony. He might base himself on any part of the Rhine below Mayence for a direct advance eastwards on Berlin. If he marched from Mayence by Frankfort, Hanau, Fulda, Eisenach, and Erfurt, he would have to pass through the hilly country now traversed by the Frankfort-Berlin railway. Though hilly, the country cannot be described as really difficult, for the valleys are open as a rule, and the hills rounded and rarely rugged. Once beyond Erfurt he would find himself on the rolling plateaux, which eventually sink, towards Leipzig and the Elbe, into the level plains of Northern Germany. From any part of the Rhine between Mayence and Wesel the advance would have to cross a more or less hilly country before reaching the Elbe at Magdeburg, and in places—the Harz, for example—the difficulties would be considerable for the movement of a great army. On all these lines the obstructions in the shape of rivers would not be serious till the Elbe was reached. Basing himself on Wesel and the Lower Rhine, the Emperor would find no mountain

The Plans of Campaign 49

barrier intersecting his line of advance across the level plains of North Germany; but the river lines, especially those of the Weser and the Elbe, would assume more serious proportions.

Should he, on the other hand, elect to advance northwards from the southern side of his re-entrant rectangular base, across the Main, he would have, before reaching the plains of Northern Germany, to pass through a difficult mountainous country of more or less rugged nature, thickly wooded, and with but few good roads, as roads were understood in Germany in 1806, before the introduction of macadam. From the longitude of Hanau to the western mountain boundary of Bohemia stretches the great Thuringian Forest, barring the way between Southern and Northern Germany, and, everywhere as far east as the longitude of Bamberg, only to be passed by many marches of considerable difficulty. Eastwards of this point, the forest narrows greatly in the Franconian Forest, which forms the connecting link between the main Thuringian Forest and the mountains of Bohemia. In this part the barrier can be traversed in three marches, or less, from the Upper Main to the Saale. Once north of the Saale, the invader would find himself in comparatively open country, where movements of troops are easy and concentration possible. During the two or three days' march through the Franconian Forest close concentration is impossible; but there were, in 1806, three good roads, on which as many columns could march with a front not exceeding forty miles. The lateral communications between them would not be good, and they would be exposed to some risk

D

of defeat in detail should they encounter a great army, concentrated on the plateaux north of the Saale, as they debouched from the Franconian mountains. This danger would, however, be very much greater in the case of an advance from the middle Main northwards, where roads through the Thuringian Forest were much fewer, and lateral communications still worse.

To base himself on the Rhine and advance eastwards or north-eastwards on Berlin would, perhaps, be easier for Napoleon than to move northwards from the Main, but it would offer no strategical advantages; for if he met and defeated the Prussians on any of these west to east lines, he would simply drive them backwards on their supports, first on Saxony and then on the Russians, whose advance from Poland was expected. To turn the Thuringian Forest by an advance from his extreme right, close against the Bohemian frontier of Austria, was no doubt a less safe movement; but, on the other hand, it offered strategical advantages of infinite importance. In the first place, the Emperor might possibly succeed in intruding with his army between the Prussians, if they decided to defend the country west of the Elbe, and the Saxons whom he saw unwillingly drifting into co-operation with Prussia. If he failed in this, he would still threaten the Prussian communications with the Elbe and Berlin, and those of the Saxons with Dresden. Were he to occupy Dresden itself, he would turn the whole defensive line of the Elbe, and, looking to the superior mobility of his own army, might still hope to be in Berlin in rear of the Prussian army, and separating it from

The Plans of Campaign

the advancing Russians, before it could reach the capital. To thus turn the forest on its eastern extremity, he would require to concentrate to his right, towards the sources of the Main, and push through the mountainous country of the Franconian Forest, forming the watershed between the Main and the Saale, and separating him from the plains of Western Saxony.

The dangers of such an advance appeared to be that, if he drew his supplies from Mayence by the line of the Main, the Prussians, by a rapid advance through the Thuringian Forest against the line of his communications, might sever him from France, and compel him to conform to their initiative. Should they, on the other hand, concentrate on the Upper Saale, there was the risk of his army being defeated in detail as it debouched from the Franconian mountains on the Upper Saale, the same danger which would have threatened a direct advance northwards through the Thuringian Forest. But in moving through the mountains east of the Thuringian Forest the Emperor would find three good roads, instead of the single bad one to which he would practically be restricted in the forest itself.

That Napoleon would advance from the Lower Rhine direct eastward against the Prussian army was never in the least probable. In the first place, as has been already shown, that plan offered no strategical advantages; and in the second place, there were, during the spring and summer of 1806, no less than six French army corps, besides the cavalry reserve, in the space between the Upper Rhine, the Inn, the Main, and the Upper Danube. The Guard alone had been withdrawn to Paris after the Peace of Presburg. To have placed this great force on the Rhine below Mayence would have involved a gigantic flank march to the left, and would have withdrawn the watch which Napoleon still thought it necessary to keep upon Austria. That country was a constant source of anxiety to him, and he could not feel sure that, if she saw his armies disappear from her frontiers, she would not, forgetting the way in which Prussia had behaved in 1805, seize the opportunity to throw in her lot with the new coalition, seeking to avenge her defeats of the previous year. She must be overawed until the march of events, and the hoped-for destruction of Prussia, should render her intervention too dangerous a move to be undertaken in the existing state of her army and her finances.

In considering any of Napoleon's schemes for a campaign, we cannot keep too steadily in mind his own saying, "Je n'ai jamais eu un plan d'opérations." He never presumed to forecast far ahead the precise course of operations after the first tactical contact. What he did was to fix his mind on a general object for attainment, and to carry out his strategical deployment so as to place his army in the best possible position for effecting that object.[1]

On the present occasion he laid down as his objective two geographical points, Dresden and Berlin; not that he committed the error of

[1] "The plan of operations must define what we wish to do, and hope to achieve, with our available resources. It cannot forecast the individual movements by which this will be effected. The first important engagement with the enemy, above all things, exercises a distinctively decisive influence on them" (Von der Goltz on the Conduct of War, p. 121).

believing that the mere occupation of geographical points was the object of war, but he saw that Dresden and Berlin were the best places to aim at in order to sever the Saxons from the Prussian alliance, to interpose between the Prussian army and that advancing from Russia, and to draw towards himself the former, whose defeat and destruction was his real objective. The shortest road, with reference to the existing positions of his army, was naturally to be chosen, and the starting-point of that was the neighbourhood of Bamberg and the Principality of Baireuth.

On the 5th September, fourteen days before he finally decided on war, we find him indicating this starting-point in a letter to Berthier. "It is necessary that, in eight days after I give the order, the whole of my armies—that at Frankfort, that at Passau, and that at Memmingen—should be assembled at Bamberg, and in the Principality of Baireuth. Send me the itinerary which each would follow, and the nature of the roads." The letter goes on to order the despatch of officers in every direction to gather the most complete information as to the country, roads, rivers, supplies, fortresses, bridges, &c., between the starting-point and Berlin, and on either side of the direct road.

So long as peace subsisted, the Emperor could draw his supplies in safety from France through Mayence, up the Main, and along the adjacent roads. Once war broke out, that line, a continuation to a flank of the army's front, would be dangerous, and exposed to be cut by an enemy moving southwards against the left of the Grand Army, through the forest.

Therefore the Emperor decided to abandon it as soon as war was declared. On the 9th September he writes to Berthier: "If I made war against Prussia, my line of operations would be Strasburg, Mannheim, Mayence, and Wurzburg, where I have a fortress; so that my convoys, on the fourth day after their departure from Mannheim, or Mayence, would be in safety at Wurzburg." Thus his line of communications with France would be thrown back south of the Main, out of reach of the enemy, until a date when the Emperor could reckon on his own movement northwards, against the Saxon and Prussian communications, forcing the enemy to abandon all idea of operations against those of the French.[1] Napoleon required fortified depôts in the advanced base on the Upper Main, from which he proposed to start. Wurzburg was suitable for one; Forchheim had to be taken as the other, though a place farther north—Königshofen, for example—would have been preferred, had it been suitable in other respects.

Napoleon, ever confident of victory, was never careless to provide for retreat in the event of defeat. An ordinary general would perhaps have sought to retreat in that case on the Rhine direct, whatever the danger from a victorious enemy moving against his flank. Not so Napoleon, whose intention was, if

---

[1] "Therefore he prepared to transfer his communications now to the line Forchheim, Wurzburg, Mannheim, which was more in his immediate rear. He was compelled to do this, for in placing his army in the best position for threatening the enemy's communications, he found himself unable to protect, without weakening his concentration, the line Mainz–Bamberg in continuation of his left flank" ("Napoleon as a General," i. 275).

The Plans of Campaign

defeated, to transfer his base from the Rhine to the Upper Danube, on which he could fall back through the friendly territory of Bavaria, and whence he could, if necessary, reach Strasburg. No clearer or better exposition of the Emperor's schemes can be found than the statement of them contained in a series of notes which he addressed, for his guidance, to his brother Louis, on the 30th September. The first note includes the following passage: "My intention is to concentrate all my forces on the extremity of my right, leaving the whole space between Bamberg and Mayence entirely unoccupied, so as to have nearly 200,000 men united on the same battlefield. If the enemy pushes parties between Bamberg and Mayence, I shall not be disturbed, for my line of communications will be established on the small fortress of Forchheim, and thence on Wurzburg. It will be necessary for you, therefore, to direct the most important messengers you have to send me to Mannheim, whence they will go direct to Forchheim, and reach me with the greatest safety. The nature of events which may occur is incalculable, for the enemy, believing me to have my left on the Rhine and my right in Bohemia, thinking, moreover, that my line of operations is parallel to my front, may have a great interest in outflanking my left, in which case I can throw him back upon the Rhine." True to his great principle of concentration on a single object, the Emperor was about to advance with his army in three columns in the smallest area compatible with the nature of the country and the communications in front of him. Thus, if attacked in any direction, he would be able to concentrate for battle in the shortest possible time.

The note proceeds to show how he proposed to deal with the possible advance of a Prussian raid into France, across the Rhine, beyond his own reach. "Employ yourself in putting Wesel in the best possible state of defence, so that you may, should circumstances demand it, be able to pass back your whole army by the bridge at Wesel, and move up the Rhine to restrain raiding forces from passing that barrier. By the 10th or 12th October there will be at Mayence the 8th corps of the Grand Army, 18,000 or 20,000 strong.[1] Its orders will be to avoid being cut from the Rhine, whilst making incursions as far as Frankfort; but, in case of necessity, it will retire behind the Rhine, leaning its left upon your troops."

The second note goes on: "The observations in my first note above are mere precautions. My first marches will threaten the heart of the Prussian monarchy, and the deployment of my forces will be so rapid and imposing that it is probable that the whole Prussian army will fall back on Magdeburg, seeking by forced marches to defend its capital. It is then, but then only, that you will have to launch an advanced guard to take possession of the Mark, of Munster, of Osnabruck, and of East Friesland, by means of mobile columns which could fall back, if necessary, on a central point. The result would be that the enemy would be able to draw neither

---

[1] The Emperor's expectations in this respect were disappointed, for, owing to delay in the arrival of reinforcements, Mortier had but three French infantry regiments on the date named.

The Plans of Campaign

recruits nor supplies from the country, whilst you, on the other hand, could derive some advantages from it. You must understand that the bulk of your forces should not go far from Wesel, so that from that point you may be able to defend your kingdom and the coasts of Boulogne, should circumstances so require. For the first period of the war you are merely a corps of observation—that is to say that, until the enemy has been thrown beyond the Elbe, I only count on your corps as a means of diversion to amuse the enemy till the 12th October, the date on which my operations will be fully developed; also to prevent the penetration into France or Holland of any hostile corps which may be cut off with no resource but to throw itself into those countries; or, finally, in the case of a great misfortune, such as a great battle lost, that you should be able to defend Wesel and Mayence with your own army and the 8th corps of the Grand Army (which will remain always near Mayence), whilst I execute my retreat on the Danube, and, at the same time, to prevent the enemy from passing the Rhine to pillage my State."

The third note deals with the possibility of invasion by the English, which Napoleon thinks more probable in the direction of Hanover than on the coasts of France or Holland. Should the English and Swedes attempt a diversion in Hanover, they might muster 25,000 men. In that case there need be no further fear for the French and Dutch coasts, and the central reserve of 8000 men at Paris could in ten days, with the aid of wheeled transport, be carried to the reinforcement of Louis, who would also call up the rest of his own army from Zeist, his central camp near Utrecht. In case of urgent need, the 8th corps could march down the Rhine from Mayence, raising the army of Holland to 40,000 men, a force ample to preclude any possibility of the English and Swedes making their presence felt on the main theatre of war. The fourth note deals with the event of a great French victory, placing at the Emperor's mercy the country west of the Elbe. Then would be the time for the 8th corps and part of the army of the north to occupy Cassel, in the genuine neutrality of whose Elector Napoleon refused to believe. "The Elector wishes to be neutral; but that neutrality does not deceive, though it suits me." The writer's concluding advice is couched in these terms: "Never expose your corps and do not risk your own life, since you command only a corps of observation. The least check suffered by you would disquiet me; my measures might be disconcerted by it, and such an event would leave without direction the whole north of my Empire. On the other hand, whatever may happen to me, I shall act more freely with the knowledge that you are behind the Rhine; even if I experienced a great disaster, I should beat my enemy, had I but 50,000 men left, because, free to manœuvre, independent of any line of operations, and feeling secure as to the most important points in my State, I should always have resources.[1] It is possible that the actual

[1] Count Yorck remarks on Napoleon's intention to use the Danube as a line on which to retreat if necessary. He quotes Jomini to the effect that if the Prussians had dreamed of an

The Plans of Campaign

situation is but the commencement of a great coalition against us, the full extent of which will be disclosed by events."

The last sentence points to the possibility of a renewal by Austria of the war in which she had been so heavily defeated. This possibility Napoleon had constantly in mind, up till the date when the victory of Friedland and the Peace of Tilsit finally removed it. From the autumn of 1806 till the summer of 1807, he was constantly striving to chain Austria to neutrality. It is to Eugène Beauharnais, the Viceroy of Italy, that he discloses his plans for forcing on Austria an attitude of neutrality, which he could hardly hope to ensure on other grounds than that of fear. In a letter, dated 18th September 1806, he inculcates on the Viceroy an attitude of watchfulness, tempered by conciliation. Austria's professions were uniformly friendly, but she was busy repairing the losses of her army, and, whilst it was unnecessary and unwise to irritate or alarm her, it was most necessary to have everything ready for the defence of Northern Italy, in case she should take advantage of the Emperor's having his hands occupied elsewhere. The supreme command of the army of Italy was bestowed on Eugène, who, if the worst came to the worst, might be reinforced by 40,000 men from the army of Naples, which was entirely separate

attempt to sever the line to the Danube by Saalfeld, Schleiz and Hof, they would have left open Napoleon's best and most direct line from Saxony to the Rhine, by the Leipzig–Frankfort road, and the others *viâ* Cassel to Coblentz, Cologne, and Wesel. "On the eve of Jena Napoleon's strategical position, considering his chance of a twofold retreat, seems to have been as carefully secured as is possible in the uncertainty of human affairs" ("Napoleon as a General," i. 300).

from that of North Italy. It had, however, depôts in the north, and the men in these were, for the present, made over to Eugène. He was also given control over seven regiments in Piedmont and the corps in Istria; the latter was to be secretly withdrawn to Friuli. The fortresses of Venice, Mantua, Palmanuova, Osoppo, Legnago, and Peschiera were to be put in a proper state of defence and garrisoned. For the purpose of manœuvring between these fortresses, and of containing the Austrians in the event of war, Eugène would still have 40,000 men, without counting the army of Naples. Marmont, in Dalmatia, was to leave a garrison in Ragusa and collect the rest of the 2nd corps towards Zara, whence he could either threaten Croatia or move into Italy to the Viceroy's assistance. These armies would compel the Austrians, should they declare war, to maintain a large portion of their army on the southern frontier, far from the main theatre of war.

The only remaining point in Napoleon's scheme for the defence of his Empire is the protection of the French coasts against a possible invasion of the English. As has already been said, this danger would cease should England, as was more probable, direct her efforts to the invasion of Hanover; for Napoleon calculated the extreme strength of an English expeditionary force at 25,000 or 30,000 men, too small a force to permit of division.

The scheme for the defence of the French coasts, should they be threatened, is sketched in a letter to Cambacérès of the 30th September. After mentioning that Louis is charged with the

The Plans of Campaign

defence from the Moselle to the coast, and Kellerman with that between the Moselle and Switzerland, the Emperor points out that he has 8000 infantry at Paris, and 2000 cavalry at Moulins and Amiens. Should the English attempt a landing near Boulogne, they would find there 15,000 men well entrenched. To the assistance of these Louis would march, 6000 National Guards would be available at St. Omer, not to mention the local gendarmerie. Lastly, the 8000 men in Paris and the 2000 cavalry could be promptly moved up, the former being conveyed to the Somme in carts for the purpose of saving time.

The attempt might be directed against Cherbourg. In that case the forts were sufficiently guarded by one regiment stationed there. To support it there would be the National Guards of the neighbourhood, a small force to be brought up from Pontoy, and the 8000 men who could be sent from Paris. At the worst, the enemy could do nothing more than burn Cherbourg, and a frigate which was on the stocks there.

If Brest were the point threatened, it would be held by all the garrisons of the 15th military circle, in addition to 10,000 sailors. The workmen (many of them ex-sailors) could be armed, and the central reserve sent up from Paris, as well as troops from Bordeaux and Nantes.

The difficulties of landing, and the uncertainty of being able to re-embark in the winter storms of the Bay of Biscay, were a sufficient guarantee for the immunity from attack of Bordeaux and Belle Isle. As for Toulon, there were troops enough in the neighbourhood to render it safe against 40,000 men. In conclusion, the Emperor considered that an expedition by sea against the exposed French coast was improbable in the winter.

Here we have the whole scheme, offensive and defensive, explained with Napoleon's usual lucidity and simplicity. Complicated concentric attacks found no place in his strategy, the essence of which was concentration. Like Frederick the Great, Napoleon was hampered by no government imposing conditions and restrictions on his clear apprehension of what was necessary. In other respects he was in a position very different from that of the great Prussian. The latter had sought to build up a strong kingdom of moderate dimensions in face of the jealousy and opposition of the older European powers; Napoleon had already established such a power beyond all probability of molestation, and was now guided in his strategy by his desire to build up an Empire of the West, constructed on the ruins of Europe, to be followed by its extension to the East. Where Frederick merely sought to save his kingdom from destruction, or to wrest a province from Austria, it was sufficient for him to strike a blow which would compel his enemy to sue for peace on reasonable terms. Napoleon, looking for much more, required the entire destruction of his enemy's fighting power. Frederick sought to live and let live, Napoleon to batten on the substance of the existing powers of the whole world. In 1806, his aim was the effacement of Prussia by the capture or destruction of her whole army. That, as we shall see in the later stages of this war, was the goal which he indicated to his com-

PRINCE LOUIS FERDINAND
(By permission of the Berlin Photographic Company, 133 New Bond St., London, W.)

The Plans of Campaign 63

manders in their pursuit of the Prussian army after Jena; that was the one great reason why he could never have rested content with a straightforward advance from the Rhine, or through the Thuringian Forest, which, with his overwhelming force, must probably have ended in victory, though not necessarily in total annihilation of the enemy's army.

Turning now to Prussia, we find her in a position similar to that of Frederick. She neither hoped nor wished to overrun and destroy France; her object would be attained by a victory which should curb the ambition of the Emperor, compelling him to confine his rule to reasonable limits, and to abandon his schemes for the subjugation of central and eastern Europe.

When the Prussian Government first resolved, on the 7th August, that war could not be avoided, they appear to have been ignorant of the position of Napoleon's great army in South Germany, though it is difficult to understand how they could be so. Possibly the arrival of the Imperial Guard at Paris, which could not have escaped their ambassador's notice, induced the belief that the whole army was following it.

In their ignorance of the distribution of the French army, the Prussian military advisers had to consider its possible advance from any of three directions:—

1. By Hanover, by Cassel, or by Eisenach, on Magdeburg.
2. By Eisenach, by Schmalkalden, or by Baireuth, on Wittenberg.
3. By Baireuth, on Dresden.

In view of this uncertainty as to the direction

of attack, the earliest orders for mobilisation contemplated the assembly of troops at the following points:—

1. Blucher, with sixteen battalions and seventeen squadrons, was to concentrate about Paderborn and Osnabruck, and between Leer and Oldenburg, leaving only light troops on the coasts, and watching the French on the Westphalian frontier. Should the latter appear to be endeavouring to turn Blucher by Hesse, his duty would be to concentrate on Hanover.

2. The troops occupying Hanover (twenty battalions, twenty-eight squadrons) would concentrate towards Celle, Hildesheim, and Brunswick, with the exception of a small force watching Lauenburg and the coast, and another detachment at Nordheim. This army, if Napoleon advanced by Hesse, would support Blucher's retirement, or itself fall back on Magdeburg, there to offer, in conjunction with the troops on the spot, a stout resistance.

3. Ten battalions and twenty squadrons, concentrated at Magdeburg, would support the above-named columns.

4. The garrisons of Potsdam, Berlin, and other places in the Mark, would hold themselves in readiness to bring further help to Magdeburg. They numbered seventeen battalions and fifteen squadrons.

5. Kalkreuth, with eighteen battalions and thirty squadrons, assembled about Prenzlau, would be in a position to march, either against the Swedes, who were still hostile, or on Magdeburg, as circumstances might require.

6. In Silesia and South Prussia, thirty-one

The Plans of Campaign

and a half battalions and seventy squadrons would mobilise as rapidly as possible between Sagan and Breslau, prepared to march, if necessary, through Saxony, pushing two and a half battalions and five squadrons into the Principality of Baireuth, which, however, they were to evacuate should the enemy appear in force there. It was hoped, in this event, that the Silesian army, joined by the Saxons, would be able to form behind the Elbe at Dresden, thus menacing the right flank of a French advance on Berlin.

7. Eighteen battalions and twenty squadrons in West Prussia, about Küstrin, would be able to bring support to any of the columns requiring it.

These orders failed to provide for the mobilisation of 34,000 men and 198 guns, a failure which is strongly condemned by Hoepfner. It seems impossible to justify it, especially as in 1805 it had been rightly decided to mobilise every available man. Scarcely were the orders issued, when the Prussian headquarters embarked on a series of councils to deliberate on the plan of campaign. At the best a council of war is a poor expedient, the favourite resource of a weak commander. These Charlottenburg councils were peculiarly bad, for every one of any note was encouraged to expound his views; memoranda begat memoranda and plans of operations; worst of all, the course eventually adopted was generally a compromise, which still left each of the advising members in the belief that his pet scheme had not been finally rejected, and might eventually be adopted. Some remarkable schemes were put forward, the most extravagant of which, perhaps, was that of Colonel von Massenbach, an officer with a high scientific reputation, who throughout played the part of the evil genius of Prince Hohenlohe. This extraordinary plan, which Prince Kraft remarks would nowadays be called the utterance of a madman, contemplated an advance with the Silesian army, entirely independent of the rest, through Saxony to Hof, thence to the Danube, and back again by Bohemia to Saxony. How he proposed to effect this *promenade militaire* in the face of Napoleon, the apostle of concentration, is beyond comprehension.

Hohenlohe put forward a scheme scarcely less contrary to all the principles of good strategy. One army was to advance on Fulda, through Gotha, another on Hof, a third through the Thuringian Forest from Erfurt, with yet a fourth in reserve about Naumburg. Three weak armies with a front of ninety miles, and a reserve far behind it! Neither of these plans took any account of the enemy, or allowed for any action on his part.

The plan finally adopted was better, for it gave due consideration to the existence of the enemy, but it was not eventually carried out. Assuming that the French forces were widely scattered over South Germany from Frankfort to the Inn, it was designed to advance with the whole allied army from Erfurt, through the forest, so as to arrive in the French centre and beat its wings in detail.[1] As a matter of fact, it would have struck

[1] This resolution was formed at Naumburg on the 24th-25th September, and the advance was in progress on the 5th October ("Napoleon as a General," i. 284).

The Plans of Campaign 67

a blow in the air; for Napoleon had arranged to evacuate the whole tract on which the Prussian army would debouch, to throw back his line of communications south of the Main, and to concentrate to his right. That the Prussian leaders did not know, and their plan had at least the merit of concentration. In condemning the plans of Massenbach and Hohenlohe, we are not committing the common fault of military, and still more of civilian critics, in judging after the event. Both schemes were bad, because they violated one of the first principles of strategy by contemplating a dispersal of forces beyond the possibility of mutual support. The plan for the passage of the forest is not open to that charge, and can only be condemned on the ground of the danger involved in the passage of a difficult country, in which insufficient communications would necessitate the march of the army in a column of inordinate length with a very narrow front, thus exposing it to defeat in detail as it emerged from the forest. Had the assumption of the wide dispersion of Napoleon's army been correct, the risk would have been small, for the head of the column would have found itself exposed only to a small portion of the hostile army. It would have been scarcely more dangerous than the issue of Bonaparte's army from the valley of Aosta in 1800. When the plan was formed, the Prussian leaders were ignorant of Napoleon's preparations for concentration to the East of the forest. What was fatal in the Prussian plans was that, whilst Napoleon laid down a distinct and decided course from which no deviation was permitted, and no subordinate was allowed to press his own views, his enemies were perpetually hesitating, holding councils of war, and modifying their plans, as one inferior commander or another, for the moment, obtained the ear of the council.

To add to their difficulties, there were two distinct parties at headquarters. The Duke of Brunswick and others were sensible of the inferiority of the numbers which Prussia could expect to oppose to Napoleon's great armies, and, clinging still to the hope of being able to avert war, were anxious to avoid the precipitation of hostilities by a bold and immediate offensive. On the other hand, Hohenlohe, Prince Louis of Prussia, Massenbach, and the enthusiastic military party, believing in the assured victory of Prussia, advocated a prompt advance on a widely extended front. The King himself, perhaps, had a clearer perception of the strategical position and requirements than any of his advisers. Being, however, young and inexperienced in war, he was naturally reluctant to impose his views on men much his seniors, many of whom had served under the great Frederick.

In the last ten days of September, the Prussian army was still spread over a front of 190 miles. Ruchel and Blucher were in Hesse, from Paderborn to Eisenach, Gotha, and Erfurt; the main army was about Naumburg; Hohenlohe was in the country between the Elbe and the Mulde; the Saxons had not yet completed their mobilisation.

In the period from the 5th to the 8th October, the general position was somewhat less widely dispersed. Ruchel, about Eisenach, had outposts towards Hesse and Meiningen.

The main army, in the neighbourhood of

The Plans of Campaign

Erfurt, pushed its outposts south as far as Hildburghausen.

Hohenlohe was at Jena and Roda, with an advanced guard towards Saalfeld. Tauenzien was away on his left front at Hof, Gefell, and Schleiz.

The whole front still covered 85 miles in a direct line. At the same time Napoleon had seven corps and the cavalry reserve assembled on a front of 38 miles, facing Tauenzien's corps of 7000 or 8000 men, at a distance of three days' march. As Prince Kraft remarks, it was Napoleon rather than the Prussians who was in a position to interpose between the parts of the enemy's army.

At this juncture the interminable Prussian councils of war recommenced at Erfurt. During them, from the 4th to the 7th October, active operations, as usual, practically ceased.

At last Napoleon's real plan had dawned on the Prussian headquarters, as is shown by a letter from the King to Ruchel of the 7th October. It was seen that the Emperor was aiming at the left flank of the widely dispersed allies, and this was placed beyond the possibility of doubt on the 8th, when Müffling reported the advance of the French north-eastwards from Bamberg. Obviously the proper course now was a concentration of the whole army towards its left centre, which would bring it in turn on the left flank of the enemy's advance, forcing him to turn towards it. The time for the offensive had passed; it was no longer possible to carry the war into the enemy's country. The orders issued for the allied armies on the 8th were to the following effect :—

The Duke of Weimar, commanding the advance guard of the main army in the direction of the Thuringian Forest, was ordered to send forward some cavalry, with horse artillery, towards Schweinfurt, whilst his main body advanced as far as Meiningen, leaving a small reserve at Schmalkalden. This was in pursuance of Müffling's suggestion that the enemy's rear should be threatened by cavalry. The bulk of the main army would meanwhile move so as to reach Erfurt on the 9th, and the neighbourhood of Blankenhain and Kranichfeld on the 10th.

Hohenlohe was to draw Tauenzien towards himself, leaving only a small force to observe the enemy towards Hof. The Prince would concentrate his main body on the 9th at Hochdorf, and on the 10th, united with Tauenzien, would be on the left bank of the Saale about Kahla and Rudolstadt.

Ruchel and Blucher, sending out detachments to threaten the enemy's communications in the direction of Fulda, were to concentrate between Gotha and Erfurt, keeping in touch with the main army.

Duke Eugene of Würtemberg, with the reserve, was to move at once from Magdeburg to Halle, where he would stand ready to join the main army either towards Leipzig or towards Naumburg.

The idea of a concentration on the left bank of the Saale was correct; the only fault to be found with the orders was that, by detaching part of Ruchel's and Blucher's forces, as well as the advance guard of Weimar, against Napoleon's

The Plans of Campaign

communications, they weakened the concentration by about 11,000 men at a time when every available man should have been brought to a central point in order to compensate, as far as possible, for the known inferiority of numbers. Prince Kraft goes so far as to estimate that, allowing for the Prussian army's inferiority in numbers, in organisation, in system of supply, in equipment, and in generalship, it was not worth more than one-third, possibly even one-fourth, of the French.

CHAPTER IV

MOVEMENTS OF BOTH SIDES UP TO THE 10TH OCTOBER

HAVING traced the Prussian movements up to the 8th October, we must now bring those of the French up to the same date; thenceforward carrying on the two together.

Napoleon, leaving St. Cloud on the 25th September, reached Mayence on the 28th. There he stayed till the 1st October, awaiting the Guard, which was on its way from Paris, travelling part of the way in country carts. On the 2nd he reached Wurzburg. It was from the latter place that he issued his final orders for the advance of his army, so that it might be ready to cross the frontier the moment war should be declared. When those orders issued, on the 5th October, peace still subsisted in name between France and Prussia; but there could be no possible doubt that it must be broken within the next few days. The Prussian ultimatum, despatched on the very day Napoleon left the neighbourhood of Paris, was still on its way in pursuit of him, and was destined not to reach him till the 7th, the day on which he had decided to declare war. Seeing how anxious he was to throw the blame of aggression on Prussia, it is difficult to resist the suspicion that he already knew the tenour of the coming ultimatum, which required a reply by the 8th. It was impossible to doubt that the reply would be war, and Napoleon so arranged that on that date his army should be well across the southern frontier of the enemy.

In accordance with the orders issued on the 19th September, the French corps were rapidly reaching the line from which their advance was to commence. The Emperor's projects are explained most clearly in his letter to Soult, dated 5th October, 11 A.M., one of those demi-official letters, explanatory of the formal orders issued through Berthier, which Napoleon was in the habit of addressing direct to his marshals. "I have," he writes, "caused to be occupied, armed, and provisioned, Wurzburg, Forchheim, and Kronach, and I shall debouch with my whole army by three issues upon Saxony. You are at the head of my right, having behind you Marshal Ney's corps, at a distance of half a day's march. A day's march behind him will be 10,000 Bavarians, making altogether more than 50,000 men. Marshal Bernadotte is at the head of my centre; he has behind him Marshal Davout's corps, the greater part of the Reserve cavalry, and my Guard, making over 70,000 men. He debouches by Kronach, Lobenstein, and Schleiz. The 5th corps is at the head of my left; behind it is the corps of Marshal Augereau. It debouches by Coburg, Gräfenthal, and Saalfeld, and musters over 40,000 men. The day you arrive at Hof all these will be abreast of you."

The strength and composition of the columns

may be stated as follows, on the basis of the present states given by Foucart, and further worked out by Lettow-Vorbeck. Seeing, however, that most of these statements are for dates earlier than the 8th October, and that reinforcements were steadily coming in, it is probable that the columns were actually stronger.

RIGHT COLUMN—

	Infantry.	Cavalry.	Guns.
IV. Corps—Soult	30,956	1,567	48
VI. Corps—Ney	18,414	1,094	24
Bavarians—Wrede	6,000	1,100	18
	55,370	3,761	90
	59,131		

CENTRE COLUMN—

	Infantry.	Cavalry.	Guns.
I. Corps—Bernadotte	19,014	1,580	34
III. Corps—Davout	28,655	1,538	44
Imperial Guard—Lefebvre	4,900	2,400	36
Cavalry Reserve—Murat	—	17,550	30
	52,569	23,068	144
	75,637		

LEFT COLUMN—

	Infantry.	Cavalry.	Guns.
V. Corps—Lannes	19,389	1,560	28
VII. Corps—Augereau	15,931	1,175	36
	35,320	2,735	64
	38,055		

Grouchy's cavalry (3004) did not reach the army till the 14th October. On the other hand, we have to add about 9000 for artillerymen, engineers, &c. Napoleon's "battalion square of 200,000 men" would thus come to about 180,000 men and 298 guns, without reckoning reinforcements after the dates of the present states. Including these and departmental troops, &c., the total was probably very close to the round sum given by Napoleon.

Soult was required to be at Baireuth (Prussian territory) on the 8th. The country as far as Hof, being hilly and wooded, was unsuitable for cavalry, as was that to be traversed by the centre and left columns until they reached the more open country north of the Saale. It must not be supposed that the right bank of the Saale is a level, open plain. It is, rather, a rolling plateau of well-wooded downs at a considerable elevation above the river, which is generally deeply sunk in a valley of varying width. Through this plateau the tributary streams pass in valleys often broad and open, as is that leading from Pösneck to Saalfeld. Farther north the plateau gradually sinks into the plains towards Leipzig.

On the other hand, the country between the Upper Main and the Saale is one of forest-clad mountains rising to altitudes of 2500 feet or more. It can be traversed only by comparatively few roads leading through the valleys, whilst beyond the Saale roads are numerous—though in 1806 they were not good—and in fine weather it is possible in many parts to march straight across country. The belt of the Franconian and Thuringian forests and mountains stretches from Bohemia to the longitude of Fulda. It is narrowest in Franconia where Napoleon crossed it. It has been shown that, whilst crossing this hill tract, the army would be marching with a front of about thirty-eight miles as the crow flies, and an equal depth. During this period lateral communication between the columns would be difficult, and often circuitous. Closer connection of the columns was, owing to the position of the roads, impossible; it was only when the opener country beyond the Saale was reached that closing up would be practicable. During this preliminary stage Napoleon expressed his intention of accompanying the centre column; for it, therefore, orders could be issued daily by himself. Not so was it with those of the right and left. To them it was necessary to issue precise instructions for the whole period to be spent in the hill tract, and for their action on first debouching from it. Accordingly, the Emperor issues elaborate orders to Soult and Lannes, whilst contenting himself with much more general orders to Bernadotte. Soult was to have with him only his own light cavalry, and he is warned of the risk of pitting it against the Prussian horsemen, whose reputation was of the highest. Rather, he should endeavour to let the latter break itself against his infantry squares. Should the enemy be found in force watching the issue from the mountains, Soult was permitted to attack him, provided, first, that Ney was able to support the attack; secondly, that the opposing force did not exceed 30,000 men; thirdly, that it was not occupying a selected entrenched position. Failing those conditions, the right column would await the advance of the centre. If the enemy were not in force at Hof, Soult must be guided by the intelligence he might gather in coming to a decision to lean, down the Saale valley, towards the centre, or to take a position beyond Hof, preparatory to marching on Plauen.

Napoleon had little fear of serious resistance to this column. "According to all my information to-day," he writes, "it appears that if the enemy makes any movement, he will do so on my left, since the main body of his forces appears to be at Erfurt."

This last quoted sentence is indicated by Prince Kraft[1] as a proof of the imperfection of the Emperor's intelligence as to the enemy's movements, seeing that there were actually three armies, respectively about Eisenach, Erfurt, and Jena, the last with a strong advanced guard towards Schleiz and Hof. Still, his information was correct generally, in so far as it indicated danger to his left rather than to his right or centre.

To return to Soult's instructions, that marshal's first care, on reaching the open country at Hof, should be to seek for direct communication with the centre towards Lobenstein, Ebersdorf, and Schleiz. This duty was equally inculcated on Lannes and Bernadotte; the latter, strong in cavalry, would feel in both directions. In this despatch to Soult the Emperor indicates Dresden, not Berlin, as his objective; he requires full and early reports of all news regarding events on the great road to Dresden. He was most anxious

---

[1] "Letters on Strategy," i. 21.

Count Yorck von Wartenburg also says that the Emperor had only an imperfect knowledge of the Prussian dispositions. "On which wing his opponent was massing his main strength he did not know; and, indeed, did not care much. For he was determined to advance in the direction which most threatened the enemy's communications" ("Napoleon as a General," i. 277).

to break up the half-hearted alliance between Saxony and Prussia; possibly he thought there was still time to interpose between the Saxon and Prussian armies. He remarks that it would be a great achievement to place his army in a "battalion square of 200,000 men" about Dresden; but he adds, "however, all that demands some art and some events." It is quite certain that, with the Prussian army standing fast about Erfurt and Weimar, he would never have marched away from it on Dresden. What we would venture to suggest is that he thought it not improbable that the Prussians would commence their retreat to the Elbe as soon as he appeared on the Upper Saale; at Dresden, looking to the superior mobility of his army, he would probably find himself still able to intercept the Prussian communications with Berlin, and to interpose between them and the still distant Russians. At Dresden, too, he would have turned the defensive line of the Elbe. Perhaps when he speaks of "some events" he is thinking of an early retreat of the enemy.

Lannes headed the left column, the flank on which the Emperor anticipated an attack, the one whose direction he desired to mask as long as possible. He had already expressed his intention of entirely denuding of troops the whole space between Mayence and Wurzburg. He had found that Königshofen and Schweinfurt were useless to him as points of support; he intended to leave them in a condition not to be of any value to the enemy. Wurzburg, Kronach, and Forchheim (south of Bamberg) were his points of support; in them were collected his depôts of food and ammunition. "You must leave nothing at Schweinfurt; you must assume that, two or three days after your departure, the enemy will be there," wrote Berthier to Lannes on October 5. To mask his movement from Schweinfurt to Coburg, Lannes was to leave cavalry pickets in front of Melrichstadt and Königshofen, with orders to continue reconnoitring as if nothing was happening on the 6th and 7th, and to rejoin the corps at Coburg on the 8th.

The starting-points of these three columns were to be Coburg, Kronach, and Baireuth; they were to reach the Saale valley thus—Soult, at Hof, on the 9th October; Bernadotte, at Saalburg, on the same date; Lannes, at Saalfeld, on the 11th.[1]

The centre was thus the leading column; being the strongest, it could support, if necessary, the issue of the flank columns. The left was the exposed column, therefore it was to be kept well back; though, as a matter of fact, it reached Saalfeld on the morning of the 10th. Lannes was warned[2] that at Coburg he might expect the enemy to be moving, either by the road from Gotha or by that from Saalfeld; therefore, he was to be fully prepared, and was not to move on till he had certain news of Augereau's approach to take his place. In any case his line of retreat would be on Bamberg, by the direct main road, not by that by which he had arrived. Thus, if attacked at Coburg, he would be able to fall back on the support not only of Augereau but of the nume-

---

[1] "You will arrive at Gräfenthal on the 10th" (Berthier to Lannes, 5th October).
[2] Napoleon to Lannes, 7th October (Foucart, i. 366).

rous troops which the Emperor would have at Kronach and Lichtenfels. His zeal in reaching Coburg on the 7th, instead of the 8th, exposed him to Napoleon's censure.

On the 6th the Emperor issued to the army his customary proclamation at the commencement of a campaign:—

"Soldiers! The order for your return to France had already issued; you had drawn nearer to it by several marches. Triumphal fêtes awaited you, and the preparations for your reception had begun in the capital. But, just as we became too confident of security, fresh plots were being woven under the mask of alliance and friendship. Warlike utterances were heard at Berlin. For the last two months we have been subjected to daily increasing provocation. The same faction, the same giddy spirit which, fourteen years ago, favoured then by our internal dissensions, led the Prussians to the midst of the plains of Champagne, still rules their councils. If it is no longer Paris that they seek to burn and destroy, it is to-day their standard which they boast that they will raise in the capitals of our allies; it is Saxony that they seek to compel, by a disgraceful transaction which would range her among their provinces, to renounce her independence; in a word, it is your laurels which they seek to tear from your brows. They wish us to evacuate Germany at the sight of their arms! Madmen! Let them know that it would be a thousand times easier to destroy the great capital than to tarnish the honour of the great people and its allies. In days gone by their schemes were confounded; they found in the

Movements up to 10th October

plains of Champagne defeat, death, and dishonour. But the lessons of experience fade from memory, whilst there are men with whom the sentiment of hatred and jealousy never dies.

"Soldiers! None of you would wish to return to France by any path other than that of honour. We must re-enter it only under triumphal arches. What! have we braved seasons, the ocean, the deserts, have we conquered Europe, several times united in coalition against us, have we carried our glory to the East and the West only to return to our country to-day as fugitives, abandoning our allies, to hear it said that the Eagle of France has fled terrified by the aspect of the Prussian armies?

"Already they are at our outposts. Forward then, since moderation has failed to calm this astonishing intoxication. Let the Prussian army suffer the fate which met it fourteen years ago! Let them learn that, if it is easy with the friendship of the great people to acquire an increase of power and of territory, that people's enmity, which can be provoked only by abandoning the spirit of wisdom and reason, is more terrible than the ocean's tempests."

The action of the French cavalry at the commencement of the campaign requires careful consideration. Prince Kraft has drawn attention to the great difference between Napoleon's use of his cavalry on this occasion and that of the Germans in 1870. But the circumstances were very different also. In 1870, war having been declared many days previously, the cavalry of either side could, at the end of July, cross the frontier, and push far into the enemy's territory without fear of precipitating war. In 1806 it was Napoleon's design to pass the frontier immediately after the declaration of war, and any cavalry movement before that date would anticipate, as Prince Kraft observes, the outbreak of hostilities, and destroy a great deal of the element of surprise which Napoleon hoped to impart to his advance. Yet there can be little doubt that the Emperor to some extent mistrusted his light cavalry, at any rate, in a contest with that of Prussia. Hence we find him directing Bernadotte, if possible, to have infantry in support of it as it issued from the mountains. His advice to Soult on the same subject has already been noted.

The general scheme for the cavalry action is laid down in Berthier's despatch of the 7th October to Murat. On the morning of the 8th one regiment of Wattier's Light Cavalry Brigade, attached to Bernadotte, was to move as far as possible to the front. Lasalle, also with one regiment, would reconnoitre towards Hof on the right, and Milhaud on the left, with another regiment from Lobenstein, towards Gräfenthal and Saalfeld. In support of them, Murat would hold two of Wattier's regiments and one of Lasalle's. Lannes' Light Cavalry would push on to Gräfenthal. The objects of reconnaissance were the nature of the lateral communications between Saalfeld, Saalburg, Lobenstein, Gräfenthal, and Hof; also the situation of the enemy towards Saalburg and Hof, and especially on the great road to Leipzig.

The three parties from the centre were to pass the Saale on the 8th. Bernadotte was, if pos-

Movements up to 10th October

sible, to support them with an infantry brigade between Lobenstein and Ebersdorf; the Saale bridges, if broken, were to be repaired. The Emperor confided the work to Murat in person, as he wished to know, as far as possible, the enemy's position, and to profit by his promptitude in striking a great blow. The dragoons and two divisions of heavy cavalry were in rear; they would be useless at the front during the passage of the hill tract. That country being poor in supplies, the Emperor required his men to carry four days' food on their backs, thus rendering them independent of provision trains, which could be kept back so as to diminish to the utmost the depth of the columns. Once they arrived in the valley of the Saale, provisions would be procurable; for, looking to the Prussian system of magazines, it was safe to calculate on the country not having been exhausted by requisitions. On the 7th October the Emperor announces to Soult the receipt, that morning, of the Prussian ultimatum, which he characterises as the height of folly.

During the 8th the advance progressed, as ordered, without any fighting, beyond a few cavalry skirmishes, the most important of which was at Saalburg. That place was defended by a small force from Tauenzien's advance guard, which had fallen back on it from Gefell, whilst Tauenzien himself retreated from Hof upon Schleiz as Soult advanced. By 3 P.M. Murat was in possession of Saalburg, where the bridge had been left intact. On the evening of the 8th, the leading French corps had reached the following positions:—

Soult was at Munchberg, with light cavalry towards Hof; Bernadotte at Ebersdorf, with four companies of infantry, supporting Murat at Saalburg; Lannes was just beyond Coburg; Napoleon with the Guard reached Kronach.

On the Prussian side, Tauenzien was at Schleiz. Besides his troops there were on the right bank of the Saale 8000 or 9000 Saxons towards Auma, Boguslawski's detachment towards Neustadt, and 600 cavalry under Schimmelpfennig about Pösneck.

On the 9th October occurred the first serious collision between the armies in front of the French centre at Schleiz. When Tauenzien arrived at that place from Gefell on the afternoon of the 8th, and was just starting for Saalburg, he met his detachment falling back and returned with it to Schleiz, intending next morning to continue his retreat on Auma. He waited, however, for orders from Hohenlohe until it was too late to avoid an action with Murat's and Bernadotte's leading troops.

From Saalburg to Schleiz is a distance of about six miles, the road rising gradually along the western slope of the hills separating the Saale from the Elster as it proceeds towards Auma and Naumburg. About half-way, it reaches the large wood of Oschitz lying on the slope on its right and left.

Bernadotte, ordered by the Emperor to attack what was in front of him, directed Werlé, with the four companies in front of Saalburg, to advance on the right of the road clearing the Oschitz wood in that direction, and rejoining Drouet's division on the road beyond as the latter moved on

Movements up to 10th October

Schleiz. Wattier's cavalry followed Drouet, as the country short of Schleiz was unsuited to its action. About 8 A.M., the Prussian outposts being driven in, the wood was occupied by Werlé. Bila II. had now come up on the enemy's side with an advance guard from Schleiz. The French were still too weak to debouch from the wood, and a desultory fire was maintained on its northern edge for several hours. About 2 P.M., as they appeared in greater strength, Tauenzien decided to continue his retreat, which would be covered by Bila with a battalion and one and a half regiments of cavalry. It was not till 4 P.M. that Drouet's arrival enabled the French to attack Schleiz, which they carried an hour after, partly thanks to a turning movement to their left. Beyond Schleiz, Murat, with the 4th Hussars, was at first driven back by the Prussian cavalry. Reinforced by the 5th Chasseurs, he was enabled to drive the Prussians as far as the wood beyond Oettersdorf, though not without difficulty or without the assistance of the infantry which saved him from being attacked in rear. Bila fell back, pursued by the French cavalry.

There was still on the French left a Prussian force of one battalion, one squadron, and two guns, which Tauenzien had sent towards Krispendorf to guard his right and maintain communication with Schimmelpfennig's cavalry at Pösneck. Hobe, commanding the detachment, finding himself in danger of being cut off as Bila retired, commenced to move back. When he reached the wood about Pornitz he found himself almost on the rear of Murat's cavalry, but with an infantry battalion advancing against his right.

Attacked in the marshy wood on all sides, he suffered very heavily; his troops were forced to make the best of their way through, partly towards Tauenzien, partly towards Boguslawski at Neustadt. Many of them were cut down or taken, and one of the guns had to be abandoned.

Bernadotte reports the enemy as 8000 or 9000 strong, and says he only employed 1000 or 1200 infantry and 700 cavalry. As appears from the above account, which is based on Hoepfner's as well as Bernadotte's, all that was engaged on the Prussian side was a weak rearguard which lost about 570 men and one gun.

The French loss was trifling, that of the Prussians occurred chiefly in Hobe's detachment. Tauenzien, reaching Auma about 7 P.M., bivouacked there, his men suffering severely from exhaustion and absence of supplies. The positions of both sides on the night of the 9th were as follows:—

On the French left, Lannes bivouacked about Gräfenthal, with his light cavalry on the road to Saalfeld. Augereau was at and behind Coburg, not far enough advanced to be able to support Lannes in action next day. In the centre, Bernadotte was about Schleiz and Saalburg, the Emperor being at Ebersdorf, after witnessing the action at Schleiz. Davout had reached Lobenstein. Dragoons and heavy cavalry farther to the rear, from Bamberg to Steinwiesen, as well as the Guard cavalry. The Guard infantry was with the Emperor. On the right Soult had occupied Hof without opposition, and reported that Tauenzien had fallen back,

Movements up to 10th October

partly on Schleiz, partly on Plauen, a few troops still further east. The marshal, deciding to move on Plauen, bivouacked between it and Hof. Ney was at and behind Munchberg. Bavarians at Baireuth.

The allies were thus disposed :—

Hohenlohe, with his headquarters and main body (about 8000 men) at Orlamunde, had Prince Louis' advanced guard, of 8000 men, at Rudolstadt and Saalfeld. On the right bank of the Saale, Hohenlohe had Tauenzien and Zeschwitz (together 16,400 strong) about Auma and Mittel Polnitz, Boguslawski (about 3000) at Neustadt. Schimmelpfennig (600 cavalry) towards Pösneck. The main army was about Erfurt. There were detachments at Magdala, Jena, and Lobeda. Weimar's advance guard was between Schmalkalden and Meiningen, with detachments moving southwards towards Schweinfurt.

Ruchel was between Gotha and Eisenach, Blucher at Eisenach, Winning was out to the right at Vach, with a small detachment, under Pletz, still further on the road to Fulda.

From Winning on the right to the Saxons on the left was ninety miles, and the army, besides being thus dispersed, was weakened by the detachment of about 11,000 men under Winning and Weimar. The general reserve, under Eugene of Würtemberg, was completely out of reach near Magdeburg. Napoleon, on the other hand, was still on his front of about thirty-eight miles.

During the night, Napoleon formulated conclusions regarding the enemy's movements and intentions, which he thus explained to Soult in a letter dated from Ebersdorf at 10 A.M. on the 10th. "This is what appears to me most clear; it seems that the Prussians intended to attack; that their left was intended to debouch by Jena, Saalfeld, and Coburg; that Prince Hohenlohe had his headquarters at Jena, and Prince Louis at Saalfeld; the other column has issued by Meiningen on Fulda, so that I am led to believe you have nothing in front of you, perhaps not 10,000 men as far as Dresden." As he finished this despatch he received Soult's of the previous evening, and added a postscript: "The news which you give me, that 1000 men have retired from Plauen on Gera, leaves me no doubt that Gera is the point of union of the enemy's army. I doubt if they can unite before I arrive there."

Had Hohenlohe commanded the allied army, Napoleon's estimate of his intentions would have been fairly correct; for, influenced by Massenbach, the Prince was anxious to move leftwards across the Saale, to join Tauenzien, and meet the French advance in front. Brunswick's views were different. He proposed to concentrate on the left bank, in the triangle Weimar, Jena, Rudolstadt, in the first instance, and had directed Hohenlohe to unite his forces about Hochdorf. This order had created much excitement at Hohenlohe's headquarters, the Prince having decided to move to the right bank to the rescue of Tauenzien, and having informed Brunswick of his intention. There was a good deal of correspondence between the two headquarters, and it was not till the evening of the 9th that Hohenlohe was informed that the orders to

Movements up to 10th October

concentrate were peremptory. In one of his despatches during the day, Brunswick had mentioned that he had no intention of awaiting the enemy on the left bank, though it would not be advisable for Hohenlohe to cross to the right until the concentration was complete. The statement was just one of those which left men like Massenbach some excuse for believing that their schemes would, in the end, be accepted. Assuming that Massenbach and Hohenlohe were justified in believing that a passage to the right bank was eventually to be effected, it is easy to understand that they would be reluctant to withdraw the troops beyond the river, with the prospect of their having to retrace their steps within a day or two.

The Emperor, then, had misjudged the intentions of the Prussian headquarters; but, holding the views he did, he naturally, as he explained to Soult, desired a battle with the enemy's army as it concentrated on Gera. Hitherto he had been moving in as close a state of concentration as the nature of the country would permit; but, for battle, he required a much closer union of his corps, and he issued orders accordingly.

Soult was to move on Gera through Weida, Ney to press on to the neighbourhood of Schleiz, Lefebvre with the Guard was to march to Schleiz itself. Lannes, supported by Augereau, hurrying up by forced marches to attack Saalfeld.

Bernadotte and Murat to proceed at once to Auma to intercept the Saalfeld–Gera route.

The heavy cavalry and dragoons (d'Hautpoult, Nansouty, Klein, Grouchy), and the artillery and engineer parks, were all directed on Schleiz.

Jerome, with the Bavarians, who had blockaded the forts of Culmbach and Plassenburg, and were under orders for Lobenstein, was diverted to Hof, so as to take Ney's place in second line behind Soult. All these orders issued at 8 A.M. on the 10th. As Lannes was only timed to arrive at Saalfeld on the 11th, the concentration could hardly be completed before the evening of the 11th.

During the 10th nothing serious occurred on the line of march of any of the corps except that of Lannes, who fought an action at Saalfeld, the moral effects of which were far more important than might have been expected from the number of troops engaged on either side.

CHAPTER V

THE ACTION OF SAALFELD (OCT. 10)

THE small town of Saalfeld stands mainly on the left bank of the Saale, where that river flows from S.E. to N.W., just before it begins to turn to the N.E. at Schwarza. On the right bank there is a suburb in which the railway station now is. In 1806 the suburb was connected, as it now is, by a bridge with the main town. It is at the mouth of the open valley leading down from Pösneck. As the traveller passes the bridge from the right to the left bank of the Saale, he sees, facing him at a distance of 1½ to 2 miles, the steep wooded slopes of the Franconian mountains rising 1000 feet above the town. A few miles farther on, towards Gräfenthal, they reach an altitude another 1000 feet greater. The line of the hills runs parallel to the Saale as far as the river Schwarza, which joins the larger river on its left bank at the large village of the same name. For a mile or more to the west of Schwarza, the left bank of the Schwarza is precipitous. Then comes the mouth of the valley of Blankenburg, where the Rinne stream joins the left bank of the Schwarza. From Schwarza to Rudolstadt the Saale valley is rather closely shut in by hills rising some 800 feet above it.

From the foot of the wooded hills in front of

Saalfeld, there slopes down to the town, and the river on either side of it, a broad, somewhat steep glacis from 1½ to 2 miles broad. This glacis is by no means smooth, and is furrowed by the ravines of two or three small brooks flowing from the mountains to the Saale; the beds are dry in fine weather. The most important of them are the Siegenbach, passing the west side of Saalfeld, and the ravine which runs down through the villages of Beulwitz, Croesten and Woelsdorf. Both of these afford good cover for troops debouching from the hills towards the Saale, especially for troops employing the skirmishing tactics of the French as opposed to the rigid line formations of their opponents.

During the night of the 9th–10th October, Lannes, as already mentioned, was at Gräfenthal, about twelve miles south of Saalfeld, with his light cavalry patrolling towards the Saale valley at that place. He had only the single main road on which to advance, though, as he approached Saalfeld, he would find small roads and paths by which infantry at any rate could move to either side, and debouch through the small valleys or down the steep slopes terminating at the top of the glacis the foot of which was occupied by the enemy. Lannes' camp fires at Gräfenthal, lighting up the crest of the watershed, were distinctly visible in the clear night to Prince Louis at Rudolstadt.

That commander had at his disposal about 8300 men. The main body and the headquarters were at and near Rudolstadt; 2 battalions, half a battery, and 3 squadrons at Saalfeld; a battery at Schwarza; and at Blankenburg, Pelet's

BATTLEFIELD OF SAALFELD
(Between Garnsdorf and Beulwitz)

THE SAALE NEAR KAHLA
(Looking upstream)

The Action of Saalfeld

detachment of 1 battalion, 1 Jäger company, 3 squadrons, and half a battery, which arrived during the night from Ilmenau. The majority of the troops were Saxons. The Prince himself, aged thirty-three, has been described as the Alcibiades of Prussia. He was one of the principal leaders of the aristocratic party, one of the young military men who favoured war and believed in its hopeful prospects. He and the beautiful Queen Luise of Prussia were the chief leaders of this party. Of him Clausewitz says: "Born with excellent qualities, circumstances would necessarily have made of him a great commander if he had been prepared for it by a long war." That preparation, as will presently appear, he was not destined to enjoy. Critics after the war freely blamed his impetuosity for the first disaster, a censure which has been shown to be by no means entirely merited. For reasons, whether right or wrong, which will shortly be stated, he had resolved on meeting with all his small force the issue of Lannes' corps from the hills.

It was 7 A.M. when the main body started from Rudolstadt to support the advance guard at Saalfeld, to which place Prince Louis in person hurried forward. A French prisoner, captured overnight near Gräfenthal, had stated that Lannes was advancing with 30,000 men, a number greatly in excess of what he actually had. The Prussian outposts near Saalfeld had already been attacked as day broke.

About 9 A.M. the Prince's main body halted short of Saalfeld, and was drawn up by him for battle. His right was just behind Croesten, and Beulwitz, in front of it, was feebly occupied. The line extended leftwards to Saalfeld, in front of which town, on the road to Gräfenthal by which the French were descending, stood more infantry, partly separated from the rest by a projection of the town. Altogether there were 4 Prussian and 6 Saxon battalions, 2½ batteries, and 10 squadrons. Of these, 2 Prussian battalions, 3 squadrons, and half a battery were on the Gräfenthal road and to its right, facing Garnsdorf. The other two Prussian battalions were in second line behind the right; the rest of the cavalry partly in third line behind these battalions, partly in second line in front of the village of Graba. The position was about as bad as it could be. The Prince's line was more than two-thirds of the way down the glacis slope; the Saale was scarcely half a mile behind it, and the town of Saalfeld, with the only passage of the river close behind the left. The right was in the air; for Pelet's detachment, beyond the Schwarza at Blankenburg, could hardly be called a support, though the Prince relied much on him until Brunswick, to whom he had reported his action, should be able to send an advance guard from the main army from Hochdorf.

In his report to Brunswick the Prince speaks of a strong hostile reconnaissance from Gräfenthal, so he apparently did not expect to have to deal with Lannes' whole corps. Meanwhile that marshal had marched from Gräfenthal at 5 A.M., and the head of his leading division (Suchet's) was near the mouth of the deep wooded gorge, through which the road descends, at about 10 A.M. Two companies were sent to occupy the heights on the right of the road, whilst two battalions,

The Action of Saalfeld

with two light guns, pushed on towards the mouth of the valley, where they were received with infantry and artillery fire by the Prussian troops in front of Saalfeld. Lannes, seeing that the enemy meant fighting, ordered the light cavalry, as well as Suchet's division, to advance. The cavalry took post left of Garnsdorf, one battalion and the two guns in and to the right of the village. Covered by them, the rest of the division moved to the left by the roads through the woods on the slope, seeking to cut the enemy's line of retreat by the Rudolstadt road. Swarms of skirmishers fired upon the Prussian line during this operation, and a battery, supported by the battalion at Garnsdorf, fully occupied the attention of the left of the enemy's line. Prince Louis had, between 9 and 10 A.M., reinforced this part of his line with three squadrons, for whose action the ground was ill suited. As the French movement to the left progressed, Lannes brought another battery into action on the right of Beulwitz. The ground was admirably suited to the French tactics, enabling their skirmishers to hold the enemy whilst the infantry columns executed their flank march through the woods.

As the fire of the skirmishers extended farther and farther towards Beulwitz, Prince Louis recognised the aim of the French to outflank his right, and about 11 A.M. commenced to build up some sort of support for that flank. He could no longer resist the conclusion that he had to deal with a superior force. He sent one Prussian battalion to Schwarza, another with a field battery to hold the height known as the Sandberg. A Saxon battalion was placed on the heights between Aue and Croesten to maintain communication between the Sandberg and the troops between Croesten and Graba.

It was just at this juncture that the Prince was further disturbed by a verbal message from Hohenlohe, which must have caused him to doubt how far his action would be approved. This message will be dealt with after the battle has been described.

The Prince now thought his right sufficiently covered to warrant him in attacking with his centre. Two Saxon regiments (those of Prince Xavier and the Elector), moving forward in squares, *en echiquier*, presently arrived so that their right was level with Beulwitz.

Meanwhile, however, Beulwitz had been taken by the French skirmishers creeping up to it along the ravine, and their fire on the right flank of the Saxons compelled the latter to halt and return it. The Xavier regiment wavered and retired in disorder, followed by that of the Elector. This retreat was presently arrested, and a fresh advance against Croesten began. The French skirmishers, running short of ammunition, were unable to repulse this attack, which was made with great vigour by the Elector's regiment. By noon the French had been driven out, and Croesten was held by the Saxons.

At 1 P.M. the French again advanced against Croesten with the 64th Infantry, which had now replaced the 17th, whilst the 88th descended the heights between the Beulwitz and Siegenbach ravines, in support of the cavalry. A fierce struggle ensued, with the result that the Saxons, after a brave resistance, were once more driven back towards Woelsdorf and the Saale.

The Action of Saalfeld

During this period Reille, with the 34th and 40th, continuing to move towards the Sandberg, had debouched through Aue. The troops on the Landberg were overcome after a sharp fight, the battery was captured, and the infantry driven towards Schwarza. As the battalion between Aue and Croesten attempted to follow in the same direction, it was attacked by cavalry and badly cut up, the Saxon general, Bevilaqua, being captured.

Prince Louis, seeing his whole line of infantry in disorder, and his left now driven from in front of Saalfeld, partly over the bridge and partly back on the centre, resolved to do what he could with the five weak squadrons which he was still able to muster in the centre. Heading them in person, he charged the French 9th and 10th Hussars, who were also advancing to complete the work of the infantry. The superior strength of the French hussars enabled them to overlap both flanks of the enemy, who were, moreover, disordered by the uneven ground. The Prince, bravely fighting against these terrible odds, was attacked by Guindet, a quartermaster of the 10th Hussars. Wounded in several places, he still refused to surrender. At last a sword thrust through the body ended his life. He was killed close to where the roadside railway station of Woelsdorf now stands. The spot is marked by a decidedly ugly monument. The death of this fine young prince, the hope and pride of the military party in Prussia, drew from Napoleon the remark that his conduct in promoting the war had earned him his fate; but he had the decency to write a letter of condolence to the King.

All was now lost; the French infantry, following up the success of the hussars, pressed on over the intervening 400 or 500 yards to the Saale, across which the Saxons and Prussians were escaping in small bodies as best they could. Many were captured, cut down, or drowned, and all the guns on this part of the field fell into the hands of the French. Beyond the Saale the ground was rocky and wooded, a fact which to some extent aided the escape of the defeated troops. They were, however, pursued by cavalry right up to the bridge of Rudolstadt, which they crossed only a few minutes before Lannes' third cavalry regiment reached it by the left bank from Schwarza. Farther to the Prussian right, the battalion at Schwarza had been pursued across the Schwarza and driven on Rudolstadt in confusion. Returning from this pursuit, and being reinforced, the cavalry moved up the Schwarza against Pelet's detachment in front of Blankenburg. At the same time French infantry attacked it from Unter Wiebach. Pelet's orders to advance on Saalfeld in the early morning had been cancelled about 8 A.M., and he had remained at Blankenburg, guarding the passage of the Schwarza, without making any serious effort to create a diversion on Suchet's left. He was now aware of the defeat of the rest of the army, and covering the retreat of his half battery by his fusiliers, he fell back over the Schwarza to Stadt Ilm, whence he reached Blankenhain on the 11th, and the neighbourhood of Weimar on the 12th. The Prussians and Saxons lost, according to Hoepfner, under 2000 killed, wounded, and prisoners. Suchet claims to have

The Action of Saalfeld

taken 1500 to 1800 prisoners alone, and it is admitted that 15 Prussian and 18 Saxon guns fell into his hands.[1]

Suchet states his loss at only 172. Even if this is an underestimate, it is probable the loss was small. As a fighting force Prince Louis' corps had been practically annihilated, but the moral effects of his defeat were far greater than is represented by this mere statement. The superiority of the French tactics had been proved, even allowing for the fact that Lannes had brought nearly 14,000 men against 8000. The action had been the first serious affair of the war, and the effect produced on the rest of the army by its result may be likened to that caused by the defeat of the French at Weissemburg in 1870. The Saxons were but unwilling allies of Prussia, and the fact that they had borne the brunt of a heavy defeat, under the leadership, moreover, of a Prussian, was not likely to increase their enthusiasm for the cause. One result of the battle was shown, two days later, in the wild and groundless panic at Jena amongst the Saxons. Prince Kraft undertakes to defend the reputation of the Prussian prince against the popular tradition that he allowed himself to be carried away by his ardour into a rash action of which he became the victim.

On the 9th October he had been informed by Hohenlohe that the latter intended to cross the

[1] Prince Louis had only 2½ batteries with him. Two of the batteries had 8 guns each, the third 12 guns—total, 24; of which 8 were horse-artillery. There were also 16 guns attached to infantry battalions. Pelet had 4 guns (half a battery), which escaped with him. Thus the French took 33 out of a total of 44 guns of all sorts.

Saale on the 10th and concentrate on Mittel Polnitz. In that case Prince Louis, still acting as Hohenlohe's advance guard on the right bank, as he had hitherto done on the left, was to march on Pösneck. Hohenlohe and the Prince equally expected the main army to follow across the Saale. Louis, therefore, understood that his rôle was to cover Hohenlohe's flank march from the enemy advancing on Saalfeld, and, at the same time, to cover the movement of the main army into Hohenlohe's place until the advance guard of the main army could take Louis' place at Rudolstadt. If he were to take post on the *right* bank at Saalfeld, he could perhaps prevent Lannes from crossing and interfering with Hohenlohe as the latter marched from Kahla or Orlamunde to Pösneck, but he could not prevent him from reaching Rudolstadt before the advance guard of the main army. On the *left* bank, at Saalfeld, he hoped to effect both these objects. As the advance guard of the main army reached the neighbourhood, Prince Louis hoped to be able to retire to the right bank at Saalfeld and destroy the bridge. The information which he had up to 11 A.M. on the 10th, therefore, seems to justify the Prince, from a strategical point of view, in his determination to take post on the left bank about Saalfeld. But at that hour he received by the Saxon lieutenant, Egydi, a verbal message from Hohenlohe, in which that commander directed him to hold fast at Rudolstadt and avoid attacking the enemy. Hohenlohe also expressed a hope that the outpost had not been withdrawn from Stadt Ilm—that is, Pelet's detachment. Had the

The Action of Saalfeld

message stopped there, it is impossible to doubt that Prince Louis would have been bound, if possible, to return to Rudolstadt and avoid Lannes; but it went on to say that Hohenlohe hoped on the 10th to have his headquarters at Kahla, whence he would inspect the whole line as far as Neustadt and meet Prince Louis. This seems to have induced the Prince to believe that the march on Pösneck was still in contemplation. Prince Kraft thinks he was justified in this assumption; but, looking to the precision of the earlier part of the orders directing him to stay at Rudolstadt, it seems doubtful if this was so. Could Prince Louis have broken off the action when Hohenlohe's message reached him? It would seem that the answer to this question should be in the affirmative. Suchet's skirmishers were still only approaching Beulwitz; and it is difficult to believe that the allied left, or at any rate the centre, could not have been withdrawn behind the right to Schwarza, Pelet at the same time being drawn somewhat nearer to Schwarza to act with the troops at Aue and on the Sandberg as rearguard. If it was too late to draw in the extreme left, it could have fallen back across the Saale by the bridge at Saalfeld, and have reached Rudolstadt by the right bank, as part of it actually did after the defeat. The objections to such a separation of his forces on the part of the Prince are obvious; but it would have been a possible remedy in a desperate situation. On these grounds it seems difficult to accept as convincing Prince Kraft's vindication of the Prince's continuation of the action after eleven o'clock. At that time he was not irretrievably committed to it as regards his centre and right. It is almost impossible to defend his decision to fight on such a hopelessly bad tactical position against superior numbers.

Lannes had attacked at Saalfeld unsupported by Augereau, who wrote, so late as 4 P.M. on the 10th from Coburg, regretting that he was unable to arrive, giving as his excuse that he had no orders for his movement beyond that place. Lannes excuses his breach of the Emperor's orders, fixing his arrival at Saalfeld for the 11th, on the ground that, hearing a sharp fusillade in the direction of the centre, he thought his movement would effect a diversion. His action in attacking without the possibility of support from Augereau was certainly a violation of his orders. His assumption of responsibility was fully justified by his great success. Augereau's excuse for not following closer on Lannes' heels shows a lamentable want of initiative. It is certainly one which would never have been pleaded by Lannes himself, or by the majority of Napoleon's lieutenants. At the same time, it marks the crushing influence on initiative which was exercised by the personality of the Emperor on his weaker subordinates, and their tendency to act as mere tools in his hands.

Plan for Action at Saalfeld

Scale 0 1000 2000 3000 4000 metres.

Contours at intervals of 100′

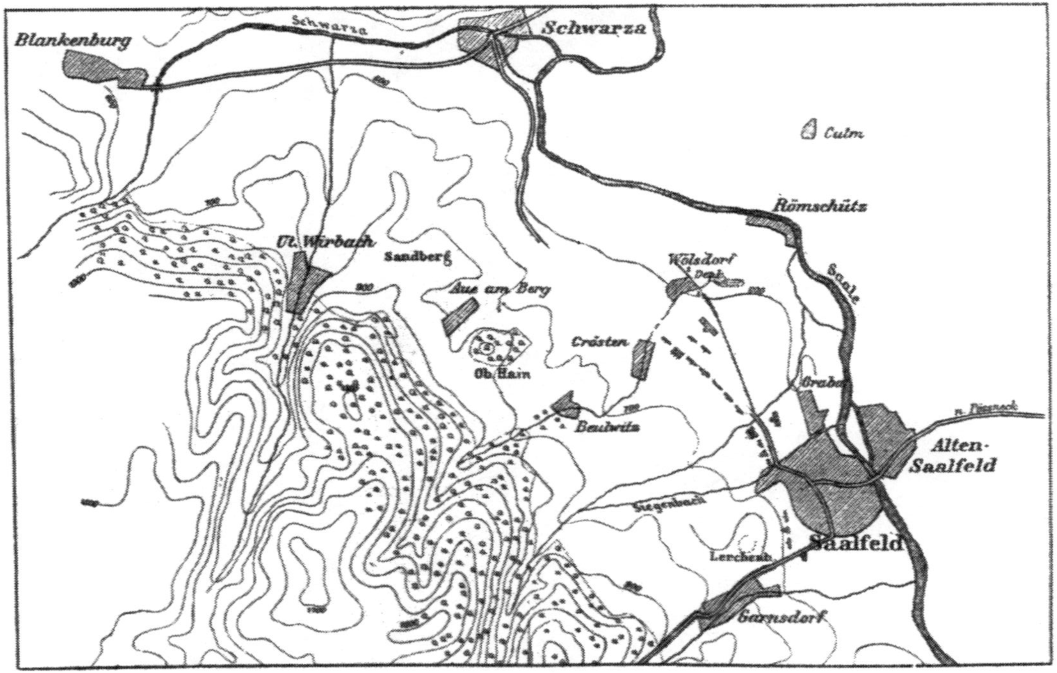

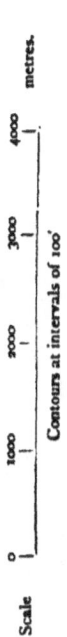

CHAPTER VI

OPERATIONS FROM THE 10TH TO THE 13TH OCTOBER

THE positions of the French army on the night of the 10th October were as follows :—

Soult was at Plauen, with cavalry at Reichenbach on the Dresden road, which appeared to be almost clear of the enemy. On his left, Ney stood between Gefell and Tanna; Bernadotte was about Auma with two divisions, Dupont's being at Posen, Wattier's light cavalry nearly up to Neustadt.[1] Murat, in front of him at Triptis, had Lasalle at Mittel Pölnitz, and Beaumont's dragoons on his left rear. Sahuc's dragoons were at Schleiz, where also were Davout and the Guard infantry. Nansouty's heavy cavalry was at Nordhalben, d'Hautpoult's at Kronach. Klein was at Lichtenfels, the Guard cavalry and artillery still at Bamberg, Grouchy in rear.

The Bavarians were at Culmbach, Lannes at Saalfeld, Augereau at and behind Neustadt on the road from Coburg to Gräfenthal.

At the same time the Allies were thus disposed. Hohenlohe still had part of his force

---

[1] North of the Saale. There are several places of this name, which must not be confused. The Neustadt mentioned in connection with Augereau is much farther south.

between the Saale and the Elster, but he had received positive orders in the night of the 9th to 10th to draw them in, and they were now on the march for the Saale. Zeschwitz's Saxons and Tauenzien had reached Roda; Boguslawski was falling back from Neustadt on Kahla, and Schimmelpfennig in the same direction from Pösneck. Hohenlohe's main body was at Jena, Lobeda, Kahla and Orlamunde. The main army was in the neighbourhood of Blankenhain, Gravert's division at Spahl, and detachments at Remda and Stadt Ilm. Ruchel was at Erfurt, with Blucher between Eisenach and Gotha. Winning was still out at, and beyond, Vach. The Duke of Weimar was at Meiningen, with infantry out as far as Königshofen and cavalry close to Schweinfurt.

The necessity for concentration had at last dawned on the Prussian headquarters. At 10 P.M. Hohenlohe received orders to concentrate with his left at Jena, his right towards Weimar. The rest of the army was to assemble at Weimar. This order reached Hohenlohe just after Massenbach had started for headquarters to urge either a general concentration at Erfurt, or a march by the left to anticipate the French on the Elbe.

The news collected on the 11th induced an entire change of Napoleon's views as to the Prussian movements. He learned the defeat of Prince Louis at Saalfeld, and that nothing had been found supporting him as far as Rudolstadt. The Saxon baggage had been captured marching westwards. Mittel Polnitz, Neustadt, Pösneck had all been evacuated; the enemy's troops were clearly making for the Saale towards Jena. There could be no doubt that there would be no attempt on his part to concentrate towards Gera, or that he contemplated a retreat beyond the Saale. Murat's reports led Napoleon to believe that the Prussians were about to concentrate on Erfurt. Thus he fell into an error opposite to that into which he had fallen with regard to the movement on Gera. He believed that he could not now reach the Allied army east of Erfurt, whereas it was really endeavouring to concentrate east of Weimar. There exists an undated note, entirely in Napoleon's handwriting, containing memoranda of distances and possible positions of his troops on different dates. This note is attributed by the editors of the correspondence of Napoleon to the 10th October, but Foucart shows that probably the first part only was written on the 10th, whilst the second part dates from the night of the 11th to 12th.[1]

The important point is that Napoleon, in the second part, calculates the position he expected his corps to reach on the 14th. The first line would consist of Augereau at Mellingen, Lannes between Jena and Weimar, and Davout at Apolda. The second line would be Ney at Kahla, Soult at Jena, and Bernadotte at Dornburg. Reserve cavalry and the Guard behind Jena. The army would thus be concentrated on a front of about eight miles from Mellingen to Apolda, the depth from Apolda to Dornburg would be about equal to the front, whilst that from Mellingen to Kahla would be about 13 miles. As Lannes is

[1] The note and the argument will be found in full in Foucart, i. 512.

noted to be at Weimar on the 15th, it is clear that a westward march was contemplated. It is also clear that the Emperor did not expect a battle till the 15th or 16th, for it was his invariable practice to concentrate for battle before reaching the battlefield, not on it. On the night of the 11th the army was facing north, with Augereau at Saalfeld, Lannes at Neustadt, Soult about Weida, Bernadotte at Gera, Ney at Schleiz, Davout at Mittel Polnitz. With the views which he now held as to the Prussian movements the Emperor, seeking a battle, must clearly change front to the west, pivoting on his left. He proposed, in the first instance, to place his army on a front extending from Kahla on the left to Naumburg on the right, a position to be gained on the 12th. On the 13th he would give a general rest to his army, every corps of which had been marching hard, some of them fighting also, since the 7th or earlier. Soult's leading division was at least 30 miles from Naumburg by the shortest route; Ney was still farther. On the other hand, Bernadotte was only about 22 miles from Naumburg, and Davout about 27. Therefore, the centre column (Bernadotte and Davout) could reach Naumburg in one long march, whilst the right (Soult and Ney) could scarcely do so, and it would save time as well as fatigue to the troops to move the original centre to the right, whilst the present right took its place. Notwithstanding the inconvenience of the crossing of the lines of communication, Napoleon decided on this measure. His orders, issued on the evening of the 11th, were thus executed on the 12th.

From 10th to 13th October

Bernadotte, marching from Gera by Zeitz, had by evening reached Meineweh, nearly half-way from Zeitz to Naumburg. Davout's leading division, marching from Mittel Polnitz, reached a point $2\frac{1}{2}$ miles short of Naumburg, his second and third were echeloned along the road from Mittel Polnitz to a distance of $7\frac{1}{2}$ miles from Naumburg. The light cavalry was in and beyond Naumburg, and down the Saale and Elster, at Weissenfels and Pegau. Sahuc's dragoons were with Davout. Milhaud, on Bernadotte's right, was at Teuchern. The heavy cavalry was behind at Auma and Schleiz. Guard cavalry still at Lobenstein. Headquarters of the Emperor and Guard at Gera. Ney was at Auma, the Bavarians far back at Steinwiesen. None of these corps had found anything in front of them. Before narrating the marches of Lannes and Augereau, it is necessary to give the enemy's positions during the night of 11th to 12th. The main army was at Weimar, on the right bank of the Ilm; Ruchel and Blucher on the left bank. Hohenlohe held Jena and Lobeda. Winning was still at Vach, with Pletz out beyond Fulda. The Duke of Weimar had begun his retreat, moving to his left and reaching Frauenwald on the 12th. The reserve, under Duke Eugene of Würtemberg, was about Halle. Lannes reached Neustadt from Saalfeld on the 11th, and now received orders to march on Jena, *viâ* Kahla. Augereau's orders, to advance to Kahla from Saalfeld, did not reach him till, in accordance with previous orders, he had arrived within two hours' march of Neustadt. Therefore, instead of proceeding by Rudolstadt direct from Saalfeld, as was apparently intended, he had to go nearly to Neustadt, there doubling back, to recross the river at Kahla behind Lannes. About 2 P.M. on the 12th, Lannes' advance guard came into collision with Prussian outposts at Goeschwitz, rather more than half-way from Kahla to Jena, and drove them in with some loss on their main body at Winzerle. The valley here is more than half a mile wide between the Saale and the foot of the hills on the left bank. Here again there was a sharp fight, ending in the retreat of the Prussian advance guard. The attack appears to have been assisted by one on the bridge of Burgau from the right bank. Lannes, from Kahla, had sent a detachment along the Naumburg road on that bank; apparently it was part of this which attacked the bridge at Burgau. The fifth corps bivouacked behind Winzerle, some three miles short of Jena.

Napoleon's movements on the 12th have been somewhat unfavourably criticised by Prince Kraft. In the first place, he thinks that the interchange of positions, between the centre and right, must have caused great confusion in the crossing of columns. A careful examination of the map appears to show that this idea is mistaken, and that to have maintained Bernadotte, Davout, Soult, and Ney in their original relative positions would, on the contrary, have resulted in the very difficulties expected by the Prince. Taking the orders issued, it appears that Bernadotte, if he started from Gera at the same time as Soult started from Weida and south of it, must have had at least three or four hours to get clear of Gera before the head of Soult's column began to

From 10th to 13th October

arrive there. As Soult was not to pass Gera without further orders (which the Emperor, himself present at Gera, could issue or withhold as circumstances required), there was clearly no need for him to cross Bernadotte's line at all. Davout's line of march from Mittel Polnitz would not cross that of any other corps, and would only be crossed by Soult next day in rear of Davout, as the latter marched to his left. Ney, marching on Roda, would equally not cross or be crossed by any other corps. Now take the case if Napoleon had kept the columns in their old relative positions. Soult would still have had to march through Gera, and then towards Naumburg, whilst Bernadotte moved westwards. The case of these two corps would have been much the same as it actually was. Ney, marching on Naumburg, would have had to follow Davout to the crossing of the road from Gera to Roda, and would therefore have been in a somewhat similar position, with reference to Davout's movement, to that occupied by Soult with reference to Bernadotte. Moreover, Bernadotte, marching from Gera to Roda, would have crossed Davout's line, and, as Gera and Mittel Polnitz are about equidistant from the crossing of the Mittel Polnitz-Naumburg and Gera-Roda roads, Davout and Bernadotte would have met at the crossing, and there would have been an inextricable confusion at that point of the two corps. Surely Napoleon's arrangement was far better than this!

Again, Prince Kraft blames the exposure of Augereau, unsupported as he marched by the left bank of the Saale through Rudolstadt to

Kahla. As a matter of fact Augereau did *not* march by the left bank,[1] though, no doubt, Napoleon intended him to do so, and thereby exposes himself to the Prince's criticism. Nor did Lannes remain on the right bank, as Prince Kraft seems to think. He crossed with the greater part of his corps at Kahla, only sending a detachment along the right bank to feel towards Naumburg. Thus, on the evening of the 12th, Augereau, at Kahla, was on the left bank, with Lannes in front of him, on the same side, at Winzerle. It is impossible to deny that their force, of not more than 39,000 men, was very dangerously exposed to attack and defeat by the Prussian army, as it actually stood. The reason for this has already been implied. Napoleon, as has been shown, believed that the enemy would not be found in force short of the Ilm. Had he realised their actual positions, it is almost impossible to believe he would have exposed his weak left wing to the great risk it undoubtedly incurred, on the 12th and 13th, of being crushed by the greater part of the Prussian army. Even with the belief he held, it would seem that an unnecessary risk was run, seeing the by no means positive character of his information.

During the 12th no very material changes occurred in the position of the allied army. Weimar, at Frauenwald, was still two long marches from the point of concentration, Winning and Pletz were still farther off; otherwise, the army was concentrated at last between Weimar and Jena, with posts on the Saale between

[1] This is clear from Foucart's book, which had not been published when Prince Kraft wrote.

From 10th to 13th October

Jena and Camburg. Demoralisation had, however, proceeded far in the ranks, and had been aggravated by the disaster of Saalfeld. On the afternoon of the 11th, as the Saxons, retreating from Roda, reached Jena, some one raised the cry, "The French are in the city." The alarm was absolutely groundless, but it produced a most disastrous panic. The troops rushed across the bridge, seeking security from the dreaded foe. Gunners cut the harness of their teams, and fled with the horses, leaving the guns blocking the streets of the suburb on the eastern bank; ammunition and provision waggons, abandoned by their drivers, added to the confusion. Hohenlohe, who had just sat down to dinner, mounted his horse and strove to quiet the tumult, but in vain. The alarm cry was echoed by the inhabitants from all sides, and it was long before this wild terror and panic were discovered to be groundless. There was not a French soldier within many miles; had there been but a handful of cavalry they would have gathered a rich harvest of prisoners, guns, and supplies. Even in the main army discouragement and insubordination had made headway. Confusion reigned in all quarters, food was not always forthcoming; the Saxons especially had already known the pangs of hunger.

It was on the 12th that Napoleon at last deigned to send an answer to the Prussian king's ultimatum. The terms of the Emperor's letter were overbearing, and expressive in the plainest terms of his assurance of victory. No king with any self-respect, or any chance of escape, could have accepted its offer of peace on Napoleon's terms. That Napoleon believed or hoped that it would procure the Prussian submission without a battle is certainly not the case. He would not even send it by one of his own aides-de-camp; he gave it to Rapp first, but recalled him, saying that that was making too much of it, and made it over to de Montesquiou, an orderly officer and aide-de-camp of Davout.[1] The bearer, whether purposely delaying or not, only reached Dornburg on the evening of the 13th, and the letter was placed in the King's hands, when his armies at Jena and Auerstädt were already half defeated, next day. On the morning of the 13th Napoleon had received reports from all his marshals except Lannes. Davout had announced the capture of Naumburg, with immense magazines collected for the Prussian army. It being the Emperor's intention to give his army a rest on this day, the only movements at first ordered were, Ney from Auma to Roda, Bernadotte to join Davout at Naumburg. Orders were despatched for the collection of a great central magazine at Auma, by moving up the supplies on the road from Kronach. The day was to be employed, by the corps not moving, in filling up stores of provisions and ammunition. The Emperor still, at 7 A.M. on the 13th, expected battle only on the 16th beyond Weimar; at 9 all was changed: "At last the veil is rent asunder; the enemy is commencing his retreat on Magdeburg."[2] Murat and Bernadotte were ordered from Naumburg to Dornburg to fill the space between Davout and Lannes, and to be able to succour the latter

[1] Rapp, 76.   [2] Napoleon to Murat (Foucart, i. 579).

MARSHAL LANNES
(From an engraving in Mr. Broadley's collection)

should he be attacked. Soult was ordered to move one division and his cavalry to Roda, the other two to Kostritz. Nansouty and d'Hautpoult were called up to Roda.

By the time the Emperor was within five or six miles of Jena, in the early afternoon, he fully expected to be attacked the same evening, or, at any rate, next day.[1] The Guard infantry were ordered to advance with all haste on Jena, Soult and Ney receiving similar orders. Napoleon now knew that Lannes was faced by 40,000 or 50,000 Prussians. If Davout and Bernadotte heard an attack on Lannes that evening, they were to manœuvre to their left to his assistance. In all the orders after 9 A.M. there is breathless haste. The Emperor had calculated the final concentration of his army for a battle on the 16th; he now found he would have to fight two days sooner, and he was not concentrated as he would wish to be.

We must return to the doings of Lannes and the 5th Corps, whom we left bivouacking about Winzerle, after driving in the enemy's advance guard. At daybreak on the 13th the marshal, in the midst of a thick mist, picked his way cautiously along the valley to Jena and the road from Weimar, which reaches the Saale at that town.

It often facilitates description of a locality when it is possible to compare it with some well-known place in the reader's country. There is a strong resemblance in many general features between the country about Jena and that in the neighbourhood of Dorking. With a few imagi-

[1] Berthier to Lefebvre (Foucart, i. 585).

nary alterations Dorking and Box Hill can be made very closely to resemble Jena and the Landgrafenberg. In the first place, it is necessary to substitute for the railway line from Reigate to Guildford a river of perhaps the dimensions of the Thames just above Reading, flowing from the direction of Guildford towards Reigate. The gap in the plateau north of Dorking, represented by the valley of the Mole, must be reduced to a comparatively narrow gorge, which would then stand for the Muhlthal, down which, to the Saale, flows a small brook, and through which winds the road leading generally downwards from Weimar to Jena. The country to the south of the railway must be imagined as a plateau generally resembling that actually existing to the north. Finally, suppose Dorking to lie close under Box Hill at the corner of the valley leading to Leatherhead, and the resemblance between the two places will be complete. From Jena there leads up to the Landgrafenberg a steep road to a height about equal to that of Box Hill. Then there are 400 yards or so of easier slope, and finally the height is crowned by a knoll which was formerly known as the Windknolle, but, since 1806, has been known as the Napoleonsberg. The plateau beyond that we will describe presently.

When Lannes' men reached Jena on the morning of the 13th October, they found the town scarcely held by the enemy, and had no difficulty in establishing themselves in it. The skirmishers of Suchet's division, which led the advance, at once began to push up the steep wooded slopes of the Landgrafenberg. Presently the rattle of musketry showed that they were in contact with the enemy. Instantly Reille with the 40th of the line was sent to their assistance. The height was gained, and a precarious foothold was obtained on the angle of the plateau as Tauenzien's advance guard, which had feebly defended the steep slope, fell back to the line between Lutzeroda and Closewitz. Lannes, standing on the Windknolle, as the mists were dissipated by the increasing heat of the sun, gazed upon a grand though alarming scene. Before him lay an army, which he rightly estimated at about 40,000 men, ranged in three lines between him and Weimar. As he watched the sun sparkling on the long lines of bayonets, sabres, and cuirasses he must have realised to the full the peril of his situation. Tauenzien's force, about Lutzeroda and Closewitz, was alone more than sufficient to sweep back, down the precipitous hill by which they had ascended, the handful of infantry Lannes had. For hours he could not hope to be more than one-fourth of the strength of the great army which appeared to be on the point of surging forward to overwhelm him. But Lannes' personal courage was equalled by his confidence in command; he had no thought of retirement. Suchet's men were hurrying up, and, even without artillery, he hoped to be able to hold on. Fortune indeed favoured him. He was right in believing that the enemy contemplated sweeping him in ruin into the Saale, and had the attack, as Hohenlohe was preparing to make it, been delivered, the result was almost a foregone conclusion. Just at this juncture, however, Hohenlohe's evil genius once more misled him. Massenbach had, after the vicious practice of the Prussian staff, been summoned to headquarters to receive an explanation of the plans which had now been decided on.

Clausewitz, discussing the strategical situation of the Prussian army on the 13th October, looks upon it as by no means a hopeless one. It stood on the left flank of the French line of advance to Berlin. If Napoleon continued his march on the capital, the Prussians would be able to operate against his communications. This case may be dismissed at once, for Napoleon was the last commander in the world to neglect the enemy's army merely for the sake of occupying territory which, with victory over the main army, must necessarily fall into his hands, and without victory would be useless and dangerous. There were two other alternatives. The Prussian army might await Napoleon's attack across the Saale. In that case the strong line of the river, if properly defended, would be an obvious advantage. The other alternative was to make a flank march towards Leipzig, seeking to head off the French about that city. Even in this case the Saale would be of great advantage in covering the right of the flank march, provided the passages at Dornburg, Camburg, and Koesen were firmly held; for the Saale is "a river deeply sunk, and offering few points of passage," at least in this part of its course. This last alternative was the one accepted.

Clausewitz says all three plans were discussed, grimly adding that even if the best were chosen,

From 10th to 13th October

it was safe to be ruined in execution in the confusion and irresolution prevailing at the Prussian headquarters. Whatever might be thought of the flank position in the abstract, the same author says that it was not a desirable one to be held, against a very superior foe like Napoleon, by an army which was not very sure about what it was doing or intended to do. It had been decided then that the main army should march on the 13th by the left bank of the Ilm, making for the passage of the Unstrut, at Freiburg; beyond that river it would be joined by the reserve under Duke Eugene of Würtemberg, moving from Halle. The right flank of the march was to be protected by seizure of the defile of Koesen on the 13th.

Ruchel (without Blucher, who led the cavalry of the main army) was to wait at Weimar till joined by the Duke of Weimar, who could only reach Ilmenau on the evening of the 13th, and would then still be 28 miles from Weimar. The united forces would then follow the main army. To Hohenlohe the part assigned was the covering of the whole of this movement, by means of his 38,000 men, in the triangle of which Weimar, Jena, and the mouth of the Ilm indicated the angles. He was to play a purely defensive rôle.

On the rebellious Massenbach the defensive nature of Hohenlohe's part seems, as Prince Kraft surmises, to have been impressed with such force as, at last, to reduce even him to passive and blind obedience to the letter of his orders. He failed to see that the observance of the strategical defensive by no means excluded a tactical offensive. Thus, when he found Hohenlohe about noon bent on attacking Lannes and driving him into the Saale, as he could so easily have done, Massenbach related his orders, and maintained that the contemplated attack would be a violation of them. Hohenlohe, whilst vehemently asserting that it would be the right course, as it undoubtedly was, allowed himself to be over persuaded by his quartermaster-general. The movement being abandoned, Hohenlohe's army quietly returned to camp, in the space between Isserstadt and Capellendorf, leaving Lannes and Napoleon, who reached the Landgrafenberg in person about 4 P.M., to fix themselves firmly in their dangerous position.

The Emperor, whilst rightly accepting Lannes' estimate of 40,000 or 50,000 as the strength of the army before him, wrongly thought—and he continued so to think till the morning of the 15th—that he had before him the whole of the Prussian army. He was entirely ignorant of the march of the King, with Brunswick and the main army, beyond the Ilm.

The whole of Lannes' corps, except the artillery, reached the plateau in the afternoon; the Guard infantry arrived in the evening. These were all the troops the Emperor had on the plateau as night fell.

During the afternoon and evening he was busily engaged in reconnoitring the enemy's position; so far did he go forward that, as he returned in the dark, one of his own sentries, mistaking the party for Prussians, fired upon him. He was restless and anxious; for it cannot be doubted that he realised the danger of his position should he be attacked in great force before his reinforcements could reach him. He must have known that 40,000 or 50,000 men did not represent the whole or even half the strength of the Prussian army ; and, for all he knew, the rest might even now be moving east from Weimar towards him. He himself pointed out the positions to be occupied by his troops.

After supping with the generals present on the plateau, he started downhill on foot to see that all was well with the artillery and ammunition on the steep ascent from Jena. He was furious at discovering that the head of the artillery column had in the dark mistaken a narrow ravine for the road. So narrow was it that the axle-boxes of the leading guns were jammed in the rocks on either side. The whole column was stuck fast, unable either to advance or retire.

Angry as he was at the mistake, and at the absence of the general in command of the artillery, he wasted no time in recriminations. Once more he was the artillery officer. Assembling the weary gunners, he provided them with tools fetched from the park in rear, and with lanterns, and set them to work to hack a way for the guns. Himself holding a lantern, he urged on the work. Tired as they were, the men laboured under the eyes of the Emperor without a murmur, until at last the obstacle was removed, and the long column began to move slowly on.[1]

What a scene for the brush of a Rembrandt! It is easy to picture, as one walks down the steep road from the Landgrafenberg to Jena, how the artillery column might stray into one of the small ravines which here and there run parallel to the

[1] Savary, *Mémoires*.

road, which is said to be still very much as it was in 1806.

The Emperor slept but little, visiting the outposts more than once in the night. What rest he took was in a rough straw lean-to, put up for him by the grenadiers of the 40th in their midst.[1]

[1] Suchet's report (Foucart, i. 589).

CHAPTER VII

THE BATTLE OF JENA

AS Napoleon and Lannes, on the afternoon of the 13th October, stood surveying the situation from the Windknolle—rightly so named as the breeziest point in the neighbourhood—they saw, just to their right, the road from Jena to Apolda running a point or two to the west of north. It almost exactly bisects the angle formed by the Muhlthal on the left leading towards Weimar, and the valley of the Saale between Jena and Koesen. It passes along a sort of saddle of only 200 or 300 yards width. From either side of it a valley runs down—that on the left just in front of the village of Cospeda to the Muhlthal, that on the right to the Saale valley at Lobstadt, a village occupying much the same position in reference to Jena that Betchworth occupies in respect of Dorking. Beyond Cospeda, somewhat to the right, is the village of Lutzeroda; and beyond that again, to the left, is the great wood of Isserstadt, with the village of the same name at its farther extremity, about 2¼ miles as the crow flies from the Windknolle. On the right is seen the village of Closewitz, at the head of the ravine leading down to the Saale, situated about a mile from the Windknolle and some 200 yards to the right of the Apolda road. That road, after passing near Closewitz, mounts the slope of a broad down called the Dornberg, the rounded top of which is some 100 feet higher than the Windknolle, and therefore shuts out the view towards Apolda. Lutzeroda is just visible over the left slope of the Dornberg. It is only as it sinks down towards the left that it becomes possible to see the country beyond, towards Isserstadt and Schwabhausen, where the main body of Hohenlohe's army was encamped. It was on to the Dornberg, and to Closewitz and Lutzeroda, that Tauenzien retired when he had so feebly allowed himself to be driven from the Landgrafenberg by Suchet's infantry. He still held the most defensible position on the plateau; for beyond the Dornberg it becomes a mere rolling country, perfectly open, without any considerable slope, and with nothing but unfenced fields, which in October were bare of all crops but potatoes and turnips. As it reaches the top of the Dornberg, the Apolda road has on its right a large wood, the Pfarr Holz. Beyond this on the right there is a clearing and then another wood, the Loh Holz, which almost adjoins the woods which fill the Rauthal, the valley leading up from Lobstadt in the Saale valley to Closewitz. The Rauthal, starting upwards from Lobstadt, is at first not very steep; then it becomes much steeper, and is entirely filled with woods. Rather more than half-way up to the plateau the valley bifurcates, the branch to the left (as you mount) going to Closewitz, whilst the other leads along the eastern edge of the Closewitz wood in the direction of the village of Rödigen.

On the left of the spectator standing on the

The Battle of Jena 123

Windknolle is the deep Muhlthal, separating the plateau on which he stands from that of Lichtenhain, south of Jena. Up the Muhlthal runs the road to Weimar from Jena. As the Muhlthal mounts to the broad saddle joining the two plateaux, the road, in 1806, zigzagged up, and was called the Schnecke ("snail"). It left Isserstadt well to its right; nowadays it is carried up the heights to that village, instead of proceeding direct to Kotschau and Weimar. It forms the southern boundary of the triangle of which the other two sides are the Saale, between Jena and Koesen, and the Ilm, between Weimar and Koesen. The general slope of the plateau is downwards towards Weimar and the Ilm, the latter river being mostly much less deeply sunk than the Saale.

There are two more features of the plateau north-west of the Dornberg which played a considerable part in the battle, and therefore require some notice. The first is the long valley originating near the village of Krippendorf and gradually becoming deeper and deeper as it runs north-east past Alt Gönna, Lehesten, Nerkwitz, and Neu Gönna to the Saale a short way above Dornburg. The second is another shallower valley passing across the Weimar road between Hohlstadt and Frankendorf, and descending to the Ilm at Apolda. With these two exceptions, the plateau beyond the Dornberg is an almost featureless plain till it drops suddenly to the valley of the Ilm. It has several substantial villages, which have perhaps grown in size and prosperity since 1806; otherwise it appears, from a comparison between modern and older maps, to be just as it was one hundred years ago. No railway traverses it; there are some new metalled roads, it is true, but roads in this open country in dry weather are of little importance from a military point of view. The woods which were growing in 1806 are still the same now, and the whole scene cannot differ materially from what Napoleon saw when he had gained Lutzeroda and looked westwards towards Weimar, eight or ten miles away.

Hohenlohe's main body was encamped facing the Weimar road between the Schnecke and Capellendorf. The Saxon infantry were on the left between the Schnecke and Kotschau, with the cavalry just west of Isserstadt. The Prussians were in the space between Kotschau, Klein Romstadt, and Capellendorf, with some hussars as far forward as Hohlstadt. The extreme left wing was formed by Tauenzien's rearguard, chiefly Prussians, whom Suchet had driven off the Landgrafenberg to Closewitz, the slopes of the Dornberg, and Lutzeroda. Napoleon from the Windknolle could see these latter clearly; the camps of the main body were only partially visible over the wood of Isserstadt.

Towards 3 P.M. Hohenlohe received intelligence which led him to believe that the enemy was advancing to the plateau from Camburg and Dornburg. Taking a brigade of 4 battalions, 21 squadrons, and 2 batteries, he marched for Dornburg, only to find that it was as yet unoccupied, though large quantities of supplies had been ordered for Bernadotte. These he took or destroyed, and leaving a cavalry outpost in Dornburg, ordered the rest of the

The Battle of Jena 125

force, under Holtzendorf, to occupy the villages on the plateau above, so as to be ready to meet the enemy should he debouch from either Dornburg or Camburg.

In Dornburg had been captured Montesquiou, carrying the Emperor's letter of the 12th to the King. Having no trumpeter with him, he was at first treated as a prisoner, and the letter was not forwarded to the King till late at night, and reached him only next morning. It was not till 9 or 10 P.M. that Hohenlohe returned to Capellendorf. Tauenzien had been left with 13 battalions, 8 squadrons, and $1\frac{1}{2}$ batteries to hold the line Closewitz–Lutzeroda against Lannes, whom Hohenlohe persisted in considering as a mere advance guard. The Prince was persuaded that nothing serious, especially in Tauenzien's direction, would occur on the 14th.

On the French side, as Lannes' corps reached the plateau, it was disposed across the angle, with the left of Gazan's division resting on the ravine in front of Cospeda, and the right of Suchet's on the wood in front of Closewitz. The French and Prussian outposts on this line were almost touching one another. Behind Lannes' divisions, the infantry of the Guard bivouacked in squares on the Windknolle. With the Guard were Lannes' light cavalry. The artillery as it arrived was placed in the intervals. Lannes had 28 guns; of the Guard artillery only 14 guns had so far arrived. Of infantry there were about 24,000, and of cavalry some 1500. Augereau, marching in the early part of the night from Kahla to the Muhlthal, would be available in the early morning on the battlefield. Ney could only reach it early with his advanced guard of 3400 picked troops, Soult only with St. Hilaire's division. The rest of these corps marched through the night, but could not be expected before at earliest 11 A.M. At that hour, too, the arrival of d'Hautpoult's and Nansouty's heavy cavalry, and Klein's dragoons, might be looked for. Thus, if the Emperor found himself compelled to oppose the enemy in the very early morning with but 25,500 men, he could rely on having 55,000 by nine or ten o'clock, nearly 80,000 between eleven and twelve, and 96,000 soon after the latter hour. Further, he believed that by 4 P.M. another 55,000 men of the corps of Davout and Bernadotte, the third dragoon division, and Lasalle's light cavalry would be on the enemy's left flank and rear. This latter expectation was not realised, and would not have been formed had the Emperor not been ignorant of the march of the main Prussian army behind the Ilm.

Even though he had to fight two days before he expected, Napoleon was thus able to unite on one battlefield 150,000 men out of the 165,000 whom he had, exclusive of the allies. Nevertheless, he was not on the 13th concentrated for battle as he would have wished to be. He had to impose enormous tasks on many of his troops; 15,000 of them could not possibly reach the battlefield. Here fortune once more favoured him; for, had he been concentrated, the Prussian main army would have escaped, for the moment at least, and his success would have been but half what it actually was.

The Battle of Jena 127

The whole of Hohenlohe's army amounted to but 38,000 men, with $12\frac{1}{2}$ batteries, and it was so distributed that it came into action only piecemeal. In Napoleon's immediate front was Tauenzien, with about 8000 men; away to Tauenzien's left was Holtzendorf, in the villages above Dornburg, with 5000 men. The remaining 25,000 men were away on Tauenzien's right rear.

Napoleon's orders for the approaching battle were issued during the night, and were thus worded: "Marshal Augereau will command the left; he will place his first division in column on the Weimar road, as far as a height[1] by which General Gazan brought his artillery on to the plateau; he will keep such force as may be necessary on the left plateau,[2] on a level with the head of his column; he will have skirmishers opposite the whole of the enemy's line, at the several issues from the heights; he will debouch, with his whole corps, upon the plateau as soon as General Gazan advances, and will forthwith march, according to circumstances, to take the left of the army.

"At daybreak Marshal Lannes will have all his artillery in the intervals, and in the order of battle in which he passes the night.

"The artillery of the Imperial Guard will be placed on the height,[3] and the Guard will be behind the plateau,[4] ranked in five lines, the first

---

[1] Apparently about the ravine leading up to Cospeda.
[2] That meant is the Lichtenhain plateau beyond the Muhlthal.
[3] The Windknolle.
[4] That is, behind the Windknolle, on the comparatively gentle upward slope of 400 yards or so before the Windknolle is reached from Jena.

composed of chasseurs, crowning the plateau. The village which is on our right[1] will be bombarded by the whole of General Suchet's artillery, and immediately afterwards attacked and carried. The Emperor will give the signal; all must hold themselves in readiness at daybreak. Marshal Ney will be placed at daybreak at the extremity of the plateau, so as to be able to mount on to it and carry his troops to the right of Marshal Lannes so soon as, by the capture of the village, he shall have room to deploy.

"Marshal Soult will debouch by the road which has been reconnoitred on our right,[2] and will hold himself always in contact, so as to take the right of the army.

"The order of battle, for the marshals generally, will be to form their troops in two lines, not counting that of the light infantry; the distance between the two will not exceed 100 toises.[3] The light cavalry of each corps will be so placed as to enable each general to utilise it according to circumstances. The heavy cavalry, as soon as it arrives,[4] will be placed on the plateau, in reserve behind the Guard, ready to move as circumstances may require.

"The important point to-day is to deploy on the plain; after that,[5] such dispositions will be

[1] Closewitz. [2] The Rauthal. [3] Two hundred and fifty paces.
[4] It could not arrive before 11 or 12 o'clock.
[5] The word used is *ensuite*, which can only mean thereafter. General Bonnal holds that Berthier made a mistake, and wrote *ensuite* instead of *donc*. The latter word would be used in the sense of consequently. It seems difficult to see why this assumption should be made, except for the purpose of supporting the General's theory that Napoleon did not intend to fight a general action on the 14th.

BATTLEFIELD OF JENA (Looking west from the Napoleonsberg)

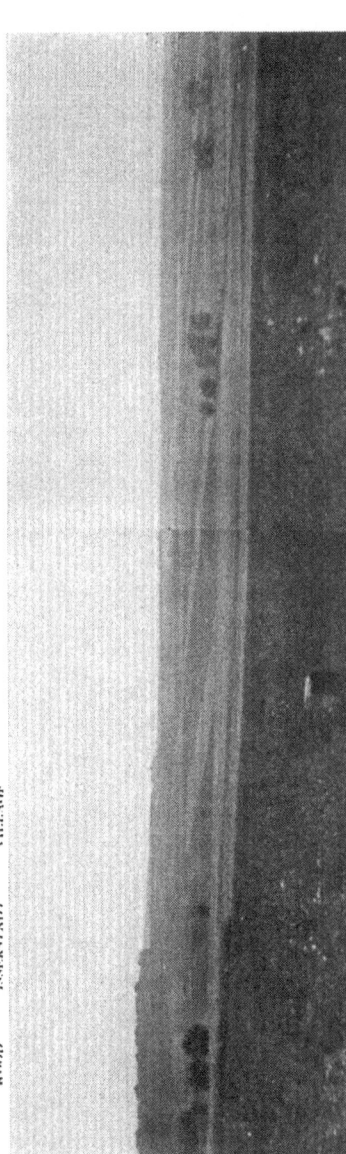

BATTLEFIELD OF JENA (Part of Prussian main position from the west)

made as may be demanded by the movements of the enemy, and the forces he displays, with a view to driving him from the positions which he holds, and which are necessary for our deployment."

The orders for Davout and Bernadotte will be dealt with later on in detail. Here it is only necessary to say that they aimed at bringing these two corps on to the left, and rear, of the Prussians at Apolda. At 4 A.M. Lannes received his final instructions verbally from the Emperor. The early part of the night was clear, with a slight frost; towards dawn there descended a mist, so thick that it was impossible to see more than a few yards. At 6 A.M. daylight was scarcely perceptible through it, but it was essential to the French to make an early start in opening a space for their deployment, before the enemy could overwhelm them in their cramped position, the front of which, the Emperor said, was scarce sufficient for the deployment of four battalions.

Napoleon, riding amongst Lannes' troops, addressed them in the terms by which he so well knew how to excite their enthusiasm. He told them that the enemy, cut off, was struggling, not for victory, but for mere existence. Shame on the corps which should allow him to cut his way through! His words were received with enthusiastic cheers and cries of "*en avant*." Tauenzien, too, was preparing to attack. During the night his light troops had occupied Closewitz, Lutzeroda, and the line between them, the main body being on the heights in rear. At 6 A.M. the troops in rear moved down to the support of the light troops. The line commenced, on its right, at the point where the Liskauer Thal bifurcates towards Isserstadt and Lutzeroda. Lutzeroda was strongly occupied. Behind the centre, midway between Lutzeroda and Closewitz, the reserves were posted. The line continued, in front of Closewitz, along the left bank of the Rauthal, being strengthened on its extreme left by two battalions on the right bank of the farther branch of that ravine, in the wood of Closewitz known as the Zwatzen Holz. Three squadrons of hussars were behind the left wing, the rest of the cavalry, with the one and a half batteries and the Saxon regimental guns, on the slopes of the Dornberg, behind Lutzeroda.

The first shot appears to have been fired by Tauenzien's artillery about six o'clock as he commenced to advance. His forward movement was almost immediately checked by a heavy musketry and artillery fire, which at this stage must have been somewhat random, for the mist rendered any deliberate aim impossible. The Saxon battalions at Lutzeroda even came under the fire of their own batteries in rear, and had an ammunition waggon blown up by it.

Lannes' corps moved forward, partly in line and partly in column, the whole front covered as usual by dense swarms of skirmishers. In the obscurity it was natural that men should unconsciously follow the slope of the ground, and as they moved the whole of Lannes' corps, especially Suchet's division, insensibly tended towards the hollow in front of Closewitz, losing heavily in the close formations resulting. A gap

The Battle of Jena 131

was thus opened on the left of the corps. It was difficult to get men forward when they were uncertain what lay in front of them, and it was not till 7.30 or so that Claparède's brigade, leading Suchet's advance on the right, could even see the outline of the Closewitz woods. When they did so they pushed rapidly on, driving Tauenzien's first line back on its supports, and winning the wood after a bitter struggle. Closewitz was also taken, and in the meanwhile Lutzeroda had fallen into the hands of Gazan's left.

As Lannes' corps pushed straight to its front, the corps of Soult on its right and Augereau on its left had been mounting the steep slopes with their leading divisions. Soult, with St. Hilaire's division in two columns, had started from Lobstadt. The left column moved by the road up the Rauthal, the right by the ravine leading from Zwatzen, the light cavalry still farther on.

As the left column reached the bifurcation of the Rauthal, it divided and followed both branches, the left half going behind Suchet's right through Closewitz and driving the extreme left of Tauenzien towards Hermstadt.

In the same period Desjardins' division of Augereau's corps, using the road as well as the hills on its right, had come up through Cospeda, and turned to its left towards the Isserstadt wood.

It has already been mentioned that a gap had been formed on Gazan's left. This the Emperor filled with a battery of twenty-five guns, drawn partly from the Guard, partly from Gazan's, and partly from Desjardins' division.[1]

[1] Fourteen guns of the Guard, seven of Desjardins', and four of Gazan's division (Foucart, i. 663, *n*.).

Hohenlohe, meanwhile, had for some time after the sound of the fight at Closewitz reached his ears refused to believe in its importance. He was annoyed with Gravert, who had begun to move to his left into a position about Gr. Romstadt, facing the direction of Tauenzien. As message after message reached Hohenlohe from Tauenzien describing the severity of the attack, the Prince at last realised that his left was being seriously menaced. He sent orders to Tauenzien to fall back into second line towards Klein Romstadt, whilst Gravert's cavalry covered his retreat. The Saxon infantry, with Boguslawski on its right front, was moved to a position at right angles to the Weimar road on the heights above the Schnecke. Dyherrn's brigade formed a reserve about Isserstadt, having the Saxon cavalry on its left rear.

Tauenzien, receiving his orders about 8.30, at once began to fall back before Lannes. As Suchet, with the leading French division, moved out of Closewitz, he found his left flank threatened by three battalions of grenadiers drawn up on the slope of the Dornberg. Wheeling to the left two battalions of the 34th, he met the grenadiers in front whilst Gazan's right-hand regiment attacked them in right flank. They were driven back into the Isserstadt wood, where the defenders of Lutzeroda had already taken refuge. In this combat two of the guns behind Lutzeroda were taken, the rest moving back on the ravine between Krippendorf and Alt Gonna. Here twenty-two of them fell into the hands of Suchet's troops. The latter, as they advanced on Vierzehnheiligen, met Gravert's cavalry, now

supporting Tauenzien's retreat. Though part
of Claparède's brigade reached the windmill on
the right of Vierzehnheiligen, and Reille with
the 40th appears to have even entered the
village, they were compelled by superior forces
to fall back, and the battle came temporarily
to a standstill. In addition to the fact that
Lannes was not strong enough to advance
farther without the support of Ney and Soult,
neither of whom had yet arrived in line, a fresh
danger began to appear on Suchet's right rear.
Holtzendorf, cantoned in the villages above
Dornburg, when he heard the commencement
of Tauenzien's action, issued orders for the
assembly of his force about Rodigen. As they
gradually came up he found himself, at about
9 A.M., some three miles from the left of Tauenzien (now on a level with Vierzehnheiligen)
and separated from it by the interposition of
Suchet's division. It was open to him either
to cut his way through direct to the main line,
or to join it by a circuitous route through Stobra
and Hermstadt. He chose the bolder, but, as
it happened, impracticable course. Hohenlohe's
orders to him to fall on the French flank did
not reach him till much later, being delayed
on the way. It was about 10 A.M. when
Holtzendorf was ready to advance. Meanwhile
Wedel's brigade of Lannes' corps, hitherto
acting as reserve, had been faced to the right
in a crotchet behind Suchet's right, between
Alt Gonna and Closewitz, whilst Soult's infantry
columns were converging on the woods (Pfarr
Holz and Loh Holz) west of Rodigen, and had
already filled them with skirmishers. Holtzendorf

moved his four battalions in echelons at two hundred paces from the right, which was directed on Lehesten. Two regiments of cavalry and a horse artillery battery guarded the left and rear; behind the right were a field battery and a battalion of Schimmelpfennig's hussars. The impossibility of advance against Wedel and St. Hilaire being soon brought home to Holtzendorf by the heavy fire from the woods, retreat on Stobra was resolved on through Lehesten and Nerkwitz. As it was in progress, Guyot's light cavalry (the 8th Hussars and 11th Chasseurs) on Soult's extreme right bore down upon Holtzendorf's left and rear. The two cavalry regiments there (one of which was of cuirassiers) were defeated by Guyot, and the whole of Holtzendorf's left was driven in on his right. A total rout was only saved by the firmness of the grenadier battalions on the right. As it was, the horse artillery battery lost in the Nerkwitz ravine all its ammunition waggons. Holtzendorf fell back on Stobra, which he reached about 11.30. He arrived at Apolda about 2 P.M. and remained separated for the whole day from the Prussian centre.

About 11 A.M. the position was this: Lannes' two divisions, Suchet's leading on the right, stood between Krippendorf and Vierzehnheiligen, facing the latter village. On their left was the twenty-five gun battery, between which and Gazan's left Ney had now pushed his advance guard of rather less than 4000 picked troops.[1]

---

[1] Ney's orders, it will be remembered, were to come into line on Lannes' right. It seems probable that the Emperor modified these

The Battle of Jena

With his customary eagerness for the fight Ney had forced himself almost in front of Gazan.

Farther to the left, Desjardins had for the moment captured Isserstadt, but had been driven back some distance into the wood by Prussian fusiliers.

On the side of the Allies, Holtzendorf, as already narrated, was retreating on Stobra. Gravert's cavalry was at and on both sides of Vierzehnheiligen. His infantry was advancing on the village. The cavalry had had a sharp action with Ney's light cavalry to the (Prussian) right of Vierzehnheiligen. Ney's men had driven them back first with the loss of a horse artillery battery, the teams of which they cut loose. Charged by fresh Prussian cavalry, they had been forced to leave the guns, which the Prussians were equally unable to move in the absence of teams. As Ney's men were borne back they were supported by one of Lannes' hussar regiments, and the Prussians, faced also by Ney's grenadiers in square, again retired.

orders when he saw the gap formed between Gazan and Desjardins by the leaning to the right of Lannes' corps.

General Bonnal, the author of *La Manœuvre d'Iena*, seeks to show that Napoleon never intended to carry the battle of the 14th October beyond the acquisition of space for deployment. He holds that Ney's impetuosity forced the Emperor's hand, and prevented the breaking off of the engagement for that day. It seems incredible that, even before Ney's arrival, it was any longer possible to break off. If Napoleon wished to do so, which seems very doubtful, Hohenlohe was bound to renew the battle in furtherance of his orders to protect the retreat of Brunswick's army. It seems unnecessary to bring a charge against Ney which the Emperor himself does not seem to have put forward (*La Manœuvre d'Iena*, par le Général H. Bonnal, pp. 424, 430). Davout, in his account of the Emperor's orders of 10 P.M. on the 13th, distinctly speaks of his master's intention to attack the Prussian army *to-morrow* (14th).

On the right of the Prussian cavalry were four battalions of the reserve, now placed under the command of Cerrini. Dyherrn's brigade was behind Vierzehnheiligen, the Saxon cavalry behind Isserstadt. The Saxon infantry, under Zeschwitz, were on the heights above the Schnecke, with Boguslawski on their right facing Heudelet's division of Augereau's corps. In all this line the two villages of Vierzehnheiligen and Isserstadt, with the wood in front of the latter, were the only points of support. Between Isserstadt and Vierzehnheiligen is merely a line, not a position.

Once more, soon after eleven, the advance of the French centre commenced. Vierzehnheiligen was again captured by the 40th of Suchet's division with the aid of Ney's voltigeurs. This point of support was thus transferred from the Prussians to the French. Between it and the Isserstadt wood were the rest of Ney's advance guard; in front of Krippendorf the rest of Suchet's division. Wedel was marching across behind them to assist Desjardins in the Isserstadt wood. Ney's two divisions were just reaching the field, Marchand's presently replacing the exhausted advance guard. The first brigade of d'Hautpoult's cuirassiers [1] and Klein's dragoons were also on the field. The Guard was in reserve between Lutzeroda and Krippendorf, and with them was Napoleon himself.

Hohenlohe was now preparing for the attack, and, as Gravert's infantry arrived, the Prussian and Saxon cavalry extended the line left of Vierzehnheiligen, and it was terminated by

---

[1] The second was not yet up (Foucart, i. 666, *n.* 1).

The Battle of Jena 137

Kollin's half battalion of infantry and one squadron. Gravert's infantry, arrived in front of Vierzehnheiligen, began solemnly, as if on the parade ground, to deploy for the attack. "The fatal method of that epoch," says Von der Goltz, "was to halt and form within the zone of the enemy's effective fire, forming line in order to act by the regulation fire of masses." Harassed by a galling fire from the swarms of skirmishers in and on either side of Vierzehnheiligen and unable to return it, the Prussian infantry was already shaken and demoralised before it was ready to begin volley firing. Even when it did begin, the fire had but little effect on the French skirmishers, adepts as they were in finding cover in the gardens and potato fields or behind the walls of the village.

Fully exposed in their close formations to the effects of the enemy's fire, the Prussians gallantly held on in front of Vierzehnheiligen for nearly two hours. As the right of Suchet's division, led by Lannes in person, endeavoured to attain the left flank of the Prussian infantry, Hohenlohe replied by pushing forward his cavalry and the extreme left of his line, so that by 12.30 it circled forwards along the line of heights above the Krippendorf valley. But St. Hilaire, of Soult's corps, set free by the retreat of Holtzendorf, was now at liberty to extend Lannes' right, thus threatening the Prussian left.

In the meanwhile matters had been going even worse for Hohenlohe in the direction of Isserstadt. At first Desjardins, forced to detach his second brigade to the assistance of Ney, could make little progress with the first. Presently the latter, reinforced by a regiment from the second and by Wedel's brigade, was able, after a long, hard fight, to force the enemy from the Isserstadt wood and through the village. The 7th Chasseurs then charged the Saxon cavalry behind the village, at first with success. They should have been supported by the 20th Chasseurs, but though Augereau's report says they were so, it does not appear to be correct that the 20th ever charged.[1] The 7th were forced to retire on the infantry. Thus, about 12 or 12.30, Hohenlohe found himself in a most unfavourable position. His left was being turned by Soult's advance. His line had been pierced at Isserstadt by Desjardins, who had thus separated the Saxons at the Schnecke from the rest of the line. His division was moving partly against the left of the Saxon infantry, partly against the right of Hohenlohe's centre. Hohenlohe's troops in front of Vierzehnheiligen, exhausted by many furious but futile attacks on the village, were standing in squares in front of it, suffering terribly from the fire of the French skirmishers, as well as from artillery fire. Guns had been lost at Isserstadt, and Cerrini, on the left of it, was retreating, partly in consequence of the enfilading fire of French batteries from the direction of Vierzehnheiligen.

As soon as Hohenlohe realised that a great battle was about to be fought, he had sent an urgent request for help to Ruchel at Weimar. The message had reached that commander about 9 A.M., when he was listening to the sounds of

[1] Foucart, i. 654, *n.* 2.

heavy firing, not only in Hohenlohe's direction, but also in that which the main army had taken. Ruchel's mission was to gather in the corps of the Duke of Weimar before he left the town; but he rightly decided that he would be carrying out his orders in their spirit by giving the desired aid to Hohenlohe. He had been asked to send what troops he could spare; he replied that he was coming at once with the greater part of his force. In fact, leaving a small detachment in Weimar, he moved with something over 15,000 men out of the town, by the road to Jena, so early as ten o'clock. It is far from clear how his march came to be so slow that at noon there were no signs to be seen of him from the Prussian line at Vierzehnheiligen. He took four hours to cover the distance from Weimar to Capellendorf, not more than six miles. What, then, was Hohenlohe to do when he found his infantry line holding, with ever-increasing difficulty, its position behind the Isserstadt–Vierzehnheiligen line? Some counselled retreat; Gravert was for doggedly holding on as they were. Once more Massenbach gave his opinion; this time it was perhaps wiser than usual. To wait passively in the present position was, he said, fatal. The only thing to be done was to make a supreme effort with the entire strength of the still powerful cavalry, supported by the other arms, to drive back the enemy, and thus gain time for Ruchel to arrive. His advice was not taken, or at any rate not acted on, and the line remained in its position, suffering more than the best troops could be expected to bear for long. Already one regiment on the left, which had shown symptoms

of breaking, had only been held in place by
immense exertions, even by violence, on the part
of the officers. Young Eberhard, the junior
officer of the Sanitz regiment, a mere child still,
seized the colours, shouting to the men, "See!
here is your standard; it you *must* follow." He
fell, pierced by many French bullets, still clinging
to his colours. In vain his heroic effort, and those
of many others; the men could stand no more.
Regiment after regiment began to fall back. For
half-an-hour some sort of order was maintained;
but by two o'clock the whole left and centre, from
Isserstadt to beyond Vierzehnheiligen, was a confused mass of panic-stricken fugitives. Arms
were thrown down, guns abandoned; men yielded
themselves prisoners in hundreds to the pursuing
French. As the line began to yield, Napoleon,
directing the battle from the slopes of the Dornberg, let loose on the fugitives the great mass of
cavalry which he now had in hand. Murat, with
the light cavalry of Lannes', Ney's, and Augereau's
corps, wielding contemptuously a riding-whip
instead of a sabre, led the pursuit. The heavy
cavalry, and Klein with two of his dragoon
regiments, thundered in a yelling, cheering,
excited mass, behind Murat,[1] through the space
between Isserstadt and Vierzehnheiligen. On
the right, beyond the latter village, Soult's light
cavalry, reinforced by another of Klein's regiments, rolled down on the Prussian left. Here
the pursuit was to some extent checked by the

[1] Murat had in the centre eleven regiments of cavalry—viz.
three of Lannes', two of Ney's, two of Augereau's light cavalry,
with two of Klein's dragoons and two of d'Hautpoult's cuirassiers.
Two more of Klein's regiments had gone to the right of Soult, and
one to the left of Augereau.

The Battle of Jena

remains of Tauenzien's advance guard, standing in support at Klein Romstadt, but there was no such support for the Prussian right; for Cerrini's and Dyherrn's brigades had both been utilised in the first line.

Onward towards Weimar passed the defeated Prussians and the pursuing cavalry. Behind them the French infantry rapidly marched, still in perfect line, cheered by the music of their drums and bands. For more than two miles the carnage continued, till the broken army poured in mad flight down the slope beyond Gross Romstadt into the valley of Capellendorf. Here at last the pursuing cavalry were brought to a temporary halt by the sight of fresh troops moving to the attack. The arrival of their own infantry had now to be awaited.

What the cavalry saw, pushing its way with difficulty through the disordered masses of Hohenlohe's infantry, was the corps of Ruchel, so long in vain awaited by the Prussian prince. When he reached Umferstadt, Ruchel received a fresh and more urgent call from Hohenlohe. "It is well," he replied; "I am coming in all haste." Near Capellendorf he received peremptory orders to support the main army in its distress at Auerstädt. It was too late for that; Hohenlohe it might still be possible to save. Then came Massenbach with the tidings that Hohenlohe's battle was as good as lost. To Ruchel, inquiring in which direction he could best help, Massenbach replied, "Now only through Capellendorf." Fatal advice! for it was hopeless to expect victory for this puny force, moving up the slope of the valley against the great line of victorious French, now rapidly nearing Gross Romstadt.

Ruchel still had to arrange his plan of attack. To Tauenzien, falling back in some sort of order from Klein Romstadt with the left, he sent an urgent request to hold fast with all the troops he could collect. From his own troops he posted three reserves, on the heights behind and on either side of Capellendorf. Already the crowd of fugitives was pouring down into the valley, disordering and demoralising Ruchel's men. His main body passed the bottom of the valley in two columns, one through Capellendorf, the other to the left of the village. Then they were deployed for attack in echelons on the centre. Hohenlohe, who had performed prodigies of valour, had during the earlier part of the retreat taken post in a square of the Winkel regiment, which, spurred by the presence of the general, alone maintained its formation. Leaving this, Hohenlohe now took over the command of Ruchel's corps. The Saxon cavalry, under Zeschwitz II., had covered the retreat through Gross Romstadt as far as possible. It was now halted and joined to Ruchel's cavalry to advance on the flanks of the infantry. On the left it met, and drove back on their infantry, the light cavalry of Soult, supported by one of Klein's regiments.

With the steadiness of the parade ground, Ruchel's troops started on their march up the hill from Capellendorf to Gross Romstadt in echelons of two battalions each, the centre leading. From the crest in front there poured a stream of shells, round shot, and bullets, launched against them by the batteries of Lannes,

The Battle of Jena

Soult, Ney, and Desjardins, and the infantry of Wedel. Great lanes were torn in the closely formed Prussians; the greater part of the officers were either killed or wounded, or lost their horses. Ruchel himself, dangerously wounded near the heart, but staunching the blood with a handkerchief, refused to leave his post. As the hill was mounted, Klein's dragoons charged down it. Met by the Saxon cavalry of Ruchel's right, they were driven back behind the infantry. Once more Ruchel's infantry moved forward. The French skirmishers were driven in, and it was only as the Prussians got within 200 paces of the guns that they saw line upon line of fresh infantry moving against their front, or outflanking them on either wing. They halted and opened fire; but ruin stared them in the face. Over the crest and down the slope charged the French infantry in overwhelming force, carrying all in confusion before them, and repeating the scenes of the pursuit of Hohenlohe. Guns, waggons, prisoners, fell into the hands of the victorious French at every step forward, as they pushed before them towards Weimar the disorganised rabble which was all that remained of Hohenlohe's and Ruchel's infantry.

We must now return to the doings of Zeschwitz I. with the Saxon infantry and Boguslawski's detachment at the Schnecke. Against their front and right flank had advanced Heudelet's division of Augereau's corps. One brigade, in touch with Desjardins' left in the Isserstadt wood, had turned to its left half-way up the ascent to Cospeda, and moved along the slope towards the Liskauer Thal. As they scrambled up the farther bank, through the vines and bushes, they met the Saxons. At the same time the other brigade, which had moved by the Muhlthal, began a similar fight on the slopes at and beyond the Schnecke. Boguslawski's men, on whom fell the brunt of the attack, contesting the ground step by step, were steadily forced back on the two Saxon brigades drawn up across the road at the top.

When Isserstadt fell, about noon, into Desjardins' hands, half his division issued from it towards the Saxon left. Outflanked thus, the Saxons were compelled to fall slowly back, fighting bravely, but entirely separated from the Prussians on their left. So late as 3 P.M. they were still not farther back than the point, about equidistant from Isserstadt, Schwabhausen, and Kotschau, where the road makes a slight bend. So closely were they followed by Heudelet's infantry that De Ségur relates how he almost rode into the head of the Saxon column, in the belief that they were French.

The end was at hand. Zeschwitz I., in the smoke and confusion of battle, had failed to perceive that the French main line was at Capellendorf, in his rear, with its back to him. Ruchel's attack and defeat had lasted but half-an-hour, and Klein's dragoons, led by Murat in person, now returned upon the rear of the unfortunate Saxons, whilst d'Hautpoult's cuirassiers descended on their left flank, and one of Klein's regiments, which had been sent to the French left about noon, charged their right from the direction of Schwabhausen. Attacked on all sides at once, the two Saxon brigades and

The Battle of Jena

Boguslawski had nothing left but surrender. Not less than 6000 men yielded themselves prisoners to Murat, whom De Ségur describes smiling triumphantly as he gathered in this great harvest.

Zeschwitz I. at first resolved to share the fate of his troops, but changing his mind, he put himself at the head of 300 horsemen, and charging furiously, cut his way through the French cavalry to Hohlstadt, where he met his brother Zeschwitz II., who still held the Saxon cavalry together. The two brothers then took post between Frankendorf and Umferstadt, endeavouring to cover the retreat of the Prussian right through the latter place. They executed more than one charge in this neighbourhood, in the vain endeavour to stem the pursuit. Meanwhile the Prussian infantry about Umferstadt had been ridden down by part of Murat's cavalry which, after the surrender of the Saxons, had gone round to the left of the Weimar road. This cavalry the brothers Zeschwitz met as they fell back on Umferstadt, and were compelled by it to seek safety in the direction of Dermstadt, where they crossed the Ilm.

The flight of the Prussian centre and left continued in ever-increasing disorder. Ruchel's force made for Ulrichshalben, where what remained of it crossed the Ilm.

A last endeavour to gain time was made outside Weimar at about 4 P.M. The French were now moving in four columns, thus: (1) the left column passing through Umferstadt towards Ober Weimar, and turning in part to its right about half-way between these places; (2) a column on the main road; (3) another to the right of this, through Sassenborn, where it turned leftwards; (4) the right column on Dermstadt. As the second column neared the large wood of Webicht, it found Cerrini's Saxons standing across the road, close to the wood, with a rearguard of infantry and a few guns, under Wobeser, some hundreds of paces out. Behind them, in the wood, were the rest of Wobeser's Prussians, and on their right rear a confused mass of Prussian infantry and cavalry. Wobeser's men were those whom Ruchel had left behind in Weimar. These dispositions had just been made by Hohenlohe when he heard of the ruin of his right wing. He at once decided to retreat through Weimar. Just as the Saxons were preparing for this the fire of the French skirmishers in their front redoubled, and French cavalry were seen approaching from the right. The Prussians behind Cerrini promptly broke and fled in the same wild confusion as before. The Saxon infantry fought bravely, but, cannonaded and overwhelmed by infantry fire in front, and charged in flank by cavalry, resistance was hopeless. A gallant charge by Major Oppen checked the French cavalry, and enabled the whole of the infantry to escape, with some semblance of order, to Weimar. Some resistance was offered at the Weimar bridge, which, however, was carried without much difficulty.

This was the last episode of this eventful day. Bernadotte was now at Apolda, and before him Holtzendorf had, about 3 P.M., retreated across the Ilm at Ulrichshalben. The rest of the

The Battle of Jena 147

53,000 men whom Hohenlohe and Ruchel had opposed to the 96,000 of Napoleon were a hopeless, helpless mass of panic-stricken fugitives. Of the 96,000 French not more than about 54,000 had been actually engaged. The losses of the Prussians and Saxons in killed, wounded, and prisoners it is impossible to compute. The losses in the actual battle are inextricably confused with those in the subsequent retreat. Napoleon, as usual, much understated his own losses, which he calculated at 4000 men. Complete returns of the losses in the various corps are not available, but the following figures are stated in the reports of some of the commanders :—

Suchet	2570
St. Hilaire	580
Soult's cavalry	275
Ney's advanced guard	600
Desjardins	704
Total	4729[1]

Seeing that these are the admitted losses of about 34,000 out of the 54,000 French engaged, it would be safe to put the total losses at not less than 6500 men, after allowing for the fact that the losses above stated are those of the corps most heavily engaged.

That evening the Duchess of Weimar insisted on doing the honours at a strange supper party. In the morning she had entertained the Queen of Prussia, returning from Auerstädt, only to escape from Weimar as the news of the disasters began to come in. The

---

[1] See Foucart, i. pp. 635, 642, 650, 662.

Duchess's guests of the evening were Murat, Rapp, and De Ségur,[1] on whose jubilations over the victory her presence imposed considerable restrictions. Murat, the pinchbeck Bayard, prided himself on his courtesy on such occasions; Rapp was a gentleman by nature, De Ségur by birth as well. The Duchess, therefore, was treated with consideration, which, however, can have been but a poor consolation for her fears and grief. The streets all around the palace were littered with corpses, wounded men, guns, waggons, and all the other wreckage of a broken army.

[1] "An Aide-de-camp of Napoleon," 289.

CHAPTER VIII

THE BATTLE OF AUERSTÄDT

WHILST Napoleon, on the plateau above Jena, was fighting a battle the issue of which was never doubtful once he had gained space for the deployment of his vastly superior numbers, Davout, far away to his right, was engaged in a more glorious struggle, in which the relative proportions of numbers were reversed. Napoleon, for his own glorification, chose in his bulletins to count the two battles as one; though the distance between his right, at Closewitz, and Davout's left, near Hassenhausen, was fully thirteen miles as the crow flies, and there was no more tactical connection between the two actions than there was, in August 1870, between the battles of Wörth and Spicheren.

The main Prussian army had started from Weimar on the 13th, as ordered, to march for the Lower Unstrut, expecting to meet the reserve, under Duke Eugene of Würtemberg, advancing from Halle. But the prevailing confusion resulted in so many delays that the army bivouacked for the night about Auerstädt, some distance short of the defile of Koesen, the seizure of which was absolutely essential as a protection for the right flank against the French, who were known to have occupied Naumburg in force. No attempt seems to have been made to seize this all important defile and passage of the Saale, which, on the contrary, was occupied by Davout on the night of the 13th–14th. The outposts of the leading division (Schmettau's) extended no farther than Gernstadt. Behind Schmettau were the divisions of Wartensleben and the Prince of Orange, the former with outposts watching the Ilm and the Saale about Sulza. It was not till midnight that Kalkreuth's reserve encamped behind the division of Orange, whilst Blucher's light troops were not up before 2 A.M.

The strength of the army thus assembled is given by Lettow-Vorbeck and Hoepfner as 52 battalions, 80 squadrons, and 16 batteries, numbering 39,000 infantry, 9200 cavalry, and 1600 artillerymen. Altogether there were 49,800 men, with 230 guns, of which 136 belonged to the artillery and 94 were attached to the infantry.

The French force, which was destined to meet in mortal combat this army, consisted of the single corps of Davout, who gives his own numbers as 26,000, of whom not more than 1300 or 1400 were cavalry, and whose artillery numbered but 44 guns.

Instead of this inferiority of 1 to 2 the French would have had a slight superiority but for the action of Bernadotte in not only refusing himself to support Davout, but also in dissuading such of the reserve cavalry as were available from doing so.[1] It will be more convenient to deal

---

[1] Sahuc's dragoon division had been placed at the disposal of Davout (Napoleon to Berthier, 12th October—Foucart, i. 515), but that marshal notes that it was withdrawn from him by Murat on the 13th (Davout to Napoleon, 14th October—Foucart, i. 672). Savary (ii. 287) says Bernadotte stopped the cavalry from joining Davout.

BATTLEFIELD OF AUERSTADT
(Looking west from south-west of Hassenhausen)

BATTLEFIELD OF AUERSTADT
(Hassenhausen from Brunswick's Monument)

The Battle of Auerstädt

with the case of Bernadotte presently, after Davout's battle has been described.

The latter marshal, it will be remembered, had received orders on the afternoon of the 13th to manœuvre to his left should he hear an attack on Lannes in progress; if there were no such attack on the 13th he was promised further orders during the night. The original of those orders is not forthcoming, but their substance has been preserved in Davout's history of the operations of his corps. They reached him at 3 A.M. on the 14th, being dated 10 P.M. on the 13th, from the Emperor's bivouac on the heights of Jena. They clearly indicate the writer's ignorance of the movement of the enemy's main army on the left bank of the Ilm; for they require Davout to march on Apolda, where he would come upon the rear of the Prussian army. Provided only that he took part in the battle, which Napoleon intended to fight on the 14th, Davout was left a free hand in the choice of his road to Apolda. The Emperor only knew the country from the map, and wisely left details to the man on the spot. The orders, in so far as they concerned Bernadotte, will be dealt with later. Here it suffices to say that Bernadotte took no material part either in Napoleon's or in Davout's battle.

Davout's shortest way to Apolda from his position at and south of Naumburg lay over the bridge at Koesen. Thence the road rises steeply, by a zigzag in one place, along the face of the hill leading to the plateau on the left bank of the Saale, a plateau corresponding to that of Jena, but separated from it by the Ilm, and not so high above the Saale as is the

Landgrafenberg. Just before the top of the hill is reached, the Napoleonsberg (Windknolle) can be clearly seen, twelve or thirteen miles to the south, making a distinct feature in the landscape. Arrived at the plateau the road turns from south to due west, and falls by the gentlest of slopes for nearly two miles to the substantial village of Hassenhausen. The plain over which it passes is almost absolutely flat and featureless. There is no village on it, no fence, no wood until, away to the left, the woods are seen which clothe the steep bank of the Saale and, farther on, of the Ilm. The junction of the two rivers is at the railway station of Gr. Heringen, about two miles south of Hassenhausen. Like that of Jena the battlefield of Auerstädt is to-day, save for the metalling of a few roads and the plum-trees now lining them, exactly as it was in 1806. No railway crosses it, and even Hassenhausen appears to have expanded only by two or three houses on the south side of the road.

From the west side of Hassenhausen the whole battlefield can be seen and understood. The road thence goes on, sunk for the first 300 yards, due west down the gentle slope of an open valley. At the bottom of the slope, about a mile from Hassenhausen, lies the village of Taugwitz, and just beyond it, on the farther side of the brook which drains the valley, is Poppel, about 100 feet lower than Hassenhausen. A mile north-east of Poppel, Spielberg marks the head of this valley. Below Poppel the brook flows south by east to Rehausen, a mile off; then it doubles back south-westwards for rather

The Battle of Auerstädt 153

more than a mile, and finally turns again to the east round the end of the Sonnenberg to join the Ilm. Thus Hassenhausen is in the centre of a rough crescent of heights, of which the horns project on the right past Spielberg, on the left to the Sonnenberg. Straight on beyond Poppel from Hassenhausen are Lisdorf and Eckardsberga. To the left, on the road to Apolda and Weimar, which turns south-west at Poppel, are Gernstadt and Auerstädt, the latter hidden from view by the downs over which the road passes above the former.

Hassenhausen has orchards and fences on its west side, and the road, as it passes along its southern edge, is sunk some ten or twelve feet, forming a ready-made entrenchment.

On the north-west, beyond Spielberg, the battlefield is bounded by wooded heights. A small brook, the Liesbach, flows eastward through Lisdorf into the main valley at Poppel, or perhaps it should be considered as the main brook and the branch leading down from Spielberg as a tributary of it.

On the evening of the 13th some of Davout's chasseurs, reconnoitring the Weimar road some three or four miles from Koesen, had been repulsed by Prussian cavalry, and the marshal had then occupied Koesen with a battalion of infantry.

First Period of the Battle—up to 9 a.m.

Before daybreak on the 14th both forces were in motion. On the French side the 25th Light Infantry, preceded by a squadron of chasseurs, passed the Koesen bridge, followed half-an-hour later by the rest of Gudin's division. The same thick morning mist which pervaded the battlefield of Jena had descended on that of Auerstädt. Davout, accompanying his advance guard, sent out his A.D.C., Colonel Burke (or Bourke), with a small detachment of chasseurs, to endeavour, by the capture of prisoners, to obtain definite news of the enemy. That officer, pushing on through Hassenhausen, encountered no vedettes or advanced body, until he suddenly stumbled in the mist, near Poppel, on the whole of the Prussian advance guard of 600 cavalry led by Blucher. The latter promptly charged, and, though the French were of course compelled to a rapid retreat, they succeeded in capturing a few of the enemy. The French cavalry fell back on the 25th Light Infantry which was now approaching Hassenhausen. That infantry regiment was on the right of the road, with the 85th of the line on its left. Behind the 25th was the 21st of the line, and behind the 85th the 12th.

Blucher, after driving back Burke, following him through Hassenhausen with the leading squadrons of his cavalry and some infantry, at once found himself under artillery fire from a battery about 700 paces to his left front. He was now reinforced by more cavalry and a horse artillery battery, which at once engaged the French guns. Unable, however, to match the French artillery, the Prussian battery soon endeavoured to withdraw. Attacked in the operation by French skirmishers, against whom its escort was unable to defend it, it lost five out of its eight guns, and the French 25th Light Infantry pushed its victorious advance into and to the right of Hassenhausen, which village was strongly occupied by skirmishers, the main body of the regiment taking post on the right of it. On the left of the village the 85th was drawn up.

Blucher, after his ejectment from Hassenhausen, had moved off to his left, seeking to outflank the French right, and sending back to the Duke of Brunswick for more cavalry. Schmettau's division was now being arrayed in front of Poppel for an advance on Hassenhausen; the French skirmishers were already in the pastures of the intervening valley. These skirmishers were driven back on Hassenhausen, on which village it was of supreme importance to Davout to maintain his hold. Between it and the edge of the plateau there was no point of support should he be driven back before the arrival of his 2nd and 1st divisions. He had already marked Blucher's movement threatening his right flank, and had, to support the 25th Light Infantry, moved to the right the 21st, followed by the 12th. About 8 A.M. the storm broke upon the squares of the 25th and 21st. Blucher, leading in person ten squadrons, which he now commanded, charged furiously from the direction of Spielberg, hoping by the violence of his onslaught to break the French defence. He had six squadrons of cuirassiers and four of dragoons and hussars, some 1150 men in all. For the moment he seemed to be succeeding. The squadron of chasseurs, whom he first encountered, gave way before him, and it looked as if the infantry squares too must go down before the weight of the cuirassiers. But now came a great change. The French squares steadily poured their fire into the charging cavalry, which was also fired upon by a 10-gun battery which Davout had moved up. General Reitzenstein of the cuirassiers was severely wounded, and his misfortune produced a panic amongst his men. Nevertheless, the attack was renewed more than once, only, however, to meet with the same stubborn resistance. In the last attack the right of the Prussian cavalry rode into the fire of their own horse artillery battery, and, to add to their difficulties, they now perceived in the distance the advance of the 108th French infantry, the leading regiment of Friant's division, which, as it arrived, Davout promptly hurried to the support of his hard pressed right. Blucher's horse was shot under him, and his temporary disappearance was, no doubt, a further discouragement to the already badly shaken cavalry. By 8.30 A.M. that cavalry had reached the point at which they could no longer hold firm, and they soon broke into a wild confused flight towards the woods beyond Spielberg. Blucher, now remounted on a bugler's horse, and the other Prussian officers, shouting to the men that no one was pursuing them, in vain endeavoured to stay the panic and reform the regiments. Utterly broken, the cuirassiers and dragoons continued their mad flight.

If Blucher had performed prodigies of valour and exerted himself to the utmost in his attack on the French right, Davout had done no less in encouraging the defence. Moving from square to square, encouraging and exhorting the men,

The Battle of Auerstädt 157

he was rewarded by witnessing Blucher's complete repulse ; but he, nevertheless, realised that Gudin's division was in imminent danger. Whilst its right flank had been attacked by Blucher, its front had been approached by Schmettau's infantry, which, however, was waiting, before making a general advance, for the support of Wartensleben's and Orange's divisions. The former had at the start got into confusion in Auerstädt, where several roads converged on a single bridge, and it was, in consequence, much delayed.

SECOND PERIOD—9 TO 10 A.M.

It was about 9 A.M. when Schmettau was reinforced by the arrival of Wartensleben on his right. Davout, too, had now got up the whole of Friant's division, which he moved to Gudin's right. Two battalions of the 111th and one of the 108th, joining the right of the 21st, captured the horse artillery battery left behind by Blucher's fleeing cavalry. The rest of Friant's division (five battalions) moved on Spielberg.

Schmettau's men had already suffered heavily from artillery and infantry fire during Blucher's cavalry fight, and as they moved forward with their right on the main road the loss continued and increased. The French skirmishers, ensconced in the houses and orchards of Hassenhausen, in the hollow roads about it, and behind the hedges on their right of it, were able to do much more damage than they suffered. In front of Schmettau the fight went badly for the Prussians. Friant with his infantry, towards and beyond Spielberg, captured that village after a severe fight, whilst his victory was completed by a charge of the three regiments of Vialannes' light cavalry—all that Davout had. Schmettau again and again attacked Hassenhausen, and Gudin's right beyond it. Each time he was repulsed by the steadiness of the French infantry, and he now saw his left flank exposed by the steady advance of Friant from Spielberg towards Poppel.

The French left, south of Hassenhausen, was, during this period, very hard beset. As his right was strengthened by Friant, Davout again moved back the 12th to support the 85th, which stood alone south of the village, at the same time sending the 21st to relieve the exhausted defenders of the village itself. The 12th was almost too late; for, as it reached the hollow road behind the village, it found the 85th being forced to a position on the edge of Hassenhausen along the road.

At this time the Prussian main line was in the shape of a hockey stick, the handle pointing east by south across the plain in the direction of the Ilm, the curve close up to the south-west corner of Hassenhausen, and the toe reaching a point almost north of the village. The 12th occupied the road just east of the village in continuation of the line of the 85th. The pressure of the overwhelming superiority of Wartensleben's numbers was more than these two regiments could stand against in the open. When, however, they found themselves able to utilise the support of the houses and of the hollow road, they were able at last to bring Wartensleben's triumphant advance to a standstill.

The Battle of Auerstädt 159

At ten o'clock Gudin's position was one of extreme peril. He had, it is true, repulsed all Schmettau's attacks on his right wing; Schmettau had been mortally wounded, and the king himself had had a horse killed under him. The Duke of Brunswick too had been carried off the field mortally wounded by a bullet passing through both his eyes. Of this wound he died on the 10th November near Altona. The spot where he fell is marked by a monument 100 yards south of the Hassenhausen-Taugwitz road, and about midway between the two villages.

On the other hand the French regiments on the right had, at times, been almost driven back into the village, his resolute hold on which alone saved Gudin from destruction. His left wing had been forced back to the line of the road, and Wartensleben was swinging his right round, so that his front now lay in the line from Hassenhausen to Saaleck. The gap between his left and Schmettau's right had been filled by Lutzow's brigade of the division Orange, the other brigade (Prince Henry of Prussia) moving to support Schmettau's left against Friant's turning movement.

On the open plateau, on Wartensleben's right and front, had been collected nearly the whole available cavalry under Prince William of Prussia, including such of Blucher's advance guard as that general had been able to rally after their defeat north of Hassenhausen.

Third Period—10 a.m.

Again, in the nick of time, Davout received his last reinforcements, by the arrival of Morand's division, which was now marching in column by the road to Hassenhausen. There was no time to be lost, and as the head of the fresh division nearly reached Gudin's extreme left on the road, the whole began to move by regiments to the left of the road against Wartensleben and the cavalry. The division was short of one battalion of the 17th, left to guard the bridge at Koesen. Davout and Morand now led the 13th Light Infantry and two light guns against the Prussians, already close up to the south side of the village with a battery and numerous infantry. These the 13th charged, driving them back towards the slope running south from Hassenhausen. Pursuing too hotly, the French found themselves almost surrounded, and compelled to fall back again to the left of the village. The rest of the French column was simultaneously advancing across the plain south of the road. In first line came the 51st and 61st, under General de Billy, who here lost his life. In second line was the 30th; the first battalion of the 17th moved on the left rear, along the edge of the Ilm valley. On these advancing lines there descended the Prussian cavalry, led by Prince William. Had there been the same unity in command of that cavalry as existed in the great charge led by Murat at Eylau, it might have fared ill with Morand's men as they moved forwards. But no one on the Prussian side seemed to know who commanded; every cavalry leader acted as seemed to him best. Some regiments were in column, others in line, and instead of the whole body sweeping forward in a succession of waves, each regiment attacked separately, without any common direction or

The Battle of Auerstädt

object. With admirable promptitude the French battalions, forming square, poured a steady fire into their assailants. The latter, unsupported by the infantry, could do nothing against the squares, and their isolated attacks soon died out, leaving Morand at liberty to move on to the destruction of the Prussian infantry south of Hassenhausen.

The 51st reached the top of the slope leading up from Rehausen, suffering fearful losses at short range from the Prussians defending it. At last they succeeded in driving back the enemy, who abandoned their guns. Simultaneously the 61st, on the left of the 51st, as it pressed on through a heavy artillery fire, charged by cavalry supported by infantry, was only saved by the timely arrival of a battalion of the 30th. Yet another desperate attempt to outflank Morand's left was made by a strong Prussian force from Sonnendorf. The greater part of it, including four battalions of Royal Guards from the reserve, advanced along the Sonnenberg, whilst three companies moved above the Ilm. This attack was met and repulsed by the 30th, and the one battalion of the 17th led by Morand himself. As the Prussians fell back through Sonnendorf, Morand gained possession of the whole projecting horn of the crescent-shaped heights on the left bank of the brook, and found himself on the right flank of the Prussians fighting in front of Hassenhausen. On the opposite flank, Friant had meanwhile been making steady progress. He had, after a long and bitter fight, gained the village of Spielberg. Thence he had sent forward the 108th against Poppel, and he now found himself opposed by Prince Henry's brigade of Orange's division, which had gone to Schmettau's left when the other division (Lutzow's) joined the right. Poppel was occupied, but recaptured by the Prussians. Again attacked and turned, it was a second time taken by the French. Friant's 48th was moving still farther to the right, towards Lisdorf. Thus by noon, whilst Gudin was still at Hassenhausen, Morand and Friant were enfilading with their artillery fire and threatening the retreat of Schmettau, Orange, and Wartensleben. Gudin now pressed on against the Prussian centre, which had fallen back 700 or 800 yards from Hassenhausen. Taugwitz was stormed, and by 12.30 the Prussians began to retreat. Before the retreat had degenerated, as at Jena, into a panic, succour was brought by Kalkreuth with his two reserve divisions, less the four battalions of Guards defeated on the Sonnenberg. That general drew up his forces on the heights of the right bank of the Liesbach. His left comprised two infantry regiments and a battalion of grenadiers; on their right was Blucher's now rallied cavalry. Even this position was enfiladed by Morand and Friant, but Kalkreuth was able to show a bold front sufficiently long to cover, to some extent, the retreat of the three beaten divisions. Then he fell back to the line of heights running south-east from Eckardsberga behind Gernstadt, his left occupying an advanced position on the wooded height (Puck Holz) between Eckardsberga and Lisdorf. Here his left was exposed to the attack of Friant from Lisdorf, whilst Gudin moved against his centre and right. Davout now ordered Petit,

The Battle of Auerstädt 163

with 400 men of the 12th and 21st, to storm the (French) left of the wooded height between Eckardsberga and Lisdorf, whilst Friant attacked it in front. As Petit's men, holding their fire, moved with fixed bayonets up the slope, the whole of Friant's division attacked the Prussian left. Kalkreuth's men once more gave way, abandoning twenty guns.

The whole army was now in more or less disordered retreat, though the disorganisation was by no means so complete as that of Hohenlohe's army. It would soon have become so had Davout possessed the means of following up his victory in a great body of cavalry; but his sole force of this arm consisted of only three regiments of Chasseurs, who had already had hard fighting and had lost heavily. The infantry was exhausted by a long day of marching and fighting, and by 4.30 P.M., when it had occupied Eckardsberga, it could carry the pursuit no farther. The light cavalry on the right did what it could, following the Prussians in front of it as far as Buttstadt, which Vialannes entered on the heels of the enemy.

If Davout failed to rout the main army so completely as did Napoleon that of Hohenlohe, he nevertheless gained a very notable victory against almost double his numbers. According to his own account, he took 115 guns and 3000 prisoners, besides inflicting a loss of 15,000 killed and wounded. Hoepfner admits the capture of 57 guns, not including those of the infantry, so that there seems no reason to doubt Davout's statement, which is accepted by Lettow-Vorbeck as regards the guns. As at Jena, it is hopeless to estimate the losses in killed and wounded on the side of the vanquished. Davout's losses were proportionately enormous, being stated by him at over one-fourth of his entire force—over 7000 out of 26,000. It must be noted that Lettow-Vorbeck is inclined to put Davout's strength at about 29,000 men.

Gautherot pinxt. Lauderer sculpt.

MARSHAL DAVOUT
(From an engraving in Mr. Broadley's collection)

CHAPTER IX

STRATEGY AND TACTICS OF THE FIRST PERIOD OF THE WAR

THE campaign with which we are dealing is divided naturally into two great and widely different periods. The first includes the strategical movements of both sides ending in the great tactical events of the 14th October; the second comprises the relentless pursuit and destruction of the remains of the armies which Napoleon had shattered at Jena and Davout at Auerstädt. The first period ended in the afternoon of the 14th October, when it became clear that both battles were irretrievably lost to the Prussians.

At the risk of some repetition, it seems well, before proceeding to the second period, to make a general survey of the strategy and tactics of the first.

In the valley of the Saale, and on the plateau of Jena and Auerstädt, the army of Prussia and Saxony, generally in a state of dispersion, encountered that of Napoleon, which exceeded it in actual numbers present by from 20 to 25 per cent. In addition to its numerical superiority, the French army had the advantage over that of the allies in a superior organisation, in a more up-to-date system of tactics, in a method of subsistence more suited to its requirements, and in a better armament, as regards the infantry at least. Whilst the allied army enjoyed no unity of command, was exhausted by useless marches and countermarches—the result of its organisation and command—that of Napoleon was moved in accordance with the uncontrolled, and always decided, will of the Emperor alone. When Prussian commanders, torn by uncertainty as to what was their best plan, were constantly seeking to improve their schemes of operation, were holding councils of war which never decided anything definite, Napoleon had laid down, without regard to the opinions of others, the general lines of his operations, on which he kept his eye constantly fixed.

Once he had settled what was the best general plan he could find, he refused to be turned from it by minor events, or to attempt to find a better scheme from moment to moment. The Prussian generals showed no such fixity of purpose. One scheme was set aside for another at every sign of a change in temporary circumstances; every officer of reputation was allowed to have a hand in the deliberations; there was a perpetual setting aside of a good plan in favour of the best. Napoleon, having settled on a good plan, preferred to carry it through consistently; the Prussians, with a good scheme, abandoned it in favour of an attempt to find the best.

Whatever may be said in favour of the Prussian commanders, no one would think of placing them as generals in the same class with Napoleon, towering as he did, in military ability, far above all contemporary leaders—above all those of the past, as most consider. If he surpassed them

Strategy and Tactics 167

as a designer of campaigns, he did so in a still greater degree in the execution of plans drawn up in the cabinet. Here it was that he reaped the advantage of the youth and energy of his subordinate commanders. Von der Golz may be correct in his statement as to the energy remaining in some of the older Prussian generals, but in the end it is impossible to put on the same level the activity of 60 or 70 years and that of 35 or 40. How is it possible to expect the same indefatigable activity from Winning at 70, from Kalkreuth at 69, or from Hohenlohe at 60, as was found in Davout, Lannes, Murat, Soult, and Ney at 36 or 37?

With all these advantages, even if we do not go quite so far as Prince Kraft, the value of the French army must be reckoned as far exceeding that of its opponents.[1]

In considering the strategic plans of the opposing chiefs, the most noticeable point is the extreme simplicity of those of Napoleon as compared with the complication of those of the Prussians. The Emperor sought, by keeping his army concentrated in such a manner as to enable it to unite for battle within 48 hours or less, to be able to meet the storm in whichever direction it might break. This is the meaning of the "battalion square of 200,000 men" of which he so frequently speaks. The Prussian generals, instead of this, sought to foresee and

---

[1] Prince Kraft arrives at his estimate of the French numbers as double those of Saxony and Prussia by including in the former Mortier's corps, the army of Holland, and the whole of the German contingent. If that mode of reckoning the French strength is adopted, it would seem fair to include, on the other side, the troops in Hanover, West Prussia, and Silesia.

make provision for meeting every possible circumstance in many directions. The result was dispersal over a very wide area—so wide that it was impossible for them to concentrate in anything like so short a time as the French. When Napoleon's army was moving in a square of 38 miles through the hills, the Allies were scattered over a front of between 80 and 90 miles. As soon as he reached the open country beyond the Saale, the Emperor drew his army still closer together. The Prussians were never properly concentrated. Even on the 13th October, Weimar's and Winning's detachments were at a distance from the main army which rendered their co-operation within a reasonable period impossible.

Napoleon based his scheme partly on the element of surprise. It was necessary for him, if possible, to carry his army through the difficult country south of the Saale before his enemy could have time to concentrate and meet him in full force as his three columns debouched from that tract. The influence which that desire may have exercised on his use of his cavalry has already been discussed. When the true direction of his march was ascertained at the Prussian headquarters, about the 7th October, it was too late.

If there is one point which this campaign brings out more clearly than another it is the truth of the saying that no general, however great, escapes errors. The greatest is he who makes the fewest.

Napoleon in this campaign made many mistakes, but their evil consequences were avoided by the excellence of his arrangements for concentration in any direction at the shortest notice. He was hopelessly wrong in his diagnosis of the Prussian intentions on the 10th, when he believed that they were about to concentrate on Gera. He was again wrong in believing that they were retiring on Erfurt, and that he would not be able to reach them before the 16th.[1] By this latter error he was led into a great risk in exposing Lannes and Augereau, as he did on the 12th and 13th, to defeat in detail beyond the Saale. He appears not to have appreciated the strength of that river line, which he had never seen, and of which his intelligence officers do not appear to have brought out the full importance.[2] Again, owing to the same error as to the Prussian position, he had his army in a far less concentrated condition than he would have had he expected battle on the 14th. Yet, such is the influence of fortune in war, the fact that Davout at Naumburg was not in close contact with the centre resulted in the defeat of the main Prussian army as well as that of Hohenlohe.

It is impossible to avoid the conclusion that the position of the two corps (Lannes' and Augereau's) on the left bank of the Saale on the 13th October was one of extreme peril, the existence of which was clearly manifest to the Emperor. To see that this was so it is only

---

[1] On this subject see "Napoleon as a General," i. 290, &c.

[2] This does not agree with the statement of General Bonnal that the manœuvre of Jena was based on the fact that "the Saale is a river deeply sunk, offering few points of passage" (*La Manœuvre d'Iena*, p. 431). It seems doubtful if the passages are quite so rare as General Bonnal would have us believe. As one passes along the Saale valley by rail from Koesen to Saalfeld, easy fords are seen in several places, especially between Jena and Saalfeld. They probably existed in 1806.

necessary to look at the urgent terms of his orders of that day—a day on which he had calculated on giving his army a rest before launching it on the final effort towards Erfurt. By his failure to throw Lannes and Augereau back over the Saale, Hohenlohe, acting under the baneful influence of Massenbach, lost his one chance of inflicting a severe reverse on the French. His success, if he had gained it, would not have saved the defeat of Prussia in the end, even if it had resulted in the destruction of Lannes' corps and the defeat of Augereau; but it would probably have prevented the fearful catastrophe of Jena and Auerstädt, and enabled the King's army as well as his own to reach the Elbe.[1]

From the position of Hohenlohe's corps on the eve of Jena, it would appear that he expected the French advance from the south, over the plateau on the left bank of the Saale, not from the east across that river. If that were the belief entertained at headquarters, it appears to have been a mistake to leave so large a proportion as half (Hohenlohe and Ruchel) the Prussian army to cover the retreat of the other half. That it was Hohenlohe's belief seems almost certain when we consider how he persisted, even when Lannes' attack had commenced on the 14th, in believing that it was only that of an advance guard. Even then he did not believe in the prospect of a great battle that day. Napoleon

[1] Count Yorck says Napoleon believed the Prussians to be at Erfurt. One of his corps might have been defeated, but that would only have given him information, and not seriously injured him. Had Lannes been cut up on the 13th, that would not have altered the result ("Napoleon as a General," i. 301).

Strategy and Tactics 171

had not believed in it till he received, on the 13th, Lannes' report of what he saw before him from the Landgrafenberg. The Emperor even then fell into the error of believing that what lay before him was not half, but the whole of the Prussian army. He was totally ignorant till the morning of the 15th of the march of the other half towards the Unstrut.

The absence of Bernadotte from Jena as well as from Auerstädt is inexplicable, except on the ground of his own selfish and jealous character. Never had commander a better chance than he had of turning the hard-won success of a fellow-general into an easy and overwhelming victory; but then the laurels must have been shared with Davout, which was not what Bernadotte could bear, especially as the lion's share would have fallen to Davout. The Emperor's orders are not forthcoming in original, which must be admitted to be *primâ facie* suspicious. They are, however, clearly given in Davout's history of the operations of the 3rd corps, and Davout is generally reliable and honest. The orders were addressed to him, and he says they ran: "If Marshal Bernadotte is with you, you can march together; but the Emperor hopes that he will be in the position indicated to him at Dornburg." These orders Davout says he communicated to Bernadotte in writing. Bernadotte himself admits receiving them at 4 A.M. on the 14th. (See his despatch of 21st October —Foucart, ii. 200.) On the other hand, he ignores the order to march with Davout if he was still himself at Naumburg, and confines himself to an exposition of the difficulties of getting from Dornburg (where he arrived at 11 A.M. on the 14th) to Apolda. Looking from the Saale up the valley leading from Dornburg to the plateau, there seem few difficulties, certainly none such as Soult had in the Rauthal. Besides, we know that Hohenlohe on the evening of the 13th went down to Dornburg with a brigade and up again, all in a few hours, apparently without any difficulty. What Bernadotte says might seem to point to the absence of any such order to march with Davout. The Emperor answered him on the 23rd October (Foucart, ii. 243) as follows: "However, according to a very precise order, you ought to have been at Dornburg, which is one of the principal passages of the Saale, on the same day as Marshal Lannes was at Jena, Marshal Augereau at Kahla, and Marshal Davout at Naumburg. In case you had not executed these orders, I had informed you during the night that, if you were still at Naumburg, you should march with Marshal Davout and support him. You were at Naumburg when this order arrived; it was communicated to you; but, nevertheless, you preferred to make a false march in order to turn back to Dornburg, and in consequence you did not find yourself in the battle, and Marshal Davout bore the principal efforts of the enemy's army." To that letter Bernadotte could have replied, if the case were so, that the orders to support Davout if both were at Naumburg had not reached him. He did not do so, and the presumption must therefore be that he *did* receive them, as Davout says he did. The orders were certainly clear enough, and it seems impossible to find any excuse for Bernadotte's reading the latter part, merely expressing a hope that he was at Dornburg, as a direction to march at that late period by a circuitous road, instead of by the straight one to Apolda.

It is on these despatches, written within a few days of the event, and not for publication, that the *affaire Bernadotte* must be judged, and they seem conclusive against him.

The utterances of St. Helena and the statements of memoir writers are of much less value, though perhaps worthy of record. Napoleon, at St. Helena, in his notes on the memoirs of Bernadotte, says that marshal demanded to lead the way if he marched with Davout. The latter objected that, Bernadotte's corps being in rear of him, it would cause confusion if it passed to the front. Bernadotte insisted on having precedence, on the ground that his corps was No. I. while Davout's was No. III.! With reference to this last astounding statement, it is noticeable that in Berthier's despatch of 21st October 1806 (Foucart, ii. 186), conveying the first written censure of Bernadotte's action on the 14th, he says the Emperor "is not accustomed to see his operations sacrificed to useless points of etiquette of command." Napoleon added, at St. Helena, that he had signed the order for Bernadotte's trial, but had withdrawn it on personal grounds (*Mémoires pour servir*, &c., viii. 215). He had no particular affection for Bernadotte; in fact, he disliked him, though he admitted his ability. But it will be remembered that in his youth he came very near marrying Bernadotte's future wife, and he always had a strong affection for her.

Rapp relates that the day after the battle Napoleon remarked to him at Jena: "Bernadotte has behaved badly. He would have been enchanted to see Davout fail in that affair, which does him (Davout) the greatest honour, all the more so because Bernadotte had rendered his position difficult" (Rapp's Memoirs, p. 84)

Savary gives Napoleon's remarks about Bernadotte thus: "That is so hateful that if I send him to a court martial it is equivalent to ordering him to be shot; it is better for me not to speak to him about it. I believe he has enough honour to recognise that he has performed a disgraceful action regarding which I shall not bandy words with him" (*Mémoires de Duc de Rovigo*, ii. 292).

Had Napoleon been correct in his assumption that he had before him the whole Prussian army, the effect of his orders to Bernadotte and Davout would have been their union on the battlefield with the centre and left, in the same way that the Prussian armies united at Königgrätz sixty years later. To fix the point of union of his corps on the battlefield itself was contrary to Napoleon's practice; he generally aimed at concentration for battle short of the field, though of course Bautzen was an example of the contrary. That was what his orders of the 12th had sought; but the concentration was to be for a prospective battle beyond Weimar. When, on the 13th, he discovered that his great battle would have to be fought two days earlier than, and a day's march to the east of where he had expected, it was too late to concentrate short of the battlefield. He was compelled to adopt the system, afterwards used against him at Waterloo, in that case also used in consequence of the stress of circumstances.

He brought on to the field at Jena, by the afternoon of the 14th, about 96,000 men. Of these, four divisions of infantry, besides the Guard and the heavy cavalry of Nansouty, were not engaged. The 54,000 men actually engaged more than sufficed to destroy Hohenlohe and Ruchel, and it was partly owing to the rapid drift of the battle towards Weimar that the remainder did not arrive in the fighting line. Had the whole Prussian army been, as Napoleon believed, with Hohenlohe, the battle would perhaps have come to a standstill in front of Vierzehnheiligen. In that event, the whole of the 96,000 French would have been sufficient at any rate to hold the Prussians until 54,000 more men, under Davout, Bernadotte, Lasalle, and Beaumont, could fall on their left flank.[1] It would not have been possible in any case for 15,000

[1] Foucart, i. 671, who calculates times of arrival thus :—

About noon.

	Infantry.	Cavalry.
III. Corps—3rd Division and Cavalry .	8,500	1,300

About 2.30 P.M.

	Infantry.	Cavalry.
III. Corps—2nd Division . . .	7,500	—
I. Corps—3rd Division and Cavalry .	5,800	1,500

About 4 P.M.

	Infantry.	Cavalry.
III. Corps—1st Division . . .	10,000	—
I. Corps—2nd Division . . .	5,600	—
Beaumont's Dragoons . . .	—	2,600
Lasalle's Light Cavalry . . .	—	1,100
Total	47,400	6,500

men[1] to reach the battlefield at all. This again would not have happened but for Napoleon's error as to the place where he would meet the enemy for the great decision.

The crucial period for Napoleon at Jena was the commencement, when he had to gain room for the deployment of his corps as they advanced. Once he had gained this, there was no longer any doubt. Here, had Hohenlohe been alive to the situation, the Prussians had their best chance. A position of which the centre is the Dornberg, the right the Isserstadt wood, and the left beyond the Rauthal, with Cospeda and Closewitz occupied as advanced posts, is by far the strongest on the battlefield. Had Napoleon found the whole of Hohenlohe's army so posted instead of only Tauenzien, his deployment would have been much more difficult than it was.

In the French tactics at Jena there is nothing to be very specially remarked, except Napoleon's use of twenty-five guns to fill the gap on Lannes' left. No attempt at a general turning movement was made, for the simple reason that that duty had been assigned to Davout and Bernadotte.[2]

The Prussians played into the Emperor's

---

[1] Foucart, i. 671. The 15,000 men were the following:—

	Infantry.	Cavalry.
I. Corps—1st Division	7000	—[1]
Grouchy's Dragoons	—	2500
Sahuc's Dragoons	—	2600
Guard Cavalry	—	2800
Total	7000	7900

[2] There were, of course, special turning movements, such as that by Soult, of the Prussian left at Vierzehnheiligen, and the surrounding of the Saxons at the Schnecke.

Strategy and Tactics 177

hands throughout. Hohenlohe's persistent disbelief in the approach of a great battle resulted in his army being widely dispersed and exposed to defeat by sections. First, Tauenzien was exposed, without support, to the attack of 25,000 French against his 8000. Just as he was defeated, and unable to do more than effect his own retreat, Holtzendorf's 5000 men coming up were equally exposed to defeat at the hands of St. Hilaire's division, supported by Wedel's brigade. The next stage was the defence, by about 23,000 Prussians and Saxons, of the line from beyond Vierzehnheiligen through Isserstadt to the Schnecke, again unsupported, till it was too late, against double their numbers.

Ruchel, arriving very late, was equally unable to stem the pursuit with his 15,000 men.

In the Vierzehnheiligen line the two important points were that village itself and the wood and village of Isserstadt. Vierzehnheiligen fell at an early hour into the hands of the French for the second time, never to be retaken by the Prussians. Isserstadt, captured by Desjardins by 10 A.M., was retaken by the Prussians. When they were ejected from it once more, the line was broken and the Saxons at the Schnecke were separated from the centre and the right. Instant retreat was their only chance of safety. They held on, probably because they were unaware of their separation from the centre. As the Prussians fell back the Saxons became completely isolated, and it was inevitable that they should be surrounded as soon as Desjardins and Murat were able to turn to the left.

Ruchel's attempt to restore the battle by an

offensive movement was hopeless. The most he could hope to do, and of that even there was but a faint chance, was to make a stand on the Weimar side of the Capellendorf valley, acting as rearguard to the disordered, fleeing masses of Hohenlohe.

The Prussian attacks on Vierzehnheiligen were a good example of the impossibility of succeeding with the parade-ground tactics of the Seven Years' War against the new tactics of the French. The unhappy Prussians, attempting solemnly to form line before opening fire, were decimated by the fire of the French, ensconced behind the walls of the village and the gardens, or hidden in the furrows of the potato fields.

At Auerstädt the Prussian tactics betrayed the same weaknesses as at Jena. Blucher's cavalry was defeated before Schmettau was able to arrive to its support. Schmettau, in turn, was half defeated before the arrival of Wartensleben. Both those generals had shot their bolt, and failed, before they received any assistance from Kalkreuth's two reserve divisions.

Davout, on the other hand, displayed all the qualities which even Napoleon could expect from the commander of an isolated corps fighting against double its numbers. He saw at once the incalculable importance of holding fast in Hassenhausen, the only point of support he had on the plateau. To that village Gudin's division held with the tenacity of the bulldog. At one moment, just before the arrival of Morand's division, Hassenhausen was practically all that Davout held, except for Friant's division, which was more or less isolated on the right.

Strategy and Tactics 179

As his troops came up, Friant's division first, then Morand's, Davout hurried them forward to rebuild his line right and left of Hassenhausen. But he was not content with a mere passive defence of Hassenhausen, for he boldly sent a large part of Friant's division to the right to turn the Prussian left wing, an operation which succeeded perfectly. As Morand, after the repulse of the cavalry and Guards on the Sonnenburg ridge, pushed forward his left, Davout was in the extraordinary position of outflanking an enemy nearly double his own strength on both wings.

In neither battle did the dreaded Prussian cavalry greatly distinguish itself. At Jena the Saxo-Prussian cavalry numbered, according to Lettow-Vorbeck, 92 squadrons, 10,500 men. The French cavalry engaged [1] were 51 squadrons, 8450 men. The Allies' cavalry did what Napoleon expected of it, expending much of its strength in futile attacks on unbroken infantry. Even against French cavalry on equal terms it gained no marked success. The Prussian cavalry proved inferior to that of Saxony; the latter kept together to the end of the battle, long after the Prussian had been completely broken up.

At Auerstädt the Prussian superiority in cavalry was immense—over 9000 against 1300; yet it was ruined, mainly by its attacks on infantry. Blucher's 10 squadrons, north of Hassenhausen, were shattered by Gudin's and Friant's infantry squares. A very large cavalry

[1] Omitting Nansouty's cuirassiers and one of d'Hautpoult's brigades.

force charged Morand at the most favourable moment, when he was moving into line. But the attack, having no unity of purpose or command, failed completely.

As for artillery, the French guns at Jena were about equal (108 to 104) to the Allies' regular artillery, but the latter was increased by 71 infantry guns. Nevertheless, everywhere the French artillery carried the day. Napoleon's use of a massed battery of 25 guns, on Lannes' left, has already been noticed.

At Auerstädt, Davout had but 44 guns; he captured 57 of the Prussian regular artillery alone. The total Prussian strength there was 230 guns (136 regular, 94 infantry).

PLAN FOR BATTLES OF JENA AN[D]

EXPLANATION OF PLANS OF TH[E]
POSITIO[N]

BATTLE OF JENA.

French infantry
" cavalry

Prussian infantry
" cavalry

PRUSSIANS.
B.—Boguslawski.
Cer.—Cerrini.
D.—Dyherrn.
Gr.—Gravert.
Hz.—Holtzendorf.
Pc.—Prussian cavalry covering Tauenzien's retreat.
Pl.—Prussians at Isserstadt, in wood, and at Vierzehnheiligen.
Sc.—Saxon cavalry.
Sl.—Saxon infantry.
Ta.—Tauenzien retreating on Gr. Romsdorf.

FRENCH.
A1.—Augereau's first division ((Desjardins)
A2.—Augereau's second division (Heudelet)
G.—Imperial Guard and Napoleon.
H.—Part of heavy cavalry.
L1.—Lannes' first division (Suchet).
L2.—Lannes' second division (Gazan).
M.—Murat with part of cavalry reserve.
N.—Ney's main body.
Na.—Ney's advance guard.
Sc.—Soult's light cavalry.
S1.—Soult's first division (St. Hilaire).
S2, S3.—Soult's second and third division[s] (Legrand and Leval).
W.—Wedel's brigade (of Suchet's division[)]

...ERSTÄDT – 14TH OCTOBER 1806.

BATTLES OF JENA AND AUERSTÄDT.

...OUT 10.15 A.M.

BATTLE OF AUERSTÄDT.

FRENCH.
- Dc.—Davout's light cavalry.
- F.—Part of Friant's division at Spielberg.
- G.—Gudin's division and part of Friant's at Hassenhausen.
- M.—Morand's division moving into line.

PRUSSIANS.
- C.—Prussian cavalry.
- L.—Lutzow's brigade (division Orange), attacking Hassenhausen.
- PH.—Prince Henry's Brigade (division Orange) opposing Friant at Spielberg.
- R.—Reserve divisions.
- S.—Schmettau's division attacking Hassenhausen.
- W.—Wartensleben's division attacking Hassenhausen.

Rl.—Ruchel in Weimar and marching from Weimar to Capellendorf.
Bt.—Bernadotte and Sahuc marching on Dornburg from Naumburg.

CHAPTER X

EVENTS OF THE 15TH TO 17TH OCTOBER

THOUGH the campaign of 1806 was the most notable example in the Napoleonic wars of what we may perhaps call a "strategical" pursuit, the two great battles of the 14th October did not end in that immediate tactical pursuit, *l'épée dans les reins*, which characterised Waterloo. The defeated armies were allowed the whole night in which to pull themselves together; for it was not till the morning of the 15th that the pursuit really commenced, or that Napoleon issued his orders for it. As a matter of fact, the disorganisation in the allied armies was so complete that they had, by the morning of the 15th, been able to effect very little in the way of re-establishing order and cohesion. Had they been closely followed and harassed by cavalry throughout the night of the 14th and 15th, as the broken army of Waterloo was during the night of the 18th–19th June 1815, it seems almost impossible to believe that any organised body whatever would have remained. Looking to Napoleon's methods of war, to the determination which he afterwards disclosed to exterminate the Prussian army as a fighting force, it naturally, on the face of it, excites some surprise that he should have allowed a cessation of pursuit for many hours. Was it possible to do otherwise? If possible, was it safe? What were Napoleon's motives? Such are the questions which will at once occur to the student of this campaign. In the first place, it is necessary to remember the extreme exertions which were demanded on the 14th October from the men and horses of the greater part of the French army, due, no doubt, largely to Napoleon's miscalculation of the day of battle, and the consequent necessity of concentrating by forced marches. Certainly there were many troops on the battlefield of Jena who had had little or no fighting during the day; but those were precisely the men who had been exhausted by immense marches. Two of Soult's divisions had marched thirty-two miles since the evening of the 13th. Ney's troops and the reserve cavalry had marched twenty-one miles in the same period, and the latter had on the previous day covered twenty-six miles. All the cavalry had had a heavy day's work during the battle except Beaumont's 2600 dragoons and Lasalle's light cavalry, who were perhaps the only troops really capable of carrying on the pursuit at once. To them might be added the light cavalry of Lannes, Augereau, and Bernadotte. As for Davout's corps, his infantry stopped, utterly exhausted, at Eckardsberga, and his light cavalry, which got as far as Buttstadt, must have been nearly at the end of its tether.

Knowing what we now know, it seems probable that even a force of 3000 or 4000 cavalry could, without great risk, have done immense harm to the broken Prussians and Saxons during the night. But it must be remembered that Napoleon's information was very scanty. He still believed that he had met the whole Prussian army, or the front of it, at Jena. He certainly could not have believed that the 50,000 men whom he defeated there were the whole army. His eye never failed him in estimating the force of the enemy on a battlefield, and he knew that what was in front of him was not half what he had to account for. Where were the rest? He knew nothing certain of the flank march of Brunswick, or of Davout's battle. If the pursuit were pressed on, it might well be that it would encounter another 50,000 men between Weimar and Erfurt. There was no news from Davout, though the Emperor once or twice fancied he heard amidst the roar of Jena the sounds of a battle to his right. If Davout were defeated it might be necessary to move in his direction next day. Everything was uncertain until Davout's despatch came in next morning. Napoleon himself was so exhausted that De Ségur records how he lay on the ground, in the afternoon of the 14th, studying his maps, whilst the Saxon prisoners, taken at the Schnecke, defiled past him. Presently sleep overcame him, and he lay there in the midst of his Guard, who, at a sign from Lefebvre, silently formed a protecting square around him whilst he slept. Murat, arriving at Weimar at 6 P.M., wrote—"Your Majesty will pardon my scribble; but I am alone and dropping from fatigue." It took a good deal to wear out Murat or to stay his ardour in pursuit. On this occasion he was so done up that he made two attempts before he finally succeeded in writing "1806" at the head of his letter.

Taking all these circumstances into consideration, he would be a rash critic who ventured to condemn the practical cessation of the pursuit during the night of the 14th and 15th. Napoleon was the apostle of thoroughness in war; his physical and mental vigour was at its zenith at Jena, the deterioration which resulted in the failure to pursue after Dresden and after Ligny had not yet begun to appear. It seems safer to assume that the Emperor's motives were based on the exhaustion of his own troops and the uncertainty of his intelligence.

For the night of the 14th Napoleon retired to Jena, leaving the Guard to bivouac on the plateau. Perhaps, it may be thought, he would have done better to go on to Weimar. But he was still waiting for news of Davout, and that marshal was more likely to send it to Jena than to Weimar.

It was not till about 9 A.M. on the 15th[1] that Napoleon received Davout's report of the events at Auerstädt. No orders were issued for the pursuit till 5 A.M. on the 15th. In the confusion which marked the flight of the army of Hohenlohe, it was almost impossible to say which direction the main body had taken.

The positions occupied during the night after the battles by the French corps were as follows:—

Davout bivouacked about Eckardsberga and

---

[1] Foucart, ii. 6. De Ségur is clearly wrong in saying that Davout's despatch arrived at 2 A.M. The Emperor's orders of 5 A.M. on the 15th indicate his ignorance at that hour of the events of Auerstädt.

MARSHAL BERNADOTTE
(From an engraving in Mr. Broadley's collection)

15th to 17th October

Auerstädt, with Vialanne's light cavalry at Buttstadt.

Bernadotte had Drouet's and Rivaud's divisions in front of Apolda, on the road to Weimar. Dupont's division and the greater part of the artillery were still at Dornburg.

Ney himself was in Weimar; his light cavalry was beyond the town on the Erfurt road, his two infantry divisions on the Jena side.

Soult's corps bivouacked behind Ulrichshalben; Lannes' was about the junction of the roads from Naumburg and Jena to Weimar; Augereau's in and about Weimar.

The Cavalry Reserve was distributed between Weimar, Apolda, and Dornburg, with the 1st division of dragoons three miles out on the road from Weimar to Erfurt.

In the meanwhile the Prussians, and what remained of the Saxons, were dispersing in all directions amidst a scene of indescribable confusion and ruin. The King, unaware of the defeat of Hohenlohe and Ruchel, had ordered the main army to retreat on the Ettersberg heights, three or four miles north of Weimar; but no provision had previously been made for retreat in the event of defeat; neither Brunswick nor Hohenlohe had anticipated a great battle on the 14th. The King's orders were issued too late to prevent the retreat, which had already begun, of part of his army in the direction of Buttelstedt. His men had in the morning, for the most part, lightened their burdens by throwing away their food; and now, suffering the pangs of hunger and thirst, they dispersed in all directions, seeking food and drink in the villages, or digging up potatoes and turnips in the fields. Discipline was at an end, and, to add to the confusion, the superior officers were as ignorant as their subordinates, or their men, of the direction for retreat. Even Kalkreuth, the commander of the two reserve divisions, when asked by Alvensleben in which direction he should go, replied that Buttelstedt seemed the best. Plainly the King's orders had not reached him, and it was well that they had not. He, with many disorganised troops, followed that line, whilst small bodies made their way direct towards Magdeburg. The King, as he marched with the reserves to cross the Ilm near Apolda, seeking to reach Weimar, was confronted by Bernadotte's corps, and compelled to return to the left bank, with the conviction that Weimar was no longer a feasible point of retreat. It was soon after this that he at last received news of the extent of Hohenlohe's and Ruchel's disaster, and heard that they were making for Erfurt. Yet even this latter news was not altogether correct, for the remains of Ruchel's force and part of Hohenlohe's had crossed the Ilm below Weimar. Presently the two streams of fugitives from Jena and from Auerstädt began to cross one another, making the confusion worse and worse. Panic-stricken drivers, cutting their traces, made off with their horses, leaving guns and waggons strewing the whole countryside, and blocking the roads in the defiles and villages. None knew where they were going, or where the enemy was; every instant the panic was increased by false alarms of French cavalry. The King himself, meeting Blucher, despaired of the situation. "We are in a sorry plight," he said; "mayhap we shall have to cut our way through." All through the miserable night this terrible flight continued; it was not till 7 A.M. on the 15th that the unhappy sovereign was able to call a halt at Sommerda, and to make some attempt to collect and organise the broken troops which followed him, or straggled in from various directions.

Tauenzien's division, or what remained of it, reached Buttelstedt in some sort of order, only to find the place blocked in every direction with guns and transport. Hearing that the King had gone to Sommerda, the general continued his march in that direction. Hohenlohe, with a handful of cavalry, reached Schloss Vippach about 9.30 P.M., finding there the baggage of the main army. Rumour falsely informing him that the enemy was already in Sommerda, he made for Tennstadt, whence, turning northwards again, he continued his weary flight to Sondershausen, where he arrived only in the afternoon of the 15th. A considerable portion of his army had fled towards Erfurt. Thither had gone the wounded Gravert, and old Marshal Möllendorf stricken with a mortal injury. The Prussian cavalry, broken up entirely, was scattered all over the country. The Saxon horsemen, who had maintained their cohesion all through the battle, still formed an organised body, which eventually found its way to Sommerda, turning thither from the Erfurt road when news reached it of the advance of the French on the latter town. Cerrini, with all that remained of the Saxon infantry, had passed, by Buttelstedt and Cölleda, to Weisensee and Frankenhausen.

Practically, excepting the reserve corps at

Halle, the only organised body of troops remaining to the Prussians on the night of the 14th–15th was the detachment under the Duke of Weimar, for whose return from the Thuringian Forest Ruchel had been left to wait at Weimar on the 14th. The Duke, who had reached Ilmenau on the evening of the 13th, appears not to have received notice of the contemplated flank march of the main army; for on the 14th he had sent a detachment towards Saalfeld, and was preparing himself to march on Rudolstadt, aiming at Napoleon's left flank and rear. At 4 p.m. he received a jubilant message from Ruchel. According to it, both Hohenlohe and Brunswick were making good progress against the enemy, and Ruchel himself was moving to join Hohenlohe. The Duke was urged to hurry up, in order to take his part in the glorious victory which was anticipated. He decided to march from Wipfra at daybreak on the 15th for Weimar. Presently, however, he appears to have been struck by apprehensions of meeting the enemy on the Ilm, and he decided to march the same night, the 14th, as far as Egstadt before turning towards Weimar. The march was to be in two columns, the right by Heyda and Wipfra, the left by Plaue and Arnstadt. When he reached the last-named place a fresh messenger arrived, announcing the defeat of Hohenlohe and Ruchel. This news decided him to alter his line, so as to march behind the Gera river to the west side of Erfurt.

Marching all night, it was not till 11 a.m. on the 15th that he found himself on the heights of Stedten, still some distance south of Erfurt. An hour later he had heard from Mollendorf that the main army was supposed to be assembling on Langensalza. The marshal desired him to make for that place, to which he would himself follow with the troops collected at Erfurt. The French cavalry were already beginning to appear from the direction of Weimar.

We must now return to Napoleon at Jena, where he slept after the battle. His earliest care on the morning of the 15th was the issue of orders for the pursuit of the wrecked Prussian army, on whose complete annihilation he was bent. Before detailing these orders there is another subject to which attention must be given, the Emperor's attitude towards Saxony. He had failed to detach that power from the Prussian alliance before the outbreak of war; now he was in a very different position, and he had no wish to annihilate Saxony, as he was determined to do with Prussia. He saw in her a useful ally against either Prussia or Austria, and a most important factor in the constitution of the Gallicised Rhenish Confederation which he was constructing. He knew that there was little or no sympathy between Saxony and Prussia; as for Austria, she had abandoned her claims on the former state by her abdication of the chiefship of the German Empire. Napoleon had been opposed at Saalfeld and Jena by some 20,000 Saxons; of these nearly half were prisoners in his hands; many more had been killed or wounded in the two battles. In both cases the Saxon army had suffered defeat under the leadership of a Prussian general, and on it had fallen the brunt of the fighting, facts which were hardly likely to cement the half-hearted alliance. Throughout, the Emperor had refused to admit that his quarrel was with Saxony; on the contrary, he had posed as the champion of that country against the overbearing pretensions of Prussia. Now was the time to dissolve, by a politic clemency, the last ties of the ill-assorted alliance, and none knew better than Napoleon how to act in such circumstances.

In the great hall of the University of Jena were assembled all the captive officers of the Saxon army, and there Napoleon addressed them in brief, energetic terms. He urged them to tear themselves from the dominion of Prussia; he promised to treat their sovereign as a friend; and, finally, he offered them their liberty on the sole condition of their engaging, for themselves and their troops, no longer to bear arms against France.

After this public scene, he sent privately for Major Funck, the aide-de-camp of the Saxon general Zeschwitz, who had been captured when his chief broke through the surrounding French. To him Napoleon spoke still more explicitly, expressing his desire for an amicable ending to the unfortunate breach with the Elector, towards whom he evinced the most friendly feeling. The personal fascination of Napoleon, when he chose to exercise it, is universally admitted, and Funck left his presence, to communicate the Emperor's assurances to his sovereign, entirely won over by it.

It will be well here to anticipate the course of events in the dealings of Napoleon with Saxony.

When Funck reached Dresden he found the wildest confusion prevailing. In anticipation of a French invasion, the Electoral treasure had already been removed, and the Elector himself, his ministers, and all persons of importance in the capital were prepared to follow it towards Silesia. The mission of Funck, and of Thielmann—another officer whom Napoleon had, in private audience, won over—together with the treatment which had been extended to the Saxon officers, produced a complete revulsion of ideas. From the depths of despair the hopes of the Elector and his court passed to the extreme heights of optimism. They foresaw the immediate evacuation of Saxon territory by the French, and the assumption by their state of a position of neutrality. Little did they understand of Napoleon's policy then; they knew not that neutrality was unrecognised by him, or that there were but two alternatives open in dealing with him—hostility, with the certainty of destruction at his hands, or friendship, with its obligations of active alliance.

They were soon disillusioned by the arrival of French officials and troops, charged to occupy Dresden so long as a state of war subsisted between France and Saxony. Similarly, the rest of the country was occupied by French troops as that of an enemy. Leipzig, the great trade centre, was the scene of the wholesale confiscation of all English merchandise; and to complete the Elector's dismay, he found that on the day after Jena Saxony had been assessed to pay a war contribution of a million sterling.[1]

[1] The war indemnities to be paid by the hostile German states were assessed in a decree dated Jena, 15th October 1806. They varied from 100,000,000 francs in the case of the Prussian states west of the Vistula, to 100,000 francs in the case of Hildesheim. Saxony's share was 25,375,000 francs; Hesse-Cassel's, 6,000,000. The total was 159,425,000 francs (Foucart, ii. 14).

Thus did Napoleon force upon Saxony the conclusion of peace on his own terms—terms which included not only withdrawal from the Prussian alliance, but also active participation by a Saxon contingent in the destruction of the army with which it had shared the disaster of Jena. Space will not allow us to enter in detail into the negotiations which ended with the Treaty of Posen, whereby Saxony became for the succeeding seven years the vassal of Napoleon, sacrificing, for the furtherance of his insatiable ambition, her wealth, her prosperity, and the flower of her population, without any return beyond the empty distinction of being raised to the dignity of a kingdom, on a level with the newly created kingdoms of Bavaria and Würtemberg. To this was added later the Grand Duchy of Warsaw.

It was 5 A.M. on the 15th when the Emperor began to issue his orders for the pursuit of the defeated Prussians. At that time he was still but ill informed as to the direction, or directions, taken by the army which he had beaten, and which he still believed to be the main Prussian army. It was not till 9 A.M. that he heard of the stupendous success of Davout, and was able to complete his orders for all the corps. In framing them, he was forced to give some consideration to the tremendous exertions which he had demanded from his troops on the previous day. The three corps which had had the heaviest fighting were allowed as much rest as possible. Davout was only to march back to Naumburg, ready to move on Leipzig. Lannes and Augereau stood fast about Weimar. Ney's corps, with the exception of the advance guard, had not borne a heavy share of the battle; it was therefore ordered to push on, in support of the cavalry, towards Erfurt.

Soult's camp at Ulrichshalben was conveniently situated for his advance to Buttelstedt, whither a considerable body of the enemy was known to have gone. Bernadotte, who had had no fighting, was sent to Neustadt,[1] on the road to Bibra, Querfurt, and Halle, in order to cut the fugitives from the Elbe.

Murat, with half of the Cavalry Reserve, was directed on Erfurt, whilst the rest were to move, in support of Soult, towards Buttelstedt. Towards noon on the 15th, Murat arrived before Erfurt, where he found Larisch drawn up outside the town on the heights to the north, with his back to the Gera and the town. His position was a bad one, with the defiles of the river and the town behind him, and as the French appeared, he withdrew his infantry to the fortress. His cavalry, attempting to cover their retreat, was swept back by the superior numbers of Murat and driven across the river at the bridge, on which a battery, getting jammed, was captured. Within the weak fortifications of Erfurt were now collected 10,000 or 12,000 Prussians. When the first fugitives began to arrive there, it had been wisely proposed to shut them out; but some officer, whose name has not been ascertained, cancelled the order, and thus the town was full of disorganised troops, whom it was impossible to reorganise there.

[1] North of the Ilm—not to be confounded with the place of the same name between the Saale and the Elster.

The admission into the fortress of these fugitives was a fatal error. Troops in the condition in which they were are only too ready to take refuge in the fancied security of a fortified place; to get them to leave it again is quite another matter.

Marshal Mollendorf, seeing clearly that Erfurt was no place for a large force to stay in, rightly decided to continue the retreat on Langensalza, covering it with the troops of the Duke of Weimar, which had had no fighting, and were not in any way demoralised. He ordered the baggage to start at once, the cavalry to march at 4 P.M., and the infantry an hour later. The Duke, too, saw the necessity for hurrying the departure from Erfurt, and despatched his infantry and heavy artillery at 1 P.M., whilst he moved his cavalry and horse artillery on to the heights west of the town, in order to cover the march of his own column and that of the troops in Erfurt. From this position he fired upon the French cavalry as they pursued that of Larisch across the Gera, and succeeded in stopping them. Again and again he sent into the town to hurry the march of the troops in it, but in vain.

About 2.30 P.M. the French colonel Préval arrived in Erfurt with a flag of truce, demanding the surrender of the place. At first the commandant talked of holding out, but his courage soon evaporated, and negotiations were commenced. The old and sorely wounded Marshal Mollendorf would perhaps have striven to keep him up to his duty, but excitement brought on a fresh outbreak of his wounds, and he was carried from the council chamber in a faint.

During the night the capitulation was signed, whereby at least 10,000[1] Prussians and Saxons fell as prisoners of war into Murat's hands. It was not till 10 P.M. that Ney's infantry began to arrive, and the strength of Murat's cavalry can certainly not have nearly equalled the garrison. Not only was Erfurt itself given up, but the surrender included the strong forts of the Petersberg and the Cyriaxberg, with great stores of powder and ammunition. This was the first of a series of pusillanimous capitulations by Prussian commandants, which vastly increased the misfortunes of the army and facilitated Napoleon's movements. Had Erfurt held out, even for a few days, it must have detained before it a considerable body of the troops which the Emperor was now enabled to launch in pursuit towards Magdeburg.

Weimar, meanwhile, had waited outside Erfurt till nearly dark, when, finding it hopeless to expect the main body from the town, he started for Langensalza with his own troops, augmented by stragglers from Erfurt, who had come out to avoid the impending capitulation. On the 16th he continued his march to Mühlhausen, having been joined by Winning from Fulda and Vach; here he mustered altogether 14 battalions, 30 squadrons, and 3 batteries, some 12,000 men with 24 guns, besides the regimental guns. On the 17th a small detachment of his cavalry had

---

[1] This is the number given by Hoepfner (ii. 19). Murat and the Emperor in their correspondence speak of only 6000; but, in the seventh bulletin, the Emperor speaks of 6000 unwounded and 8000 wounded prisoners. Probably Hoepfner's estimate of 10,000 is not far out, including the wounded. Murat himself says, later, over 10,000.

a remarkable piece of good fortune. Wandering about in search of the main body, the Pletz Hussars came upon the first column of prisoners from Erfurt on their way to Frankfort. The French escort was insufficient; it was attacked in detail by fifty hussars, and the whole column of prisoners was released.[1]

Murat had already started for Erfurt, with the whole of his cavalry that was at hand, when he received the Emperor's orders of the early morning of the 15th.

After the capitulation he marched on Langensalza, which he reached at 7 P.M. on the 16th, to find it evacuated by the Prussians, with the exception of twenty-five hussars. Here he lost touch of the troops with Weimar. Having disposed for the moment of the enemy on his left, he now turned to his right towards Soult. With himself he had the two heavy cavalry divisions and Beaumont's dragoons, some 7000 men.

Klein's dragoons, preceded by the 13th Chasseurs, had already been despatched on the 15th towards Weissensee, whilst Lasalle's light cavalry moved on Tennstädt. Klein reached Weissensee at midnight on the 15th, Lasalle arriving about the same time at Walschleben. Sahuc's dragoons were on the march to Buttelstedt; Grouchy still far behind at Schleiz. Ney, leaving a regiment in Erfurt, had followed Murat, reaching Gr.

[1] The Emperor was extremely angry about this, and wrote plainly to Murat, whose fault it clearly was. The lieutenant in command of the fifty hussars says he released 9000 prisoners, which is probably an exaggeration. Clarke, Governor of Erfurt, puts them at 5000, which is a more likely figure (Foucart, ii. 128). Later, he said 4000 (Foucart, ii. 877). Weimar afterwards tried to gather in these prisoners again to the colours, but they dispersed, not one rejoining the army.

Fahner and Gräfen-Tonna on the night of the 16th. Murat, as well as Lasalle and Klein, had taken many guns and waggons on their march.

We must now follow the movements of Soult on the 15th and 16th. That marshal, sending forward his light cavalry at daybreak, himself marched, about ten o'clock, as soon as he had received the Emperor's orders, for Buttelstedt, where he captured large magazines, as well as abandoned guns and waggons.[1] In front of him Kalkreuth's rearguard was at Sömmerda, with Blucher west of him, both marching on Sondershausen, preceded by the King, with all the débris of the army that he had been able to collect. Frederick William had scarcely left Weissensee an hour when it was occupied by Klein, who thus found himself between the King's troops and their strong rearguard under Kalkreuth.

On the morning of the 16th, Tauenzien, riding with a few cavalry in advance of Kalkreuth from Sömmerda, arrived before Weissensee. Finding Klein there, he at once sent back to warn Kalkreuth of the presence of the French. The Prussian general, aware that he was between Soult and a force of unknown strength at Weissensee, abandoned hope of escape, and was for surrendering. Such a course was vehemently opposed by Prince August of Prussia, by Blucher, and by Tauenzien, all of whom resented the idea

---

[1] Near Buttelstedt, Soult found Ruchel apparently mortally wounded. Soult ordered his surgeon and a guard to attend the wounded general, but before they reached him Ruchel had disappeared. He recovered, and was able again to fight in Poland. Napoleon numbered him among the dead, which, notwithstanding Sir R. Wilson's censure, was, under the circumstances, not unnatural. See Foucart, ii. 59, *n*.

of surrender without fighting when they still had 12,000 Prussians. Finally, negotiations for their passage were opened with Klein, who, according to Hoepfner, had but 800 cavalry, whilst Lasalle was to the west of him with only two light cavalry regiments. The absence of any strong force guarding Klein's flanks was revealed by Prussian cavalry reconnaissances. The French and Prussian accounts of the negotiations differ, the former asserting that the Prussian leaders positively affirmed the conclusion of an armistice, whilst the latter say that Blucher and Kalkreuth, positively alleging the King's proposal of an armistice, only expressed a belief that Napoleon was entertaining it favourably.

It will be remembered that Napoleon's letter of the 12th to the King had only reached its destination during the battle of Auerstädt. In his reply the King, indeed, proposed an armistice, but when the letter reached Napoleon on the 16th at Weimar circumstances had vastly altered. The French had gained two tremendous victories, and the Prussian armies were in a condition of ruin. It was hardly likely, therefore, that Napoleon would agree to an armistice before gathering in the full fruits of his victories. Whether Klein was deceived by the Prussian representations, or whether, as Hoepfner opines, he felt that resistance was impossible with his small force, and did the best he could by wasting time in negotiations, the fact remains that both he and Lasalle agreed to let the Prussians pass. For this they were most severely, unjustly, Hoepfner thinks, censured by Napoleon in general orders. Certainly Kalkreuth's march was delayed

by the parley, and by noon on the 16th he had
only reached Greussen, when Soult, with his light
cavalry and horse artillery, came in sight. Negotiations were again commenced. Soult was still
waiting for his infantry, without which he could
not venture to attack; he was, therefore, anxious
to waste time. Kalkreuth was again for surrender, but was kept up to the mark by Blucher.
Soult declined to recognise the existence of an
armistice of which he had received no intimation
from the Emperor; but, as Kalkreuth still asserted
his belief in it, the marshal proposed conditions,
one of which provided for the surrender of Kalkreuth should the armistice turn out not to exist.
These conditions, as Soult expected, were refused,
and about 4 P.M., his infantry being now present,
he broke off the negotiations and proceeded to
the attack. Blucher's cavalry retired across the
Helde stream and through Greussen, under cover
of a small force of infantry under Oswald.

Soult had now been reinforced by Sahuc's
dragoons, detached by Murat from Erfurt, but
the fall of night prevented pursuit and enabled
Kalkreuth, escaping with little loss, to continue
his march to Nordhausen.

It was not till the evening of the 17th that
Soult again caught him up, attacking his rearguard a few miles short of Nordhausen, and
then finding him drawn up on the heights at
that place, with cavalry in the plain in front.
The latter were driven in, with some loss in
prisoners and guns, by the 8th Hussars and 22nd
Chasseurs. Legrand's division then attacked the
heights, one brigade turning them on the left.
Kalkreuth, however, retired once more, seeking

to reach Magdeburg by marching through the Harz Mountains, partly by Halberstadt and partly by Quedlinburg. On these roads he had already been preceded by Hohenlohe, now placed in command of the collection of fugitives from all corps. News had arrived of the advance of Soult, of Bernadotte's progress towards Halle, and of other French movements, rendering it by no means certain that Magdeburg could be reached at all.

Confusion reigned supreme; the starving men robbed the bakeries and magazines; discipline did not exist.

To expedite the march of Hohenlohe, the heavy artillery, some 40 guns, had been ordered to march *viâ* Ellrich, Gittelde, and Brunswick to the Elbe at Sandau below Magdeburg. Scharnhorst, who was to have gone with this column, got separated from it, and eventually Blucher accompanied it, with 300 or 400 infantry and some cavalry. Other infantry which was to have formed part of the escort got driven towards Halberstadt. Blucher and the artillery, marching all night, reached Scharzfeld next morning, only halting when they were some way on the road to Gittelde. Murat and Ney were now marching hard to join Soult, the former being on the road from Langensalza at Immenrode, and as far forward as Gr. Furra. Ney, by dint of marching all day on the 17th, had reached Sondershausen, whence, apparently, after a few hours' rest, he pushed on to Nordhausen in the ensuing night. Here we will leave the French left wing whilst we recount the movements of the centre and right.

15th to 17th October

The Emperor himself remained at Weimar till about noon on the 17th, when he moved to Naumburg. Being separated by some sixty miles from his left wing, he could only send it general instructions.

Davout had, on the 16th and 17th, remained about Naumburg, whither Lannes' corps and the Guard had also moved; detachments were out on the Leipzig road. Augereau had only been moved as far forward as the neighbourhood of Auerstädt; Grouchy's dragoons were still at Gera. The Bavarians had been moved from Schleiz to Plauen, to be followed by the Baden and Würtemberg troops. None of these corps had any fighting on the 15th, 16th, or 17th.

Bernadotte's had alone pushed to the front on this side. On the 15th he had marched by Neustadt on Bibra and Querfurt. On the morning of the 16th he arrived at Schwan, about three miles beyond Bibra, having encountered no organised body of the enemy. Here he received Napoleon's orders of 2 A.M. on the 16th, indicating as probably his best direction Nebra, on the Unstrut, on which line he would be in a position to intercept the enemy's communications from Halle to both Erfurt and Weissensee. He was aware that the King and Hohenlohe had retired towards Nordhausen and the Harz Mountains, and, as a matter of fact, he had already, on the 16th, intercepted the roads indicated by the Emperor. He was also informed that the Prussian Reserve, hitherto not engaged, was about Halle, under Duke Eugene of Würtemberg. If this news still held good, he expressed his intention of marching against Halle, requesting Davout to join him, by means of cavalry pushed on Merseburg; in the event of Hohenlohe's turning towards Halle, Bernadotte would be in a position to attack the right flank of his troops on the march. Should both Hohenlohe and Würtemberg have disappeared, the marshal would consider the possibility of surprising Magdeburg.

At 2 A.M. on the 17th, Bernadotte started from Querfurt for Halle. When he had only covered some three miles of the road, his light troops brought news of the movement of a Prussian force on his left from Eisleben on Halle. The Eisleben to Halle road approached that from Querfurt about eleven miles from the latter town. Arriving at this point before the Prussians, Bernadotte left Drouet's division to observe the column of which he had heard, and continued his march with Dupont's and Rivaud's divisions.

Duke Eugene, whose whole force then consisted of 17¾ battalions, 20 squadrons, and 4 batteries (about 16,000 men) was proceeding to Magdeburg from Brandenburg on the 10th October, when he received orders to march on Halle and Leipzig. At that time, the King hoped by marching on Leipzig, aided by the Reserve corps, to keep the enemy from marching on Dresden.

By the 13th, Duke Eugene was with his main body at Halle, with a battalion at Merseburg, and a detachment protecting Leipzig. Another regiment (Treskow's) was following, by Aschersleben, from Magdeburg. French cavalry outposts were met at, and driven off from, Merseburg on the 13th. On the 14th the Prince received the King's orders of the previous day, directing him to wait at Halle, in readiness to join the main army as it marched down the left bank of the Saale towards Merseburg. The march to Leipzig was countermanded. The force at Merseburg had already been raised to 2½ battalions.

The sound of the battles at Auerstädt and Jena reaching his ears, the Duke resolved to await further orders at Halle. None had reached him by midday on the 15th, and it was not till the ensuing night that he heard, from a wounded officer and a passing despatch-bearer, of the disasters of the 14th, and the retreat of Hohenlohe and the King on Nordhausen. Simultaneously, news arrived that Davout, with 30,000 men, was at Naumburg and Weissenfels. On the 16th, being still without orders, Würtemberg decided to call in his detachments from Leipzig and Merseburg, and to endeavour to guard the magazines from Halle to Bernburg. He sent back a detachment to Dessau, with orders to burn the bridges of the Elbe in the event of his being driven towards Bernburg.

In the evening his troops left their cantonments in and about Halle to take up a position, with their right resting on the Galgenthor of Halle, and their front facing the Saale above the town, on the heights of the right bank. The extreme left was thrown back *en potence*. Three companies remained in Halle; a dragoon regiment held Passendorf and other villages on the left bank. The 2½ battalions, arriving at 10 P.M. from Merseburg, occupied the suburbs and gates on the east of the town. A regiment of hussars was still in the angle of the Saale and the Elster. Treskow's regiment had only reached Eisleben; the detachment from Leipzig had not yet arrived. Not having yet resolved on retreat, the Duke again, at 4 A.M. on the 17th, sent a battalion and 50 hussars to reconnoitre towards Merseburg.

THE ACTION OF HALLE—17TH OCTOBER.

The town of Halle lay at the foot of, and on the slope rising about 100 feet above the right bank of the Saale, which, opposite the town, divides into several branches, across which the road from Querfurt enters the town by a series of covered bridges, the Hohe Brücke. These bridges are reached, on the left bank, across the marshy low ground, by an embankment about half a mile in length. This open low ground made a plain of considerable extent, opposite to and above the town, whilst a little below it the river, again united in a single stream, flows between steep banks.

On the north of this plain, where the high ground trends towards the river, the knolls are covered with vineyards, and farther back are the extensive woods of Dolau, just north of the village of Nietleben on the Eisleben road. The Querfurt road descends from the heights to the valley at Passendorf.

Halle itself had no modern fortifications, but was surrounded by an old wall which, towards the river, formed a double enceinte. Due north, parallel to the right bank of the river, ran the road to Bernburg and Magdeburg. From the north-eastern gate—the Steinthor—issued the roads to Dessau and to Wittenberg, *viâ* Bitterfelde on the Mulde. The south-eastern gate—the Galgenthor—was the starting-point of the Merseburg and Leipzig roads.

The Duke of Würtemberg had at his disposal, at and about Halle, about 11,350 infantry, 1675 cavalry, and 58 guns. The two divisions with which Bernadotte was approaching by the Querfurt road numbered 12,190 infantry, 1000 cavalry, and 12 guns. Except, therefore, in the matter of artillery, the forces were fairly equal; neither had seen any fighting worthy of mention as yet.

At 8 A.M. the Duke received a report that his dragoon regiment at Passendorf had been attacked by French cavalry, who were driving it in. He sent four companies, with two guns, into the plain beyond the farthest of the Hohe Brücke, whilst five more companies, with four guns, occupied the island behind it, and guarded a ford below the bridge. The Prussian dragoons were now driven back in confusion; some of them, unable to reach the bridge, had to ford or swim the river above it.[1] The Prussian commander was still doubtful if Bernadotte's attack was serious, but, as he heard from Merseburg that there was no enemy in that direction, he began to prepare for retreat on the Elbe, sending off his baggage to Dessau. A false alarm of the French started a panic in the baggage column, which fled in terrible confusion, abandoning many waggons, to Dessau.

[1] Bernadotte mentions an attack of fresh cavalry from across a ford in the direction of Augersdorf, but this finds no place in Hoepfner's account. Perhaps the cavalry were only part of the dragoons.

Bernadotte, considering that he would do well to attack promptly, before the arrival of the hostile column from Eisleben and that of the small force from Merseburg, of which he appears to have had intelligence, sent for Drouet's division, which had remained behind on the Eisleben road, and ordered Rivaud to hurry up. About 10 A.M., as Rivaud came in sight, the marshal, keeping the 96th and the cavalry in reserve at Passendorf, sent forward Dupont with the 32nd, followed by one battalion of the 9th Light Infantry and supported by three light guns, against the bridge. These regiments charged along the embankment in columns, whilst their skirmishers, right and left, dealt with the Prussians opposite them, and fired on the flanks of the defenders of the dam. Losing heavily, the Prussians were forced across the first bridge and the island, those on either side in the island being cut off and captured. The second and third bridges were captured in like manner; within three-quarters of an hour Dupont was pressing through the town from west to east. General Hinrichs, commanding in this part, was taken. Another Prussian battalion, sent forward from the Galgenthor, was only in time to meet the French in the market-place, where it was almost entirely destroyed or captured. Yet another battalion was driven back through the Galgenthor, which Dupont now occupied, as well as the Steinthor, and the edge of the town between them. He was, however, still too weak to venture on issuing from the town against the main Prussian force.

The position of the latter, south of the town,

was badly chosen. Its line of retreat, to Magdeburg and Dessau, was far beyond its right flank, completely open to the enterprises of the enemy. The Duke, hurrying across the eastern front of the town with two battalions, reached the Steinthor only just in time to stop the issue of the French on the Dessau road; that of Magdeburg was already lost.

Dupont's men, awaiting reinforcements, barricaded themselves at the two gates and along the front of the town, and kept up a steady fire on the Prussians as they moved to their right to take position towards the Dessau road.

Presently arrived Dupont's 96th and the second battalion of the 9th Light Infantry, which had taken no part in the storming of the town. At Maison's suggestion, Bernadotte had pushed forward Rivaud's division, which now also began to arrive, headed by the 8th Infantry. The last-named regiment, by occupying the Galgenthor, enabled Dupont to collect his whole division and a regiment of hussars towards the Steinthor. The gardens between the gates swarmed with French skirmishers, whose fire, from behind the cover of walls, caused much loss and annoyance to the Prussians as they moved to the heights on the road to Zorbig and Dessau.

The French now broke out vehemently from the whole eastern front of the town. At the Galgenthor and the Steinthor the strenuous fire of the Prussians could not save them from being overwhelmed, even though their artillery was able to bring a heavy cross-fire on the ground between the gates, whilst the garden walls offered good protection to their infantry. The Prussian cavalry, standing behind the Funkengarten near the Steinthor, soon found both its flanks exposed to the fire of the advancing French, and was compelled to fall back on Motzlich. As the covering forces at the two gates were repulsed, the cross-road between them ceased to be practicable for the Prussian movement towards the Dessau road. Consequently, their centre was forced and the wings were compelled to retire, partly towards Zorbig and Dessau, partly towards the Mulde at Bitterfelde, followed on both roads by the victorious French. At Motzlich the rearguard of the right wing made a stand, only retiring in good order when the rest of the column was safe through the village. At Oppin the cavalry again checked the pursuit, which here ceased, the Prussians reaching Dessau after midnight the same night. Their left wing, unable to reach the Dessau road, retired by that of Wittenberg in disordered fractions, hotly pursued by the whole of Rivaud's division and the greater part of Bernadotte's cavalry. At Rabatz the latter were driven back by the Prussian horsemen on the infantry, who stood fast, enabling the pursuit to be again continued till nightfall. At Bitterfelde the beaten left wing crossed the Mulde, burning the bridge behind it, and made for Dessau, which it reached early on the 18th. The débris of the Reserve corps, now reunited after crossing the Elbe at Roslau, burnt the bridge there and marched by the right bank on Magdeburg, which was reached on the 19th. The small force which had been sent to Merseburg in the morning of the 17th, cut off by Rivaud's advance, eventually crossed the Mulde at Duben, making direct for Potsdam and Berlin. Whilst Dupont and Rivaud were beating the main body at Halle, Drouet fought a little action by himself with Treskow's regiment, which appears to have been the column he was left to check in its advance from Eisleben to Halle. Treskow, about 9 A.M., hearing the firing at Halle, and apparently aware of the presence of a considerable French force on the road in front of him, moved to his left, round the north of the Dolau wood. Drouet meanwhile, in obedience to Bernadotte's orders already noted, had hurried along the Eisleben–Halle road. Arriving at Mitleben, he was informed of the approach of a column beyond the great wood. He at once sent a strong detachment into the wood to fall on the right and rear of this column as he himself attacked it in front. There was danger of its getting into Halle on the left rear of Dupont, thus causing embarrassment, if not disaster. As Treskow, with nine companies of infantry, a few hussars, and his regimental guns, approached the edge of the heights where they join the left bank of the Saale below Halle, he was met and forced to deploy by Maison with a company of the 8th from Rivaud's division and a few hussars. Treskow drew up his men with his right resting on a vineyard and his left on the Saale. Against this position Drouet sent the 95th and the 27th Light Infantry, with two guns. The 94th and the 5th Chasseurs were sent to reinforce the main fight in Halle; it was the former which decided the retreat of the Prussian left wing after the cavalry charge at Rabatz.

Treskow, attacked in front by Drouet with

superior forces, and seeking to regain the Eisleben road by the wood, found himself checked by the French detachment in it. He now commenced to retreat, in squares, down the left bank of the Saale towards Cröllwitz. For some time the retreat was conducted in good order, but as the rear battalion attempted to move round the head of a marshy valley it was thrown into disorder, which spread to the leading battalion. Drouet, now attacking in earnest, drove Treskow to the paper-mill below Cröllwitz, capturing his guns.

On the Ochsenberg height an attempt was made to stem the pursuit, but after losing 200 men, the whole force, save a few who escaped by swimming the Saale, was forced to surrender to Drouet.

The fight at Halle had cost the Prussians a loss of 5000 men in killed, wounded, and prisoners, besides 11 guns and 4 standards. With a loss of between one-third and one-half of its strength, it may be well imagined that the Reserve corps had lost most of its fighting value. Bernadotte gives his own loss as 800 only.

The action was certainly not creditable to the Prussian commander. The faults of his main position, with his lines of retreat uncovered, have already been demonstrated. His attempt to defend Halle and the passage of the river was half-hearted and disjointed. If he wished to hold the town at all, the force originally employed was insufficient, and the companies thrown across the farther bridge were exposed to almost certain defeat. He would have done much better to have burnt that bridge, concentrating his de-

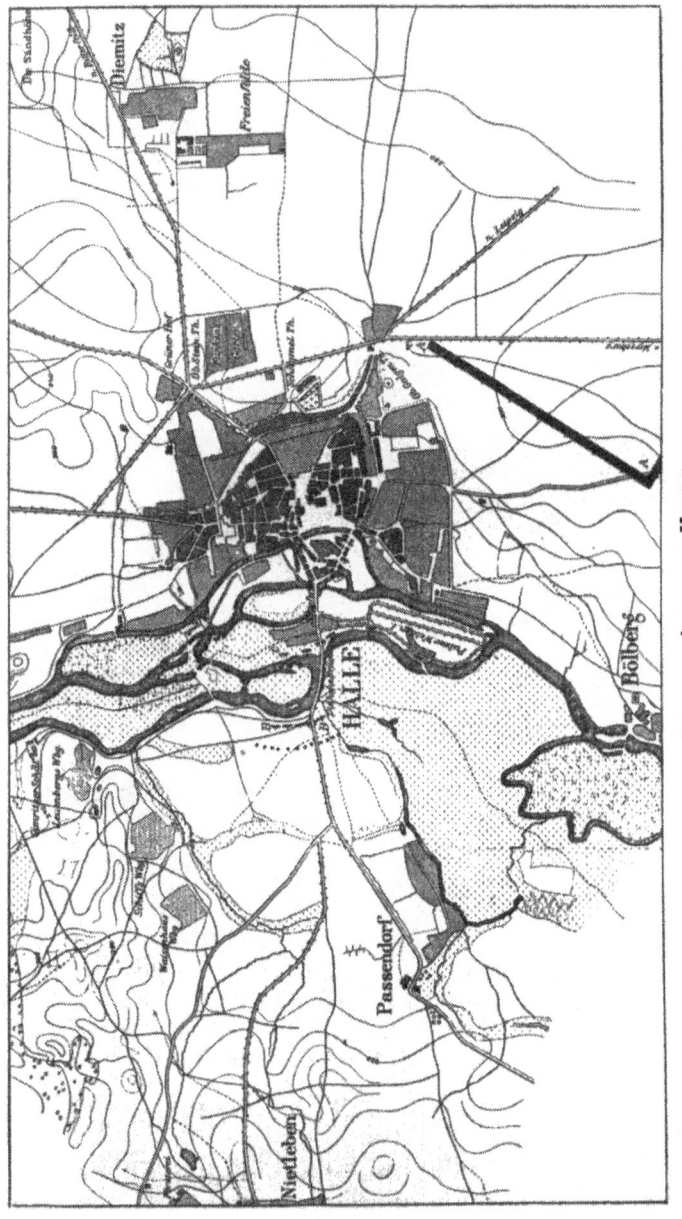

PLAN FOR ACTION OF HALLE

A-A. Main Prussian position. *B-B.* Troops beyond Hohe Brucke. *C-C.* Troops on islands.

fence in the island beyond the bridge; better still, perhaps, to have burnt all three bridges, confining his defence to the right bank. The reinforcements which he eventually sent to the defenders of the town were brought up piecemeal, and exposed to defeat in detail. With the news which he had of the defeats of Jena and Auerstädt and the retreat on Nordhausen, it seems almost impossible to doubt that his wisest course would have been, not to attempt to defend Halle, but to retreat at his best pace, *viâ* Bernburg, to Magdeburg, there to provide a nucleus of unbroken troops on which the débris of the armies could fall back and reorganise. His position, it must be admitted, was rendered more difficult by the omission to send him orders from headquarters. In the confusion his existence seems to have been forgotten there. On the night of the 17th, Bernadotte's corps, exhausted by a march of 17½ miles followed by a severe fight, bivouacked on both sides of Halle. The marshal had intended marching on Dessau next morning, but hearing that the Emperor was at Merseburg,[1] he decided to await further orders.

[1] The Emperor in reality was still at Naumburg, which he only left at noon on the 18th (Foucart, ii. 884).

CHAPTER XI

FROM THE ACTION OF HALLE TO THE OCCUPATION OF BERLIN

HITHERTO Napoleon's line of communications with Mayence and the Upper Rhine had continued to be by Wurzburg and Forchheim, and thence through the mountainous country between the Upper Main and the Saale. So circuitous a line was now very inconvenient, and the vast change in the strategical situation had rendered it possible for a more direct one to be established. In an order of the day, dated Merseburg, 18th October, the army is warned that in future the lines of communication will pass from Mayence through Frankfort, Fulda, Eisenach, and Gotha to Erfurt, a distance of about 160 miles, divided into ten stages. It practically followed the line of the present railway. Though by no means a flat country east of Fulda, there are no serious difficulties in it. All prisoners of war were to be directed on Erfurt, thence by this new line to Mayence, whilst officers, troops from France, and convoys were to follow it in the reverse direction. Wurzburg and Forchheim, ceasing to be useful, were almost denuded of their garrisons.

Let us glance at the position of affairs which rendered possible this most desirable change in the line of rearward communications. As a result of the battles of the 14th, the capture of Erfurt, and the advance of Soult, Ney, Murat, and Bernadotte, the French were in undisputed possession of the whole country between the Saale and the Elster, and as far north as Halle and Nordhausen. The principal part of the Prussian army of Jena and Auerstädt was making for Magdeburg through the Harz Mountains. The Duke of Weimar and Blucher were reported to be seeking to gain the Lower Elbe by Brunswick. The whole of the line from Mayence to Erfurt was clear of the enemy. Hesse-Cassel might be disregarded; for the Elector, who had played at neutrality whilst the result of the French operations was still in the balance, was quite safe not to join the Prussians after the disasters of Jena and Auerstädt.

With the abandonment of the southern line it was no longer necessary to keep a strong Bavarian force to watch Austria on the Inn; therefore the 2nd Bavarian division was ordered to follow the 1st, and the Baden and Würtemberg contingents to Plauen, whence they were sent on to occupy Dresden.[1]

[1] We need not in this volume concern ourselves further with this column under Jerome Bonaparte, which, when Napoleon advanced on Poland, undertook the conquest of Silesia.

The Saxon Elector, who expected that the armistice granted him by Napoleon would lead to a peace by which his neutrality would be re-established, was undeceived by the arrival at Dresden, on the 25th October, of seven Bavarian battalions, followed shortly by the rest. The Bavarians appear to have behaved in a very overbearing manner in Dresden, for we find the French general Thiard complaining of them, saying that he had been forced to curb their exactions by prescribing a scale of food, &c., to be requisitioned. The Bavarians being useful allies, whilst the Saxons were still nominally enemies, Napoleon took a much more lenient view of their conduct.

To safeguard the communications from stray bodies of Prussians, such as that which had released the column of prisoners from Erfurt, three of Klein's dragoon regiments were sent back to sweep the country between Weimar, Erfurt, Eisenach, and Nordhausen.[1]

General Clarke had been appointed governor of Erfurt on its capture. The Wurzburg battalion of allied troops was now ordered to replace the French troops of Ney there as garrison. The Emperor, already beginning to prepare for the change of line on the 16th, had ordered Mortier to occupy the principality of Fulda. Louis, with the advance guard of the army of Holland, was also under orders to advance so as to meet Mortier at Cassel.

The French army, pursuing a completely disorganised and defeated enemy, had, during the three days after the 14th, been somewhat widely dispersed, each corps being assigned a general line of advance, with directions to overthrow the enemy wherever met. It might now be supposed that the Prussians were to some extent recovering a semblance of organisation; Napoleon must begin to think of reassembling his forces. It was apparent that Magdeburg was the goal at which the force in front of Soult, Ney, and Murat, as well as the remnants of the Reserve, were aiming.

On the right Bernadotte still stood, during the 18th, about Halle; Lannes bivouacked on the right bank of the Elster, between Merseburg

---

[1] Berthier to Murat, dated Merseburg, 19th October. It is in this letter that Murat is censured for carelessness in the matter of the Erfurt prisoners.

and Halle, Augereau being at the former place. Davout was about Leipzig, to reach which place from Freyburg his 2nd division had to make a forced march of 30 miles. Grouchy was at Naumburg.

The Emperor, when at Merseburg, took the opportunity to visit the field of Rosbach, from which he caused to be sent to Paris the monument of Frederick's great victory over Soubise —a notable instance of Napoleon's pettiness. Meanwhile the three corps of Murat, Soult, and Ney were following Hohenlohe through the Harz, two columns by the Halberstadt and Quedlinburg roads, with a third between them.

On the evening of the 18th Legrand's division was at Guntersberg, with light cavalry as far as Friedrichsbrünn. In the centre the 25th Dragoons reached Hasselfelde. The left column had its light cavalry out as far as Königshof, where it captured half a battalion of the Prussian Guard and a quantity of baggage. Sahuc's dragoons were at Tanne, the divisions of Leval and St. Hilaire at Beneckenstein with the headquarters of Soult. Ney was at Nordhausen; the rest of the dragoons, Lasalle, and the heavy cavalry, behind at Ilfeld, Cremderode, and Sandhausen.

There had been no serious fighting, though guns, waggons, and prisoners continued to fall into the hands of the French. Hoepfner records that 47 guns were lost or abandoned between Nordhausen and Magdeburg.

On the 19th the pursuit towards Magdeburg was continued in the same style, the cavalry alone engaging in small combats with detached bodies of the enemy. The positions on that evening are stated by Murat, who had marched by the centre road in order not to hamper the infantry. Beaumont's brigade[1] was across the Magdeburg road at Emersleben and Neuendorf, Sahuc at Quenstadt, Beaumont (dragoon division) at Wegeleben, Nansouty at Westerhausen, d'Hautpoult at Langenstein, Klein and Lasalle at Blankenburg. Soult had one division beyond Quedlinburg, the other two at Halberstadt. Ney, following, was at Beneckenstein and Hasselfelde.

On his own side the Emperor, who was somewhat behindhand as regards news of the left column, was most anxious to secure a passage of the Elbe; to make sure of finding one, he directed Lannes on Dessau and Davout on Wittenberg. By evening on the 19th Lannes had his light cavalry at Dessau, where the bridge was found burnt, though not past repair. His infantry divisions were at Zorbig. Davout, at Duben, had found the Mulde bridge passable, and had one division on the right, two on the left bank.

Bernadotte, with his light cavalry at Aschersleben, had his 2nd division at Alsleben, the 3rd behind it, the 1st behind that. Augereau's infantry stood in front of Halle, his light cavalry five miles out on the Dessau road. The Guard was at Halle with the Emperor. These arrangements were calculated to enable the Emperor to combine his army by two marches in two great bodies, each more than sufficient to deal with

---

[1] This Beaumont was apparently Murat's A.D.C., not the commander of the dragoon division. The brigade was that of Milhaud, who had been disabled by a fall (Foucart, ii. 148, *n.*).

any force of the enemy it was likely to meet. He was at present uncertain whether he would be able to pass the Elbe at Dessau; he expected to be able to do so either there or at Wittenberg. From Halle he could, with the Guard, Augereau, and Grouchy, reach Dessau in one, Wittenberg in two marches; from either place he would be able to intercept the enemy attempting to reach Berlin by Magdeburg. His right would then consist of Lannes, Davout, and the three forces just mentioned.

By moving Bernadotte on Aschersleben, he would be able to cut off any part of Hohenlohe's army which might attempt to pass south of Magdeburg, or to assist Murat, Ney, and Soult in driving the whole into the fortress.

The Prussian positions on the night of the 19th were as follows:—

Hohenlohe was on the road from Quedlinburg to Magdeburg, between the river Bode and the latter place.

Kalkreuth was west of him at Gr. Oschersleben, about to make for Tangermunde, on the Elbe below Magdeburg. He was displeased at being put under the command of his junior Hohenlohe. The Reserve corps had reached Magdeburg by the right bank of the Elbe.

Tschammer was at Dodendorf, south of Magdeburg, on which place he was falling back from Aschersleben.

The remains of the Saxon cavalry had moved to Barby, preparatory to surrender in consequence of orders from Dresden passed on the conclusion of the armistice.

Far to the west were Blucher with the artillery column at Salzgitter, and Weimar's corps to the south of him about Osterode, Clausthal, Seesen, and Gittelde.

The King had left Magdeburg on the 18th for Berlin, whence he intended to proceed beyond the Oder, behind which river it was hoped to rally the remnants of the defeated armies, to reinforce them from Silesia and Prussian Poland, and to hold on until the Russian army, which was slowly moving forwards, could add its much needed assistance.

On the 20th Murat and Soult were before Magdeburg, in which were Hohenlohe, the Reserve corps, Tschammer, and the garrison of the fortress. Kalkreuth had on this day broken off to his left to pass the Elbe below the fortress, partly at Tangermünde, partly at Rogatz. Being now ordered to take over the command beyond the Vistula, he made over his corps to Hirschfeld. In the evening Murat sent his chief of the staff, General Belliard, under a flag of truce, into Magdeburg to demand its surrender. With incredible folly Belliard and other French officers were allowed to enter Magdeburg, and were conducted to Hohenlohe's headquarters without the ordinary precaution of blindfolding. Thus they were able to report, not only the wild confusion and disorder prevailing in the place, but also the important fact that Hohenlohe was still in Madgeburg with the greater part of the débris of the Prussian armies, and that no attempt had yet been made to push on towards Berlin and the Oder. Ney reached Halberstadt the same evening.

F. Bonneville, del. sculp

MARSHAL AUGEREAU
(From an engraving in Mr. Broadley's collection)

It must be remembered that news from the left wing took some time to reach the Emperor; the last he had heard of Soult, on the morning of the 20th, was dated from Nordhausen on the morning of the 18th. Yet he had heard enough to show him that the main Prussian army was falling back through the Harz on Magdeburg. He was somewhat exercised by Murat's report of the 17th to the effect that he had driven Weimar to his left. He presumed that Murat had gone in pursuit of that corps: "For, in the position in which we find ourselves, His Majesty can undertake no further operations till he has cleared the entire left bank of the Elbe." Magdeburg he regarded as "a mouse-trap in which there are now arriving all the stragglers since the battle." Into this mouse-trap Murat should, by scouring the surrounding country, force as many of the enemy as possible. He was, with the heavy cavalry, two divisions of dragoons and two brigades of light cavalry, to lean towards Bernburg and Calbe on the Lower Saale. Klein's two remaining regiments[1] were to be sent to Ney. Sahuc's division was already attached to Soult's corps.

Meanwhile, the three advanced corps of the right wing had acted thus on the 20th.

At midnight of the 19th–20th Davout had sent forward 100 chasseurs to endeavour to seize the bridge at Wittenberg. The leading patrol of 4 men reached the bridge at 9 A.M. on the 20th, and found there a Prussian lieutenant with 30 men, who had prepared to burn the bridge. As they saw the French, the Prussians fired the

---

[1] The other three, it will be remembered, had been ordered back to clear the country about Erfurt, &c.

bridge, laid a train to the powder magazine, lighted it, and disappeared. More French cavalry arrived a few minutes after the patrol, and the inhabitants of the place were naturally anxious to prevent an explosion which must ruin the whole town. With their willing help the fire and the train were extinguished, leaving a free passage open to Davout,[1] whose seizure of it turned back two Prussian regiments marching from Berlin to defend it. The powder magazine, with 140,000 pounds of good powder, was a valuable acquisition. Davout promptly set to work to construct a bridge-head, as he had been ordered; by 3 P.M. his whole corps was on the right bank of the Elbe. Lannes, as already noted, had found the Dessau bridge burnt, but he hoped to finish the repairs in forty hours, and had already, on the 20th, passed over his cavalry and two light infantry battalions, with two guns. The rest of the infantry were to follow early on the 21st. Thus Napoleon had secured two passages of the Elbe, ready for his crossing on the 21st. Bernadotte's light cavalry was beyond the Bode, his 3rd division on the left banks of the Saale and the Bode at their junction, the 1st behind it at Bernburg, the 2nd at Aschersleben; headquarters, Bernburg. An order of the early morning had directed him to throw a bridge over the Elbe at the mouth of the Saale, and to take two divisions to Calbe or Bernburg, leaving only one and some cavalry at Aschersleben.[2]

[1] For this account, see Foucart, ii. 171.
[2] See Berthier to Bernadotte, 20th October, 4 A.M. (Foucart, ii. 154). The despatch distinctly orders all the corps, except the troops at Aschersleben, to move "on Calbe *or* to Bernburg," not on Calbe *and* Bernburg.

Napoleon was furious when he heard of Bernadotte's positions, and at 8 A.M. on the 21st sent him orders to cross the Elbe during that day and the ensuing night. So angry was the Emperor that he, for the first time, censured Bernadotte in writing for his absence from the field of the two battles of the 14th. In the present instance the marshal does not seem to have been so much to blame. He appears to have taken immediate measures to reconnoitre a place of passage and to collect boats for a bridge. The latter was no easy matter. Even during the day of the 21st, he and Murat, whom he met at Barby, had only succeeded in getting together seven.

The Emperor's orders of the 21st only reached him at 8 P.M., on his return from Barby, and he obviously could not, even then, get his corps across during the night. He promised to do his best, sending, if necessary, part round by Dessau.[1]

The fact appears to be that the Emperor gained his knowledge of Bernadotte's doings not from the marshal himself, but from a passing aide-de-camp,[2] who naturally did not know what the marshal had done about crossing the river. Napoleon had jumped to adverse conclusions as to the action of the by no means reliable marshal. When the Emperor reached Dessau at 2 P.M., he found Lannes engaged in passing Suchet's division across the Elbe. The 2nd division could not cross that night.

Meanwhile, Davout had got two divisions over

[1] For Bernadotte's defence as regards this matter, as well as of his action on the 14th, see his despatch to Berthier, dated Bernburg, 21st October, 8 P.M. (Foucart, ii. 200).
[2] See Foucart, ii. 186, *n.* 2.

at Wittenberg, and was reconnoitring between the Elbe and the Mulde with his cavalry. With passages secured at Wittenberg and Dessau, that at Barby became of less importance, and Murat and Bernadotte were both empowered to use Dessau if necessary.

Becker, now acting for Grouchy, who was ill, was ordered to Dessau; Augereau to Wittenberg, so as to relieve the pressure on the bridge at Dessau. The Guard was near Dessau; Murat's cavalry were at Muhlingen, Barby, Calbe, Glothe, Atzendorf, &c., under orders to move to Dessau next morning. Soult was five miles short of Magdeburg, surrounding it on the left bank of the Elbe, with cavalry close up to it, and Ney was behind him.

At this time the state of discipline in the French army was very serious. If crushing defeats, followed by long marches, by scarcity of provisions of all sorts and by a general loss of confidence in superiors, had reduced the Prussian soldiery to pillage and insubordination of all kinds, victory had exercised a precisely similar influence on the French. The forced marches, which had to be executed almost daily by pursuers as well as by pursued, left a train of stragglers and pillagers, who lived upon the country, burning and robbing in every direction. Complaints by superior officers on this subject were constant. Clarke noted the ravages of plunderers at Erfurt. The commandant of Jena gives a terrible account of the pillage there, "*qui dure toujours.*" Ney, writing from Nordhausen on the 18th October, says he had been compelled to issue special orders regarding discipline, "the relaxation of which has reached such a point that the lives of officers are no longer safe."

On the 21st October Soult finds himself compelled "to take rigorous measures to put a stop to the disastrous consequences of the indiscipline existing in the *corps d'armée*. . . . The footsteps of the *corps d'armée* are marked by fire, devastation, and crimes atrocious almost beyond belief. The orders of leaders are despised, the lives of officers are often endangered, and, as a crowning evil, the resources and food afforded by the country are destroyed as French troops come on the scene." This preamble is followed by a Draconian code for dealing with marauders and the women followers, vivandières and washerwomen, who were, doubtless, the common receivers of the plunder which the soldier could not himself carry. A woman of these classes, on conviction, was to have her cart with all her possessions burnt in front of the regiment to which she belonged; then, clad in black, she was to be marched through the camps and driven from the army.

These testimonies are drawn, not from the memoirs of men like De Fezensac, who are above suspicion, not even from those of less respectable officers, looking back after many years on what they had witnessed, but from reports and orders written at the time by the commanders, of whom Soult at least cannot claim any great reputation for honesty.

However we may deplore it, we can hardly be surprised that men who had seen their homes and their country ravaged by this fiery whirlwind of unscrupulous soldiery should, when, in 1814, a reversal of fortune placed them in a similar position in France, have amply avenged their sufferings of 1806.

Napoleon had now resolved to advance direct on Berlin. He was apparently satisfied that there was no danger to be apprehended from Weimar and Blucher, who, should they risk attempts on the new line of communications, could probably be dealt with by the three dragoon regiments sent back from Klein's division. Soult and Ney, with Sahuc's dragoons and Klein's two remaining regiments, would suffice to prevent any attempt to return on the part of Hohenlohe, which was in the highest degree improbable. "Whenever you pass the Elbe," writes the Emperor to Murat on the 22nd October, "hasten in the direction of Treuenbrietzen. I fancy that to-day you will be at, or abreast of, Dessau; that on the evening of the 23rd you will not be far from the point indicated."

By the evening of the 22nd the right wing was far on its road. Lannes had his light cavalry at Treuenbrietzen itself, Suchet's division at Strauch, Gazan abreast of him at Liesenitz. The latter had passed at Wittenberg in order to relieve the crowd at Dessau. Augereau was about Wittenberg, Murat's three cavalry divisions in the angle between the Elbe and the Saale, west of Dessau. Davout was from Wittenberg to Seehausen, on the direct road to Berlin, Becker's dragoons with him on his right. The Emperor and the Guard were at Wittenberg; Bernadotte was collecting his corps at Zerbst, on the road from Barby to Brandenburg. One of his divisions (Rivaud's) was still at Bernburg collecting the arms and horses of the Saxon cavalry, who had now left the Prussians and surrendered. It would follow by Dessau. Under the impulse of the Emperor's censures, Bernadotte had, by tremendous exertions with very insufficient means, got Dupont's and Drouet's divisions across the Elbe.

Meanwhile, Soult and Ney, on the 22nd, completed the investment of Magdeburg, on the left bank of the Elbe. Ney occupied the right sector, from the Elbe above the fortress, with his corps quartered about the Halberstadt road. Soult, with his stronger force to the north-west of the fortress, guarded the left sector, watching for the missing corps of Weimar. Of this he could, as yet, obtain no news, but he did learn that Hohenlohe had escaped, for the moment, from the eastern side of the "mouse-trap"—that the Prince himself had moved towards Burg from Magdeburg, whilst part of his force (Kalkreuth's) had crossed the Elbe lower down, at Rogatz and Tangermünde.[1] Hohenlohe had indeed, on the night of the 20th, decided, in accordance with the royal orders, to endeavour to reach the Oder, an intention of which Davout had already got information on the 21st, from captured letters of Duke Eugene

[1] Soult's information as to the passage at Tangermünde was confirmed by the following letter, written there on the 20th October, and seized in the post: "MY DEAR FATHER,—How are matters with you? Have you the French yet? The greatest terror reigns here. The citizens and the peasants know not whether to remain or to flee. The King arrived here on Saturday (18th) evening at 7 o'clock and passed on; the Queen had passed two days earlier; to-day there arrived General Ruchel grievously wounded; almost everything coming from the army passes here; every instant we witness the arrival of soldiers, mounted or on foot, without any order. What will become of us Prussians? Our reputation is entirely lost" (Foucart, ii. 232 *n.*).

of Würtemberg addressed to the commander of the troops at Wittenberg.

The Prussian Prince set apart, for the support of the Magdeburg garrison, a force which he himself states at 9000 men. His cavalry passed the Elbe at 3 A.M. on the 21st, the rest of the army followed; but, what with the inevitable difficulty of getting beaten men away from the fancied security of a fortress, and with delays of one sort and another, several regiments and 39 guns got left behind to add to the contents of the "mouse-trap."[1] On the 21st Hohenlohe reached Burg, where he was joined by Hirschfeld, the successor of Kalkreuth, from Tangermünde.

Magdeburg was now left to its own resources; it was very fully garrisoned, with some 25,000 troops amply supplied with ammunition, guns, and stores of all sorts. The commandant, Kleist, was old and feeble, and found himself exposed to much opposition from the civilian population, who were naturally anxious to avoid a prolonged siege, ending perhaps with the horrors of a successful assault. Soult summoned him to surrender, and, though Kleist refused, it was not difficult to see that he only sought an opportunity to yield with honour.

Looking to the unknown strength of the force in Magdeburg, and to the uncertainty of the position of Weimar, Napoleon was bound to leave a strong force to blockade the fortress, and he had directed Soult to endeavour to find a passage immediately above it, by which he could

---

[1] This is stated by Hoepfner, and can be clearly inferred from the fact that, when Magdeburg surrendered three weeks later, it contained over 24,000 troops.

communicate with the right of the army, and complete the blockade on the right bank of the river. If possible he should select an island and fortify it. There, in the event of a serious attempt to relieve the fortress, whether by the turning back of Hohenlohe, as he found himself cut from the Oder by the Emperor's advance, or by Weimar and Blucher, Soult could take temporary refuge. He found much difficulty in carrying out these orders, owing to the scarcity of boats on the Upper Elbe. Yet the bridge was very necessary, first for the passage of Soult, should the Emperor think it desirable and safe to call him to Berlin, and, secondly, as providing another line of retreat for the army in the unlikely event of a disaster. Truly has it been said that, if Napoleon was the boldest of generals, he was at the same time the most cautious. He never, in these days at least, neglected to provide for the event of defeat, however unlikely he might think it.

On the 21st he had issued an order laying down fully the line of communications, with the stages from Mayence to Berlin. The old line from Warzburg was to be used only for troops actually on it. The new line continued from Erfurt, by Buttelstedt, Naumburg, Leipzig, Düben, Wittenberg, Treuenbrietzen, Potsdam, Spandau, to Berlin.

On the 23rd he issued a long decree, formally taking possession of all the Prussian territories west of the Elbe, and making provision for their occupation and administration. Another decree made similar provision for the whole of Saxony, dashing the somewhat unreasonable expectations formed by the Saxon Elector as to his future position.[1] With the details of the march of the French right wing from the Elbe to Berlin we need not concern ourselves, for it was uneventful and unopposed.

On the evening of the 24th the positions of the corps constituting it were as follows: Davout could proudly date his despatches from "the suburbs of Berlin." However little credit for the mighty results of the 14th had been given him in the Imperial bulletins, the superlative merit of Davout's conduct at Auerstädt had been fully recognised by the Emperor in private, and even in public at the front. As a reward the 3rd corps had been promised the proud distinction of being the first to enter the conquered capital on the 25th. We find, therefore, Davout jealously resenting Lannes' despatch of some hussars into Berlin itself on the 24th. The latter marshal's corps, the Guard and the Cavalry Reserve, were about Potsdam; Augereau south and south-west of that place. The Emperor, leaving Wittenberg on the 23rd, had slept at Kropstadt that night, reaching Potsdam on the 24th. The Corsican soldier of fortune, the man who had started life as the enemy of France, only to change his pose to that of her greatest admirer when that attitude seemed to offer him the greatest personal opportunities, was now in the favourite residence of the great King, who, whatever his faults, had strenuously and successfully striven to raise his country to the highest

---

[1] For fuller details as to the negotiations with Saxony, see *Un Allié de Napoleon*, by Bonnefons, an excellent and most interesting work.

position in Europe. The conqueror of Austerlitz and Jena gazed with interest not unmixed with reverence on the relics of the victor of Rosbach and Leuthen. Truly, in the Emperor's own grandiloquent terms, the insult of Rosbach had been wiped out, and he might well have foregone the petty satisfaction of removing from Prussia the poor relics of her former glory—the sword and the decorations of Frederick, with the colours so gloriously borne by his Guard during the Seven Years' War. But Napoleon, at his greatest, could never cast aside his desire for trivial triumphs, and the relics were forwarded to the Invalides at Paris, with an expression of the Emperor's belief that "the old soldiers of the war of Hanover will receive with a religious respect all that belongs to one of the foremost captains whose memory history will preserve."

At Potsdam, on the 24th, Napoleon received much important news and took momentous steps; but, before detailing them, it will be well to glance at what happened on the 25th and subsequent days at Berlin. On the morning of the 25th, Davout's corps passed in triumph through the capital, in whose conquest it had taken so distinguished a part. It encamped, beyond the city, on the Spree. The Emperor was still at Potsdam; it was not till two days later that he made his own entry into Berlin and took up his quarters at the palace of Charlottenburg.

Vienna he had not entered in triumph in the previous year; Berlin was not so spared the lowest depths of humiliation. The municipal authorities, headed by Prince Hatzfeldt, came out to tender the submission of the city. The Prince subsequently came as near the fate of a traitor as was possible. It appears that he had written to King Frederick William an account of his proceedings, in which he mentioned facts as to the positions of Napoleon's troops. The despatch, seized in the post, was handed to the Emperor. When, therefore, the Prince again appeared before Napoleon, he was received with angry words and looks, and ordered to at once withdraw to his estates. Later in the day, he was arrested and ordered to be tried by a court-martial as a spy. It seemed impossible that he could be saved, when his unfortunate wife managed to secure a private interview with Napoleon. For arranging this De Ségur claims the credit.[1] In the end, the Emperor handed her the incriminating letter; when she had read it, he pointed to the fire, remarking that the letter was the only evidence against her husband, a hint which she promptly took by throwing it into the flames. Whether Napoleon ever intended to execute Hatzfeldt we may well doubt. The information sent in his letter was probably public property, of little or no value to the King. The Emperor delighted in a dramatic scene, when it could serve his ends in any way, and he was utterly regardless of the feelings of others. However har-

---

[1] "An Aide-de-camp of Napoleon," p. 307.

Rapp also tells the story (pp. 107–13), and claims credit for having kept Hatzfeldt at the palace, instead of sending him to Davout's headquarters. He adds that Berthier, Caulaincourt, and Duroc had all interceded with the Emperor in favour of the Prince.

rowing the proceedings might be to the Prince and his wife, that was nothing to Napoleon if, by a little acting, he could enhance his own reputation.

It is now necessary, in order to take up the thread of events, to return to Soult and Ney, whom we left in front of Magdeburg on the 22nd October, acquainted with the movements of Hohenlohe, but unable to obtain news of those of Weimar and Blucher since their separation from the Prussian army at Langensalza and Nordhausen respectively. Blucher, marching by Scharzfeld and Gittelde, left the latter place on the 19th, and marched a short way beyond Salzliebenhalle. On the 20th he continued his march, so as to leave Brunswick to his left. During this march he held a meeting, at Wolfenbüttel, with Weimar. That general, after leaving Langensalza, had moved through Muhlhausen, and on the 19th was about Osterode. On the 20th, the day of his meeting with Blucher, his corps was about Salzgitter. The two commanders agreed that it was not possible, looking to the line of the French pursuit, for them to reach Magdeburg, and that they must strive to cross the Elbe lower down, at Tangermünde or Sandau if possible. Blucher, with a considerable start, got safely across at Sandau by boats, though he did not do so till the 24th. One of Soult's parties appears to have captured 1 gun and 120 men from the rear of his column on the 23rd.

Weimar, reaching Brunswick on the 21st, was at Konigslutter on the 22nd, where he was rejoined by a detachment which he had left behind to try and gather in the released prisoners of Erfurt. The latter having had enough of the war, gradually melted away; not one of them rejoined the colours.

The news which Weimar now received of Soult's position showed that that marshal was as near to Sandau as the Prussian corps. The latter, exhausted by hard marching and insufficient food, could not hope to rival the marching powers of the French. Unless Weimar could mislead Soult as to his real intentions, he was certain to be intercepted on the Sandau road. What he endeavoured to do was, by pushing out cavalry and light infantry to his right, to induce Soult to believe in an advance direct upon Magdeburg, whilst the main body slipped away, thus covered, to the Elbe. In this he was successful. Soult's cavalry, scouting north and north-west of Magdeburg, at last brought him news on the 23rd. A party, moving on Helmstadt, had been attacked and driven back to Erxleben by Weimar's advance guard. From prisoners it had been ascertained that the main body, 16 battalions and 4 cavalry regiments, was moving on Magdeburg. This, of course, was false; for Weimar was about to turn to his left at Helmstadt and take the road to Sandau.

Soult fell into the trap, and, on the 24th, with two divisions and some cavalry, he moved on Erxleben. He had covered half the distance when he got news of the enemy's movement to the north. He had lost the whole day of the 24th, and just given time to Weimar to get a good start on the Sandau road. The Prussian cavalry, pushed out on Weimar's right, still induced Soult to believe that Tangermünde was the point aimed at.

On the morning of the 25th he marched, with his whole corps and a large cavalry force, on Tangermünde, leaving Ney alone to blockade Magdeburg. The bridge above that place had now been completed at Westerhausen. Soult was at Tangermünde at 10 P.M. on the 25th, but found Weimar was still north of him. Soult's own account of what followed is to the effect that the enemy fled at once as he came up with their rearguard, which he found it impossible to bring to a fight.

Hoepfner tells a different story. Yorck, he says, with four or five battalions of light infantry and fusiliers, took up a position behind Altenzaum, with his left resting on the Elbe dam, on the 26th October. Here he was attacked, about 4 P.M., by Soult's cavalry, and later by infantry. He held on firmly, and, finally, after repulsing several attacks, he drove the cavalry off in confusion, and compelled the infantry to fall back on Altenzaum, whence they kept up a desultory fire till nightfall. Leaving his fires burning, Yorck fell back in the night on Sandau. The French, pursuing his rearmost troops, inflicted some loss, but Yorck succeeded in getting across the river, and sinking all the boats.

During the fight Weimar received orders superseding him in his command, which he surrendered to Winning after the passage had been completed. Yorck's rearguard action had given the time necessary for the crossing.

Soult, having now cleared the left bank of the Elbe of all important hostile forces, proposed to cross at Tangermünde, in order to pursue the troops driven across the river as they marched for the Oder. Ney alone could blockade Magdeburg.

We left Hohenlohe at Burg on the 21st October. On the 22nd he reached Genthin with his headquarters. He was now entering quite a different country from that in which he had operated nearly up to Magdeburg. There were no more mountains, but a vast undulating plain, intersected in all directions by rivers, canals, lakes, and ponds. The country was poor in resources, whilst the Prussians, driven from their magazines, had lost most of their provision trains, and were reduced to living as best they might on what the country would yield. For this their training had ill fitted them, and it became necessary, at least Hohenlohe thought it so, to split up the army into several columns for facility of supply. When, on the 23rd October, his main body reached Rathenow, he had Schwerin away on his left towards Havelberg, where his cavalry was joined by that of Blucher, which had crossed in advance of the artillery. On Hohenlohe's right, his light troops, crossing the Havel at Plaue, had reached the Rathenow-Spandau road. The rearguard was about Genthin.

At this time Bernadotte's corps, the link between Napoleon and the blockading corps at Magdeburg, had reached Deetz with Drouet's division and a regiment of cavalry; Dupont's was still at Zerbst, Rivaud's still beyond the Elbe, only able to reach Dessau that night. The whole corps was under orders to march

From Halle to Berlin 235

on Brandenburg, which Bernadotte hoped to reach on the 25th. At present his corps was no serious menace to Hohenlohe's retreat on Stettin. The real danger to him was from the army now approaching Berlin. Napoleon had been satisfied, from numerous reports received on the 22nd, that Hohenlohe had left Magdeburg for Berlin or the Oder. It was this which decided him to march on the capital. As yet, however, he had no very definite news of the direction taken by the Prussians beyond Burg. On the 24th, Lannes reported that his cavalry had had a skirmish, towards Spandau, with Prussian horsemen, apparently covering the march of a column. On the same day Savary was sent out, with a small detachment of cavalry, towards Nauen (north-west of Spandau), to search for news of Hohenlohe.

CHAPTER XII

THE PURSUIT OF HOHENLOHE AND HIS CAPITULATION AT PRENZLAU

ON the night of the 24th, Hohenlohe was with his main body about Neustadt; Schwerin, with the cavalry, was at Kyritz; Natzmer, with the rearguard, about Rhinow; Schimmelpfennig towards Fehrbellin. Blucher's artillery had just got across the Elbe at Sandau, where most of its escort, under Wobeser, had been left to keep open the passage for Weimar, still a long march behind. Blucher himself had reached Hohenlohe's camp and urged the rapid despatch of the artillery column, which he had thus far so successfully conducted, to a place of safety at Stettin. Massenbach, without taking any notice of Blucher's proposal, ordered the artillery to take a day's rest on the 25th, then to march so as to reach Rheinsberg only on the 27th. Blucher was now offered as a command either Hohenlohe's cavalry or the rearguard of Natzmer. He chose the latter. A glance at the map will show that from his present positions, with Napoleon at Potsdam and Berlin, it would be very difficult for Hohenlohe to reach Stettin unmolested, unless he could conceal his movement for at least the next two days from Napoleon, or could obstruct seriously the French advance from Berlin.

Pursuit of Hohenlohe

The plan he adopted was this. From the Elbe below Sandau to the Oder there was a continuous navigable channel running from west to east. First there was the lower Havel; then the Rhin Canal, joining the Havel to the lake about Fehrbellin; then the lake itself; then the Ruppin Canal from the lake to the Havel near Oranienburg; then another stretch of the Havel; lastly, the Finow Canal, joining the Havel, near Liebenwalde, with the Oder.

Along this stretch of water, from Fehrbellin to Liebenwalde, Schimmelpfennig was to break the bridges and guard all the passages, whilst Hohenlohe marched by Neu and Alt Ruppin and Gransee to join the Berlin–Stettin road at Zehdenick. Blucher, facing south about Rhinow, would cover the rear and right, before rejoining the main body, and wait to be joined by Weimar's corps.

On the 24th, Napoleon ordered Lannes to seize Spandau, the fortifications of which place had been allowed to fall into decay. Hasty attempts to restore them had been made after the disaster of Jena, but, as a curious instance of the way things were then done in the Prussian army, it may be mentioned that the work was entrusted to a blind and deaf engineer officer.[1] Nothing could be made of the outer fortifications, and the garrison of 900 men had retired into the citadel before Lannes arrived, with Suchet's division, on the 25th. He had not much difficulty in obtaining its surrender.

On the night of the 24th–25th, Napoleon had received a despatch from Bernadotte reporting the direction of Hohenlohe's march, with a force

[1] Hoepfner, ii. 128.

estimated at 30,000 or 35,000 men. The Emperor seems to have believed that Hohenlohe had already got past Oranienburg,[1] but he at once ordered Lannes and Murat to follow towards Zehdenick and Stettin. As a matter of fact, Hohenlohe, on the night of the 25th, had only reached Alt and Neu Ruppin and Lindow, whilst Schimmelpfennig had not destroyed the bridges farther east than Kremmin, and was making for Zehdenick. Blucher remained guarding the Rhin Canal south of Neustadt and patrolling about Rhinow, where there had been a fight with Bernadotte's advance guard. Schwerin's cavalry, and Hagen's infantry brigade, farther north, had marched on Wittstock. Bila, with light troops, was at Kyritz. The baggage, which reached Wittstock on the 25th, was directed on Stettin, *via* Strasburg and Pasewalk. Hohenlohe's plan was already ruined; for, instead of Schimmelpfennig's seizing and destroying the all-important passage at Oranienburg, it had been reached by Lasalle's light cavalry and Grouchy's dragoons. Milhaud was on the road from Spandau to Oranienburg, where Lasalle had already arrived. The heavy cavalry had not left Potsdam at noon. Savary was with his detachment at Wustermark moving on Nauen.

On the 26th, Hohenlohe proposed to march with his infantry and artillery through Gransee to Zehdenick, at which place Schimmelpfennig would cross the Havel. That general reaching Zehdenick, passed safely through about 8 or 9 A.M. He was still halting just beyond, when the arrival of the enemy was announced. Lasalle,

[1] Berthier to Lannes (Foucart, ii. 322).

reaching Zehdenick about noon, found Schimmelpfennig's rearguard still in front at his halting place. The leading French hussars were driven back, as they debouched from the town, by the rearguard under Yorck, who had promptly demanded the return of reinforcements from Schimmelpfennig, and taken position on the edge of the wood beyond Zehdenick, on the road to Prenzlau. Finding himself too weak to attack with only two regiments of hussars, Lasalle waited for the arrival of Grouchy's and Beaumont's dragoons. Supported by them, he charged the Prussian dragoons, whom he drove back, even after they were reinforced by a regiment of hussars, into and through the wood to the great clearing, about three miles along the road to Templin.

Here the French hussars, disordered by their pursuit, found themselves opposed by a fresh Prussian regiment, the Queen's dragoons, who promptly charged and drove them back into the wood. At this moment Grouchy's fresh division arrived and fell upon the Prussian dragoons, who, overpowered by superior numbers, were almost all captured or destroyed. Practically the whole of their officers, as well as their colours, fell into the hands of the French. Grouchy continued the pursuit of Schimmelpfennig till nightfall, when he took post with his vedettes close up to Templin. Schimmelpfennig's troops, as a fighting force, had been destroyed. The remnants made straight for Stettin, which they reached without further molestation.

The news of this action showed Hohenlohe

that it was no longer possible, on the 26th, for him to reach the Prenzlau road by Zehdenick. He had waited at Gransee in vain for Blucher, who eventually announced the impossibility of his marching farther than Ruppin on that day. Hohenlohe now resolved to try and reach Prenzlau by a road farther to his left through Furstenberg. He called in Beeren's cavalry brigade, and ordered that of Bila to march as his rearguard on the 27th, whilst he himself moved to Prenzlau by Lychen and Boitzenburg. He still had three brigades of cavalry on his left, where they were useless. They were ordered to Prenzlau, whilst Blucher was urged to hurry up.

On the French side, Murat, followed by Lannes, was still pressing on by the main road to Prenzlau, scouring the country to his left, and rendering it impossible for Hohenlohe to send Bila from Furstenburg to Templin, as he had intended.

On the morning of the 27th, Hohenlohe waited at Lychen for some time for the arrival of Bila with the rearguard, as well as for news of Blucher. Nothing being heard of either, he resumed his march on Boitzenburg, protected on his right by a chain of lakes. In the absence of Bila, he detached the regiment of mounted gensdarmes to reconnoitre the country beyond the lakes on his right.

Murat, meanwhile, had sent Lasalle on towards Prenzlau by Mittenwalde, whilst Milhaud's light cavalry brigade [1] went towards Boitzenburg, and Murat himself, with the rest of the cavalry, fol-

---

[1] It comprised only the 13th chasseurs and one squadron of dragoons (Murat to Napoleon—Foucart, ii. 416).

lowed the main road. Arriving at Hasleben, where he proposed to spend the night, he heard, about 4 P.M., the thunder of guns on his left, towards Wickmansdorf and Boitzenburg. Thinking that this indicated either that the enemy was trying to force a passage, or that he was retiring by the road in that direction, Murat hurried, with Grouchy's division and a regiment of hussars, towards Boitzenburg, leaving two dragoon regiments in Wickmansdorf as a support, and Beaumont's division at Hasleben. As he came up, he found Milhaud just being driven out of Boitzenburg by Hohenlohe's advance guard, after having defended himself at the bridge from 2 P.M. till 5.

Whilst Murat was holding back the enemy, the gensdarme regiment, under cover of the closing day, arrived on his rear at Wickmansdorf. Turning back with a regiment of dragoons, he joined the other two at Wickmansdorf. At the head of these three regiments he charged the gensdarmes. The result of such a combat could not be doubtful. The gensdarmes, driven upon a marsh and hemmed in, surrendered, with the exception of one section which had escaped northwards. Without infantry, Murat was unable to attempt the recapture of Boitzenburg. He was, however, at last able to write to the Emperor: "It is the advance guard of the army; no one has yet passed." The news was correct. Hohenlohe, as he approached Boitzenburg, had been met by Count Arnim, the landowner of the place, announcing the collection of supplies at his château for the famished Prussians. When they returned together, they found Milhaud's cavalry already plundering the château. The latter, as already stated, were driven out, but the advent of Murat showed clearly that the cavalry which had defeated Schimmelpfennig now barred Hohenlohe's road to Prenzlau by Templin.

Once more he decided on moving farther to his left, seeking to reach Prenzlau by Schönermark. That place he reached at 4 A.M. on the 28th, his troops exhausted by marching and by hunger, with still a five-mile march before they would reach the fancied security of Prenzlau, and the supplies collected there. Yet it was the only place, short of Stettin, where he could hope to feed and rest his famished and weary troops. Once more councils of war were held, wasting precious moments. Some thought the idea of reaching Prenzlau must be abandoned, and the Pasewalk road taken. Presently a cavalry patrol brought the welcome news that Prenzlau was still clear, at 6 A.M., of the enemy. Three hours were thus wasted before the march was resumed. Schwerin, with a cuirassier regiment and a horse battery, formed the advance guard, followed by the infantry. Two dragoon regiments flanked the march on the right; Prince August, with a battalion and a cavalry regiment, formed the rearguard. Hagen's infantry brigade, away to the left, was ordered to march to Pasewalk, where it would receive further orders.

The dispirited, starving troops could only be got forward by the utmost exertions, even violence, of the officers. As Hohenlohe, himself almost overcome by hunger, rode out of

Pursuit of Hohenlohe 243

Schönermark, he was greeted by murmurs and protests that the men could do no more.

Whilst this dreary march was progressing, Murat's cavalry, themselves not overfed, but still buoyed with the hope of victory, were also pressing on, by the Boitzenburg road, to Prenzlau. Lannes' main body was still far behind, but he, with 3000 picked men of his advance guard, was nobly responding to Murat's urgent demands for infantry.

Prenzlau, the goal for the attainment of which both parties were striving, was approached by two roads, that from Mecklenburg and that from Berlin, each of which, before reaching the town, passed over an embankment about 1500 paces long, with low marshy land on either side. The last 1000 yards or so of each embankment was covered by a small suburb stretching along the road. South of Prenzlau lay the Ucker Lake, forming an impassable barrier for several miles. North of the town the marshy river Ucker continued the obstacle, expanding presently into a lake, and extending through Pasewalk. Prenzlau was not regularly fortified, though its old walls and gates, combined with the position of the town in the neck of a defile, made it an invaluable possession to the party which should first arrive.

The Boitzenburg road, by which Murat was moving, joined that from Berlin about a mile short of Prenzlau, the Mecklenburg road entered the town 500 yards north of the gate admitting that from Berlin.

The Schönermark road, on which was Hohenlohe's army, crossed the brook, north of the Berlin road, at the head of the suburb at the entrance of which it joined the main road. As Lasalle, with the light cavalry leading Murat's advance, arrived at the suburb, he found Hohenlohe's advance guard moving into it, and he was unable to occupy it in face of the Prussian cuirassiers. But the Prussian column had become gradually more and more spread out in length. Cavalry from the right, unable to make its way through the marshy ground, returned to the road, separating the infantry and increasing the length of the column marching on a single road. The rearguard lagged behind. The morning mist lay heavy over Prenzlau, and, in its obscurity, there were perpetual alarms of the enemy's presence. As they hurried up, the troops were directed to pass through Prenzlau and provision themselves as rapidly as possible from the trains in waiting beyond the town. The protection of the passage, and of the rear, was entrusted to Tschammer with a picked force. That general posted two grenadier battalions right and left of the embankment on the Berlin road, with a company beyond the brook at the paper-mill turning its rear to the Schönermark road. A small force guarded his left flank towards the Ucker Lake, two companies were in reserve at the town gate, the battalion guns on the embankment itself.

Before any fighting occurred, a French officer, Captain Hugues, bearing a flag of truce, was brought in to Hohenlohe's headquarters. He had fallen amongst some Polish lancers, who, knowing neither French nor German, had seized him, and, in spite of his protests, robbed and ill-

Pursuit of Hohenlohe

used him. Of this treatment he loudly complained to Hohenlohe. He seems to have been a person of considerable resource, untrammelled by scruples on the subject of truth; for he proceeded to invent a wonderful tissue of lies. He said he had been sent by Bernadotte (who was nowhere within reach); that Murat with 30,000 men was on the Prussian right flank; that Lannes with another 60,000 was already between Prenzlau and Stettin; that Luchesini was negotiating a peace, and that, therefore, there was nothing for Hohenlohe but surrender. In the statement about the peace negotiations he rather overshot his mark; for Hohenlohe naturally replied that, if peace was imminent, it was certainly not the time for capitulation. Nevertheless, the Prussian general was to some extent deceived; he was quite inclined to believe himself surrounded, and, in the hopes of gathering reliable information, he sent Hugues back to Murat, accompanied by Massenbach. The extraordinary story which the latter brought back will appear later. Scarcely had these two started when Murat's attack broke out.

Lasalle led the way with his brigade against the suburb. Behind him was the whole of Grouchy's dragoon division, with three of Beaumont's regiments. A horse-artillery battery soon silenced Tschammer's regimental guns.

Murat feared that his prey would yet elude him; for Hohenlohe's column had been hurrying into Prenzlau. Sending a party to his right to see if the town could be turned by the south of the Ucker Lake, he moved one of Beaumont's dragoon brigades round to the left, by Gollmitz, to harass the enemy's rear and right flank, under the command of his own aide-de-camp, whose name was also Beaumont. As his anxiety increased lest the column should escape, he sent Broussart, with Grouchy's third brigade, across the brook, by a ford, to charge the column from that side. The attack was completely successful. Broussart rode down cavalry and infantry alike, captured eight guns, many men, and Tschammer himself, and drove the rest of Hohenlohe's corps, except the rearguard, in confusion into the town, the gates of which were shut just in time to prevent Broussart's entry. Prince August, with the Prussian rearguard thus cut off, was open to the attack of Beaumont (the A.D.C.) from the west and the divisional general Beaumont from the south. Charged again and again, the unfortunate rearguard was driven towards the lake north of Prenzlau, where, with its commander, it was forced to surrender.

Meanwhile, Grouchy's men had beaten in the gate, forced their way into the town, through it and out at the other side. There they found Hohenlohe drawing up the 9000 or 10,000 men who remained to him, not, as might have been expected, across the direct road to Stettin, but on that to Pasewalk, at right angles to the Ucker, on which his right rested. Hohenlohe at first refused a fresh summons to surrender conveyed by Belliard, Murat's chief of the staff. His position was really not so desperate as he believed it. The road to Stettin was still open, and the enemy's force consisted entirely of cavalry, supported only by a handful of Lannes' light infantry, which was all that had yet arrived. Murat had

Pursuit of Hohenlohe 247

beyond Prenzlau only Lasalle's light cavalry, Grouchy's dragoons, and a few infantry—not more than 4000 or 5000 men in all. He was actually inferior in numbers to Hohenlohe, though his troops were fresher and cheered by victory. It is difficult to believe that Hohenlohe could not still have gained Stettin with a large part of his force; but he had lost all hope. Murat, with a magnificent disregard of truth, had made Massenbach believe that 100,000 French troops surrounded him.[1]

"Now," said Murat, "will your general at last surrender?" "No," replied Massenbach; "he will never accept such hard conditions." "Very well, I will cut him to pieces," was the retort. All this Massenbach repeated to Hohenlohe, adding that the defile of Lockenitz, on the Randow, was already lost, and that he himself had seen numerous French troops far east of Prenzlau. All this story was pure imagination, and we can only suppose that Massenbach was blindfolded, and that when he passed the brook west of Prenzlau he believed it to be the Ucker. Just as Belliard was leaving with Hohenlohe's refusal to capitulate, Murat requested a personal interview with the Prussian commander. He assured the unfortunate Prince, on his word of honour, that he had 100,000 men. "There," said he, pointing in different directions, "is the

[1] "Colonel Massenbach, whom he (Hohenlohe) had sent to the enemy, and who had altogether lost his head, brought news that the enemy was advancing along the right bank of the Ucker on the Pasewalk road 100,000 strong, and that they themselves would soon be completely outflanked. In reality, only Murat's cavalry was there, and no other troops were on the right bank of the Ucker. Massenbach had mistaken a small brook, which he had crossed, for the Ucker" ("Napoleon as a General," i. 307).

corps of Marshal Lannes, there Soult's, there Bernadotte's, and here am I with many more thousands than you have." A statement in which there was scarcely a word of truth.

At this moment an explosion was heard in the distance. It was in reality a Prussian ammunition waggon blowing up, but a French officer promptly remarked, "That is Marshal Soult's signal, announcing that he has reached and cut your line of retreat." Neither Soult nor Bernadotte was within many miles of the spot! Soult in particular was only just crossing the Elbe. Hohenlohe asked for terms allowing the withdrawal of his corps. To this Murat replied that, the Emperor being determined to annihilate the Prussian army, the only conditions permissible were the following:

(1) The Prussian army to be prisoners of war, surrendering all cavalry and artillery horses. Arms might, as a concession, be piled and left, instead of being thrown down.

(2) Officers, retaining their swords and baggage, to be released on parole not to serve again till formally exchanged.

(3) The Royal Guards, on a similar promise, to be allowed to return to Potsdam, without escort, under their own officers.

(4) All other soldiers to be sent to France.

Before submitting to these hard conditions, Hohenlohe retired to consult his generals, whom, when he had assembled them in a circle around him, he thus addressed. "I have always considered it an invariable principle that a general should never surrender, and doubtless you think likewise. . . . I am bound to inform you of our position, and, at this important and decisive moment, to give the gravest consideration to your individual opinions. Our troops are harassed by the fatigue of night marches, the supplies and forage destined for our use have fallen into the enemy's hands, we have no means of procuring more on this side of Stettin. We have lost one battery, and have but five or six rounds apiece for our remaining guns. Both our flanks are turned, and the corps of Marshal Lannes is marching against us in several columns. If any of you gentlemen can see a possibility of escape, let him speak."

Beyond a few incoherent murmurs, this speech elicited no reply. Massenbach's "fantasy," as Hoepfner terms his story, had extinguished every spark of hope; no one had any proposal to make in these apparently desperate circumstances. After a short pause, the Prince continued: "This day I close my military career; I shall render a faithful account to the King, and shall request him to have my conduct investigated by a military court of inquiry. My previous actions will, I think, free me from the necessity of founding my personal reputation on the dubious basis of the useless sacrifice of several thousand lives." He proceeded to detail the terms dictated by the Grand Duke of Berg, which were received with sobs and tears, with outcries against their officers by the soldiery, with appeals by subordinate officers to their men to endeavour to cut their way through. As might be expected, these were but demonstrations of the general sense of shame and sorrow, resulting in nothing. Sadly and sullenly the arms were piled, and the whole force surrendered.

Murat stated his capture at 16,000 infantry, 6 regiments of cavalry, 64 guns, and 45 standards. Naturally, much reliance cannot be placed on the statement of a marshal who had pledged his word of honour that he had many times his actual numbers on the field. According to Hoepfner, there surrendered with Hohenlohe about 10,000 men. Nearly 1000 more had been taken in the suburb, as well as the rearguard of Prince August. The total could hardly have exceeded 12,000. Even adding the captures of the two preceding days, it is impossible that the number was over 13,000 or 13,500.[1]

For Hohenlohe's capitulation at Prenzlau it is impossible to find a justification in the existing position of affairs. Even Von der Goltz, in general an apologist for the Prince, seeks only to excuse him, not to justify his disastrous surrender—a surrender which, according to Hoepfner, was quoted as a precedent and an excuse for a pusillanimous defence by many commandants of the fortresses of Prussia. The blame is thrown, justly so, no doubt, mainly on Massenbach and his fantastic confirmation of the bombastic and unfounded statements of Hugues and Murat. There were not lacking men who openly accused Massenbach of treachery. It is not necessary to accept these accusations, formulated by his fellow-countrymen when smarting under the bitter shame of this disastrous campaign. Von der Goltz says of him that he "has well shown in his own works that

[1] Beaumont, on the 30th October, gives details of the prisoners in his charge amounting to 9534. As the regimental totals he gives are generally below Hoepfner's, it is probable there had been numerous escapes. Nearly 400 officers are not included in the return (Foucart, ii. p. 548, *n.* 4).

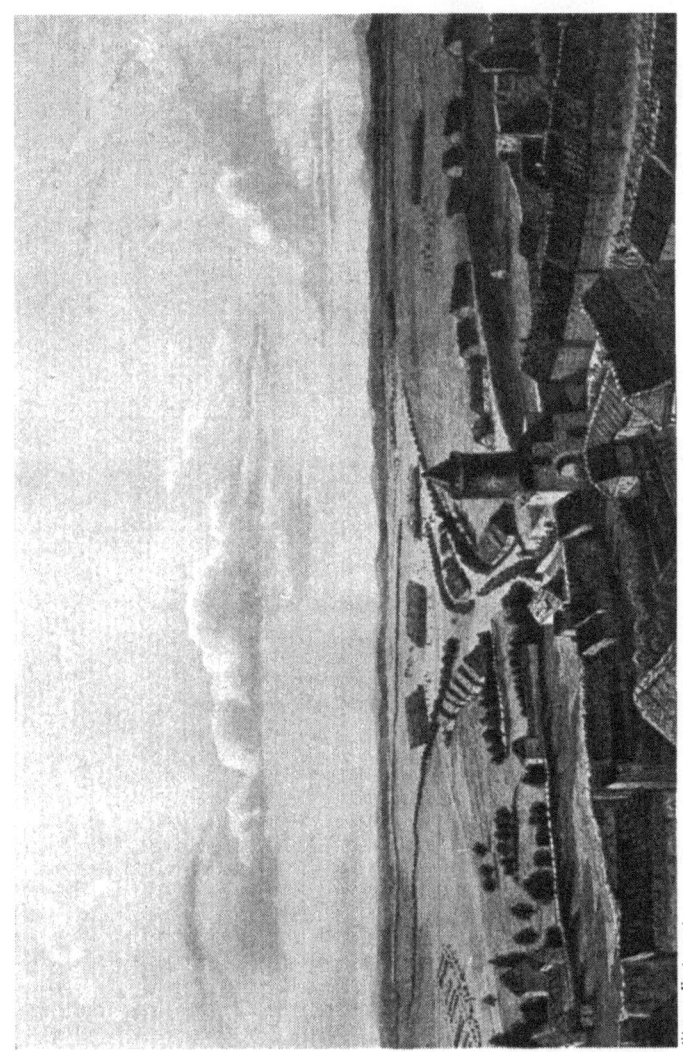

THE CAPITULATION OF PRENZLAU
(From an engraving in Mr. Broadley's collection)

Pursuit of Hohenlohe 251

he was a fantastic man and an unstable character." It is difficult to understand how he allowed himself to be gulled into believing, as no doubt he honestly did, all the fictions which he retailed to Hohenlohe as to the position, at noon on the 28th October, of Lannes' infantry. At that hour there was, with the exception of the few thousand cavalry and the handful of light infantry outside the Stettin gate of Prenzlau, not a Frenchman between the Ucker and the Oder. Weary and starving though they were, it is almost incredible that the 10,000 men whom Hohenlohe still commanded could not have won their way to Stettin without extravagant loss. To do so they required a determined leader of the stamp of Blucher, not a man broken in spirit and deceived as to facts, such as Hohenlohe at this moment was. Bila and Quitzow, with 3 cavalry brigades, Hagen, with his brigade of infantry, were approaching Pasewalk and must soon appear on Murat's flank as he pursued Hohenlohe towards Stettin. That he would have dared to follow, in the face of this threatening superiority of force, is more than doubtful.

Before describing the fate of Blucher's rearguard and of Weimar's corps, both of which were now hopelessly cut off from the Oder, it will be well to narrate the proceedings of Murat's command during the few days following the capitulation of Prenzlau. That capitulation by no means included the whole of Hohenlohe's forces, and, in pursuance of Napoleon's design for the complete destruction of the Prussian army, Lasalle hurried on, in the afternoon of the 28th October, to seize the defile of the Randow, at Löckenitz. Reaching that place by 4 P.M., he took post there, and at Berkholz, facing towards Pasewalk.

Milhaud, it will be remembered, had been detached to Murat's left in the morning, with the 13th chausseurs, and a regiment of dragoons, towards Pasewalk. Arriving at Bandelow, he heard the firing at Prenzlau on his right, and at once turned in that direction. Having witnessed the destruction of Prince August's force by Beaumont, he resumed his march on Pasewalk, but spent the night at Bandelow. Next morning he reached Pasewalk, where he found Hagen's infantry with a large body of cavalry. This force now found itself with Milhaud behind it, and Lasalle barring the road to Stettin towards Lockenitz. No attempt at resistance was made, the whole force surrendering in reply to Milhaud's summons. Hoepfner gives the numbers at 185 officers, 4043 men, and 2087 cavalry horses. Milhaud's and Lasalle's combined forces cannot have equalled half the number of the enemy.

Lasalle at once proceeded to Stettin, to the governor of which he sent a summons to surrender soon after midday on the 29th. The place was fortified, was amply stored with guns, ammunition, supplies of all sorts, and had a garrison of over 5000 men, including some of Hohenlohe's army, chiefly Schimmelpfennig's men, who had reached it. At first the governor refused to surrender. At 4 P.M. another summons was sent, which threatened that unless the place was surrendered within twelve hours a contribution of 500,000 thalers would be exacted. It was added that Murat and Lannes had 30,000 or

40,000 men before it; the truth being that there was nothing but a handful of cavalry, Lannes not getting beyond Lockenitz that day.¹

The threat produced the desired effect. During the night of the 29th–30th the governor agreed to surrender with his whole garrison. The surrender was shameful, for the place could have made a stout defence; and at the worst, if it were thought useless to defend it, the garrison could have escaped with ease across the Oder to join the remains of the Prussian army farther east. But the Prussians were utterly demoralised by their disasters, and had before them as an example the capitulation of Prenzlau. Lannes scarcely exaggerated when he wrote, "The Prussian army is in such a state of panic that the mere appearance of a Frenchman is enough to make it lay down its arms."

There still remained two or three columns endeavouring to gain the Oder, which must be swept in if the Prussian army was to be completely destroyed. Bila II., following Hohenlohe with his cavalry on the morning of the 28th, had found his right flank threatened by Milhaud's cavalry, and had turned to his left to avoid it, directing his march on Strasburg. Leaving Pasewalk to his right, he crossed the Ucker some six or seven miles below it, and marched to Falkenwalde, north-west of Stettin. Here, on the evening of the 29th, he heard of the capitulation of Hohenlohe, as well as of the nego-

---

¹ "My compliments on the capture of Stettin; if your light cavalry thus takes fortified towns, I must disband the engineers and melt down my heavy artillery" (Napoleon to Murat, 31st October—Foucart, ii. 556).

tiations in progress for the surrender of Stettin. Under these circumstances, he started during the ensuing night to march on Demmin, if possible to rejoin Blucher.

By the evening of the 30th he was near Anklam. Next morning he met there his brother, Bila I. The latter officer, commanding in Hanover at the beginning of the war, had left that town on the 20th October with the archives and treasure, under escort of one battalion and a few cavalry. Marching rapidly at first, he presently began to move more slowly; and, thanks to this and to contradictory orders, he was still in Anklam on the morning of the 31st when his brother arrived with the cavalry. His treasure, as well as that of Hohenlohe which had been detached from Lindow on the 26th, got in safety to Wolgast, where it was ferried over to the island of Usedom, and thence passed in safety beyond the Oder. During the 31st Becker with his dragoon brigade arrived before Anklam, forced the two generals Bila across the Peene, and, during the night, induced them to surrender next morning with 1100 infantry and the same number of cavalry.

Though there had been transport enough at Wolgast to pass over the treasure chests to the island of Usedom, it had not sufficed to deal with the baggage and troops arriving there. Hohenlohe's baggage had been detached on the 22nd from Genthin. On the 2nd and 3rd November all that was at Wolgast surrendered to a detachment of Becker's dragoons. The artillery column, which Blucher had so successfully led through the Harz, had already, on the 30th October, fallen

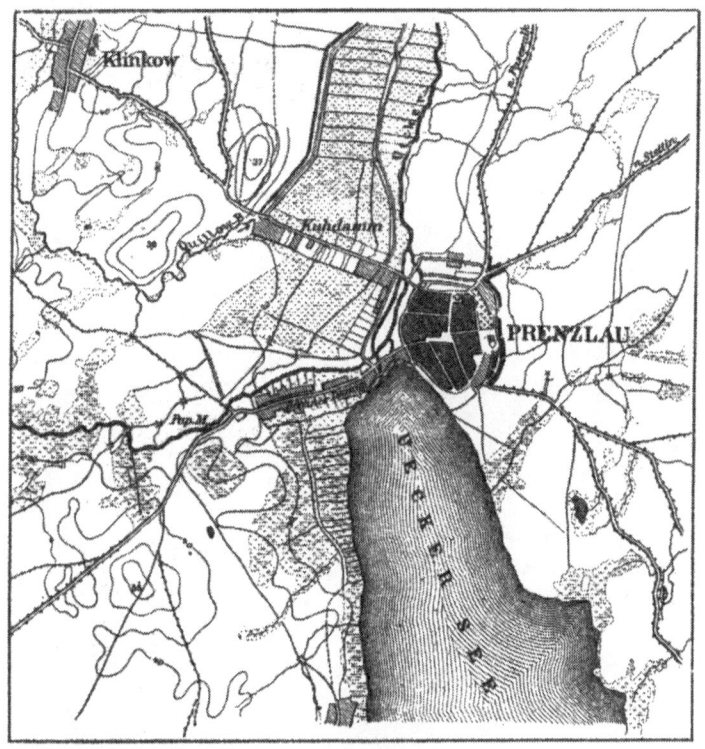

PLAN FOR ACTION OF PRENZLAU

into the enemy's hands. It had, as will be remembered, been delayed by the perverse orders of Massenbach.

At noon on the 28th, about the time of Hohenlohe's capitulation, Hoepfner, commanding the column, had passed but a short way beyond Neu Strelitz. He reached Friedland on the road to Wolgast by 5 P.M. Thence, hearing of the disaster of Prenzlau, he proceeded northwards next morning towards Anklam, but had only reached Boldekow (about five miles from Friedland) when he found himself in presence of detachments of Lannes' corps, to whom he surrendered with 25 guns, a number of ammunition waggons, and about 600 men.

Thus were disposed of all the organised Prussian forces between the Elbe and the Oder north of the latitude of Berlin, excepting the corps of Blucher and Weimar, the latter now under Winning, and the garrisons at Magdeburg and in Hanover.

CHAPTER XIII

BLUCHER'S MARCH TO LÜBECK AND SURRENDER AT RATKAU

IT is now necessary to return to the movements of Ney, Soult, and Bernadotte on the one hand, and of Winning and Blucher on the other, during the last few days of October.

Soult we left, on the 26th, on the Elbe below Magdeburg, busily preparing to cross it about Tangermünde, and to continue the pursuit of Winning, whom he had failed to intercept west of the river. This plan he had communicated to the Emperor, asking his approval, which was duly accorded, Soult being left a free hand. The blockade of Magdeburg was now left to Ney alone, with the assistance of the two dragoon regiments remaining to Klein, after the detachment of the other three to clear the line of communications. The blockade of Magdeburg will be dealt with later.

Soult crossed the Elbe on the 28th October at Tangermünde, and occupied Rathenow the same evening. There five Saxon cavalry regiments came in, demanding to be sent back to their own country.

On the 29th his light cavalry reached Dreetz, the infantry divisions Rhinow and Hohenauen. Soult's view of the situation is given in his

Blucher's March to Lübeck

despatch of the 29th. He thinks that Hohenlohe, finding himself outflanked by Murat, will turn back to Ruppin, endeavouring to rejoin Winning. At Ruppin he would encounter Bernadotte, and might then possibly move westwards towards the French left. Reading for Hohenlohe's whole corps the portion under Blucher, Soult's diagnosis was not far wrong. Holding these views, he had decided to march on Wustershausen, which he reached on the 30th, with cavalry in advance towards Wittstock and Rheinsberg. At this moment Winning was between Mirow and Speck.

Bernadotte had reached Brandenburg with two divisions on the 25th, whence, having obtained definite news of the direction of Hohenlohe's retreat, he decided to follow him. On the 26th he was at Nauen, where he learnt that Hohenlohe, instead of aiming for Oranienburg, had gone from Rathenow by Neustadt and Ruppin. He was able to announce the capture, on the Plaue Lake, of a large convoy of provisions and twenty guns seeking to reach Magdeburg. On the 27th, at Oranienburg, he received orders to move between Gransee and Badingen. On the afternoon of the 28th he reached Furstenberg, on the 29th Boitzenburg. Here the result of some cavalry skirmishes induced him to believe that Blucher was in front of him on the road, by Furstenwerder and Strasburg, to Pasewalk.

Leaving Boitzenburg on the morning of the 30th, he soon received intelligence that Blucher, abandoning the attempt to reach Pasewalk, had again turned to his left and was making for Neu Strelitz, leaving only detachments on the Fursten-

R

werder road to mask his real movement. By a forced march Bernadotte carried his whole corps to between Teschendorf and Neu Brandenburg, sending a cavalry regiment to harass Blucher's retreat on the road to Neu Strelitz. Gérard, commanding this regiment, took 400 prisoners with much baggage, and recognised that Blucher was making for Waren, in the hope of rejoining Winning.

The positions of the various corps on either side on the evening of the 30th were as follows :—

Of the French corps, Murat and Lannes were about Stettin, with cavalry out towards Anklam, at and beyond Pasewalk, &c. ; Bernadotte was about Stargard ; Soult in the neighbourhood of Wustershausen.

On the Prussian side, Blucher was between Neu Strelitz and Waren ; Winning near Mirow, almost in touch with him. It will be remembered that the two generals Bila were still at large towards Anklam.

The French corps[1] were now about to close in on Blucher and Winning, who joined hands on the 31st. Blucher, taking over command of the united force, reorganised it in two corps, each consisting of one light and two heavy divisions. The first corps, about 11,000 strong, represented Winning's force ; the second, of 10,000, that of Blucher himself.

Winning had wished to march for Rostock, there to embark and pass by sea beyond the

---

[1] Lettow-Vorbeck thus reckons the pursuing French corps : Soult, 24,375 ; Bernadotte, 15,450 ; Sahuc's dragoons, 2550 ; d'Hautpoult's heavy cavalry, 1660 ; Grouchy's dragoons, 2432 ; Lasalle's light cavalry, 785. Total, 47,252.

Blucher's March to Lübeck

Oder.[1] This scheme Blucher disapproved; his object was to keep back from the Oder as many of the French as possible, so as to give time for the Russians and Prussians to unite behind that river and organise the defence beyond it, as well as to gather in the troops from Silesia. He decided, therefore, to try to reach the Elbe about Lauenburg and Boitzenburg, to cross it there, and then either to move on Magdeburg or to join the troops under Lecocq in Hanover. Officers were sent forward to collect supplies on this route, and to prepare the means of passage of the river. Blucher's command was specially strong in cavalry, having nearly 80 squadrons, most of them good.

Bernadotte also reorganised his corps, leaving at Neu Brandenburg all doubtful men, and marching with only about 12,000 picked troops, of whom not more than 700 or 800 were cavalry.[2]

On the night of the 31st Winning's corps was between Waren and Alt Schwerin, Blucher's at the former and to the east of it.

Bernadotte was marching between Neu Brandenburg and Waren. Soult had reached Zechlin, his advance guard having overtaken the rearguard of Winning and inflicted some loss on it. Murat was at Friedland, marching up the Peene on Jarmen and Demmin, whilst Beaumont and Lasalle cleared the country on his right rear. Lannes was left at Stettin, a position of inaction which he probably appreciated as little as Ney did being left to blockade Magdeburg.

[1] Winning had actually ordered Wobeser in advance to Rostock to prepare the means of embarkation. These arrangements were cancelled by Blucher (Hoepfner, ii. 244 and 246).

[2] Foucart, ii. 533.

Blucher proposed to reach on the 1st November Alt Schwerin and Plau, with the main body of his 1st corps (Winning's), keeping the rearguard, under Pletz, between Alt Schwerin and Nossentin. The 2nd corps (Blucher's own) would at the same time be towards Kirch-Kogel with its main body; its rearguard, under Oswald, behind it towards Hohen Wangelin. The main bodies having got safely away about 8.30 A.M., Pletz started from Waren towards Nossentin, whilst Oswald took the road by Sommerstorf.

Pletz had left some 200 or 300 cavalry in Waren, against whom came Guyot, from Soult's corps, with the 22nd Chasseurs. Some parleying ensued, during which the Chasseurs managed to surround Waren and compel the surrender of this extreme rearguard. Guyot then advanced on the Nossentin road, but being charged by Prussian hussars, was driven back into Waren.

At this juncture Bernadotte's light cavalry came up from the direction of Neu Brandenburg, thus raising the French cavalry to eight regiments, inclusive of two brought up later by Savary.[1] During three hours, from 10 A.M. to

[1] Savary had been ordered with the 1st Hussars, on the 29th October, to Neu Ruppin and Fehrbellin, where he would pick up the 7th Chasseurs. His objects were to gather information, to clear the country of straggling columns, and to form a link between Murat and Bernadotte. On the 31st he reached Neu Strelitz, where he found Duke Charles of Mecklenburg, second son of the reigning duke and brother of the Queen of Prussia, himself an officer of the Prussian Guards, in which capacity he was made a prisoner of war. The Duke of Mecklenburg was also there, very nervous as to his own fate, and earnestly recommending his daughter, the Queen of Prussia, to the generosity of the Emperor (Foucart, ii. 481 and 570). From the despatch at the former page, it appears that the Emperor on the 29th believed Soult to be still on the left bank of the Elbe.

1 P.M., there had been a series of skirmishes between the Prussian cavalry and that of Soult and Bernadotte, the latter being, according to Savary, on three separate occasions driven back in confusion. Under cover of the Prussian cavalry, Yorck's infantry had taken up a position in the defile behind Jabel, flanked by a lake on either side, with marshy ground in front.

Against him Bernadotte advanced with his own and Soult's cavalry, supported by his infantry, whilst Savary, with his two cavalry regiments, now reinforced by the 9th Light Infantry, moved to his right on the Sommerstorf road, where he appears to have come on Oswald's rearguard of Blucher's corps. He was prevented from attacking it, as Bernadotte recalled him towards Jabel.

After about an hour of artillery combat Yorck withdrew from his position, under cover of the cavalry, to take up a fresh one in the great wood in front of Nossentin. Along the eastern edge of the wood ran a marshy brook crossed by a small bridge. In the wood Yorck left two Jäger companies and some fusiliers, who destroyed the bridge as soon as the cavalry had passed, and withdrew his main body to Nossentin.[1] The French 9th Light Infantry succeeded in passing the brook by fording, and got into the wood, where they were soon engaged in a severe fight, with Yorck's light infantry, now reinforced by four more companies sent back from Nossentin. The defence was stubborn, from tree to tree in the wood, every foot being hotly contested. At

---

[1] Yorck's infantry consisted of 3 battalions of fusiliers and 6 companies of Jägers, with 20 squadrons of hussars.

last the French succeeded in gaining the western edge of the wood, only to find Yorck once more drawn up at and behind Nossentin. His right rested on the Fleesen Lake, his left on the marshes north of Nossentin. The village, the hedges and ditches on either side of it, and the embankment leading to it were occupied by his infantry, the cavalry being now behind.

A French hussar regiment attempting to issue from the wood was unable to face the infantry fire, and Dupont's division was now sent forward to storm the village, the rest of the corps remaining in the wood.

After a sanguinary fight Dupont's men succeeded in driving the Prussians from Nossentin, but the cavalry attempting to turn Yorck's left found itself unable to get through the marshy ground intersected by ditches.

All three of Bernadotte's divisions were now following Yorck, who retired, still in good order, to Alt Schwerin.

Between 8 A.M. and 10 P.M. he had only retreated nine miles, and had suffered comparatively slightly. The action was certainly one of the best contested of the war, and Yorck, the man who six years later, at Tauroggen, was to lead the revolt of Central Europe against the tyranny of Napoleon, had shown himself a master in the art of commanding a rearguard. He had known exactly how long to hold each favourable position, retiring from it to a fresh one in rear in the very nick of time. Bernadotte in his despatch makes light of the fight, though he admits the bravery with which the Prussians fought. That it was not the easy victory which Bernadotte alleges

Blucher's March to Lübeck

is shown by the report of Savary, who condemns Bernadotte for attempting to push on with cavalry alone, when a little patience would have enabled him to bring up an overwhelming force of infantry. During the latter part of the fight the marshal had a narrow escape; for, in attempting to correct the direction of the 5th Chasseurs, he was overthrown and ridden over by the whole regiment. It may seem curious that so good a fight was made at this advanced period, when the general rule was for Prussian corps to surrender or yield before very inferior forces; but it must be remembered that Yorck's force was composed of troops of the corps of Weimar, which so far had not suffered defeat or been seriously engaged, except in covering Weimar's crossing of the Elbe, when it had given a very good account of itself at Altenzaum.

The Prussian numbers are greatly exaggerated by Bernadotte, who puts them at 12,000 or 14,000. Soult says 5000 or 6000; but, as a matter of fact, Yorck had not anything like even these numbers. Taking the battalions and squadrons at the average of the corps, the whole rearguard cannot have exceeded 2000 infantry and as many cavalry, with half of a horse artillery battery, besides the regimental guns of three battalions.

The severity of the fight is shown yet again by the fact that the accounts of it which reached Murat on the 2nd November were so unfavourable that, for the moment, he decided to give up his intended march on Rostock and move to his left towards Waren, in support of Bernadotte.

Later news, of the union of Bernadotte and Soult, caused him to return to his original idea.

On the night of the 1st November the positions were as follows:—

Blucher, who had refused Bernadotte's summons to surrender after the combat of Waren, was assembling his 1st corps at Passow and Grambow, with Pletz's rearguard in Alt Schwerin, which was to be evacuated at 2 A.M. The 2nd corps was at Medow and Kleisten, Oswald's rearguard to withdraw to Goldberg at 2 A.M.

Bernadotte stood at Malchow and Sparrow and in front of Alt Schwerin, which was occupied by his advance guard when Pletz evacuated it.

Savary, six miles to the right of Bernadotte, was at Hohen Wangelin and Leipen.

Soult, with his infantry, had reached Waren after a 30-mile march from Zechlin. His cavalry was with Bernadotte.[1]

Murat was at Demmin with the light cavalry of Lasalle, Grouchy's dragoons, and d'Hautpoult's heavy cavalry.

Sahuc's dragoons were at Rathenow.[2]

During the 2nd November Blucher's corps remained in their positions till noon without seeing anything of the enemy, yet one more proof of the severity of the previous day's action. By evening they had reached Frauenmark, Kladrum, Prestin, and Demen, with rearguards some way short of those places.

On the French side Bernadotte reached

---

[1] Soult, like Bernadotte, decided now to leave all his feebler men behind, and formed them into a separate battalion at Waren (Foucart, ii. 604).

[2] Sahuc had been kept behind Soult's corps during the march from Tangermünde.

Granzin with his light cavalry and Drouet's division, Benthen with Rivaud's division, Passow with Dupont's.

Soult marched to Plau with cavalry at Lübz, on Bernadotte's left.

Murat, still far away on the right, had reached Malchin on his way to Güstrow. During the whole of this day contact with the retreating Prussians was lost.[1] Soult had come to the conclusion that they were marching either on the Elbe or behind the lakes of Schwerin. Savary, still on Bernadotte's right, was on the road to Wismar, in pursuit of the Usedom hussars and two guns, which had got separated from Blucher during the fight at Nossentin on the 1st November. They were actually on the road between Sternburg and Schwerin. On the 3rd November Blucher hoped to be able to make a stand behind the line of the Stoer, south of Schwerin, for a sufficient time to enable him to replenish his provisions, previously to marching south-west, through Wittenburg, on Boitzenburg. At both the latter places much bread had already been collected by the officers sent in advance.

The fighting on this day again fell on the rearguards. Bernadotte, thinking that by marching direct to Granzin he would outflank Blucher, was disappointed to find him gone from the Lake of Goldberg, on the edge of which Bernadotte believed him to be. In this respect the French intelligence was incorrect, as will be seen from a reference to the Prussian posi-

[1] In the evening Drouet at Granzin came upon and captured part of Tschammer's regiment which had lagged behind.

tions on the night of the 2nd–3rd November, already given.

Bernadotte, arriving at Grebbin, found the enemy drawn up, prepared apparently to dispute his passage. No serious resistance, however, was made, and Pelet's division and Oswald's rearguard, which constituted the Prussian force, presently fell back on Criwitz, which was occupied by Oswald. The village, attacked by Maison with Bernadotte's advance guard, was taken after a sharp fight, the Prussians retreating in good order to the heights beyond. Again Bernadotte gives a much exaggerated estimate of his opponent's force, which he puts at 12,000 men. Bernadotte now sent Wattier forward from Criwitz with the light cavalry, supported by an infantry regiment. The Prussians, who had continued their retreat, at once brought back a regiment and a half of dragoons. Wattier, instead of promptly charging them, sent out an officer to demand their surrender, and then appears to have allowed his men to open fire with their carbines. Charged by the dragoons before he had himself got under way, Wattier was driven back in considerable confusion, until he was rescued by the fire of Pacthod's infantry. In this fight Bernadotte narrowly escaped capture by taking refuge in an infantry square. Colonel Gerard, commanding the French 2nd Hussars, was taken, as well as Bernadotte's aide-de-camp, Vilatte. The Prussians now retired upon the bridge of Fahre, where they passed the Stoer, after another combat in the defile against Bernadotte's infantry, now joined from the left by Soult's light cavalry. Bernadotte, owing to the fall of night, was unable to

T. Lawrence, pinxt.

GENERAL BLÜCHER
(From an engraving in Mr. Broadley's collection)

Blucher's March to Lübeck 267

follow the enemy beyond Muess. His rapid advance had cut off Wobeser and Usedom as they attempted to reach Fahre by the eastern side of the Schwerin Lake.[1]

Soult, meanwhile, hearing from Bernadotte that the enemy was in force at Criwitz, had marched towards that place, and at night bivouacked there and at Wessin. He had by this time been rejoined by Sahuc's dragoons. Murat, with Lasalle, d'Hautpoult, and Grouchy, had reached Güstrow.

Blucher was behind the Stoer, but he had not succeeded in holding the passage at Fahre against the enemy. His perplexity was increased by a false report that Soult, marching by Parchim and Neustadt, was already in Wittenburg.[2] If so, it was clearly impossible for him to entertain hopes of reaching the Elbe at Boitzenburg. He decided, therefore, to fall back on Gadebusch, calling in Wobeser and Usedom by Hohen-Wiecheln, round the north end of the Schwerin Lake, and sending orders to have the means of passage of the Elbe floated down it to Lauenburg. He was at this time not informed of the loss of the passage of the Stoer at Fahre. Had he known of this and of Soult's true position, he would have seen that Boitzenburg was still not an unattainable goal, by the Wittenburg road, though it might not have been possible for Usedom and Wobeser to rejoin him. His positions were, during the night of the 3rd–4th November, the 1st corps behind the defiles of Banzkow and Plate, the 2nd at Schwerin and Wittenforden.

---

[1] Usedom's was the force which Savary had been pursuing since the 1st November. It was now again cut off.

[2] Hoepfner, ii. 262.

Early on the morning of the 4th, Blucher assembled his 1st corps at Bleese, with rearguard at Welzin, his 2nd at Gr. Brütz, with rearguard at Wittenforden. During this day he was joined by a dragoon regiment, a battalion of fusiliers, and a company of Jägers, which, under Colonel Osten, had come up from Hameln by Boitzenburg.

During the 4th the pursuit was not conducted with any great vigour by Bernadotte and Soult. Their overworked troops required some relaxation. Soult, moving by Plate and Pampow, captured 200 or 300 stragglers, and, in the evening, had reached Gr. Welzin, Perlin, Dummer, and Walsmuhlen. Bernadotte merely moved his corps to Lankow, a mile or two beyond Schwerin, which latter place Murat reached the same evening.

Blucher, meanwhile, had been successfully rejoined by Wobeser, who had received, at Hohen-Wiecheln, the order to march on Gadebusch. Of Usedom there was no news.[1] He

[1] When Wobeser and Usedom were cut off from Schwerin by the advance of Bernadotte, Wobeser sent an officer with a verbal message to Usedom, requesting him to march towards Wismar to join him (Wobeser). The message was misunderstood by the bearer, who delivered it as a request to Usedom to march to Wismar. Usedom arrived there at 11 A.M. on the 4th, and, of course, found no trace of Wobeser. Then he proposed to gain Swedish Pomerania, and had already started when he received the order to march on Gadebusch. Turning back once more, he found Wismar already occupied by Savary, when he reached it at daybreak on the 5th. Savary had heard of the presence of Prussian baggage, under a small infantry escort at Wismar; also of Usedom's whereabouts. The baggage had been detached from the army to facilitate the march to the Elbe. The whole surrendered to Savary, who puts his capture at 700 cavalry, besides baggage and a few infantry (Foucart, ii. 717). Hoepfner (ii. 270) gives the cavalry as only 367 horses, of which but 100 were fit for use. Savary then went to Rostock, where he took twenty-four Swedish ships but no troops (*Mémoires*, ii. 308).

eventually fell into the hands of Savary. Blucher's perplexity was now great; his army had been reduced by losses in action, by desertions, and by privations, to 16,000 or 17,000 men, all of them exhausted by hard work and short supplies; his cavalry was still numerous and he had nearly 100 guns, though artillery ammunition was running very low in the 2nd corps. His infantry, with worn-out boots, were almost barefooted. He lacked money, bread, and fodder for the horses.

Behind Gadebusch he had the strong position protected in front and on the left by marshes, which had been the scene of a battle between the Saxo-Danish army and that of Sweden in 1712; but, with his army in its present condition, it seemed hopeless to fight a battle against the superior forces of the French. With Soult moving, as Blucher believed, between him and the Elbe, he had no hope of reaching that river, even at Lauenburg. There remained two places only where he could hope to find sufficient resources to enable him to refit, to some extent, his shattered corps—Hamburg and Lübeck—both of them free cities. Lübeck, by far the nearer of the two, still had the remains of its fortifications, and would supply provisions and clothing, possibly also powder, in abundance. Thither, too, the Swedish corps from Lauenburg had retired, and might possibly give a reinforcement in men. On Lübeck Blucher resolved to retire. His 1st corps was to march by Roggendorf to Herrenburg, the 2nd to the same place by the main road. On the march a battalion and forty hussars were detached by Ratzeburg to bring in the supplies and arms collected there to Lübeck. Arriving at Herrenburg, Blucher found it unsuitable for the assembly of his corps, and decided to push on to Lübeck, leaving only Oswald's rearguard behind. The march from Roggendorf had been delayed by waiting for Pelet with his four squadrons of dragoons and half a horse artillery battery. Eventually he had to be left to himself. On the French side, Bernadotte, marching by Gadebusch, came there upon the Prussian rearguard, which he drove before him. Following the enemy, the 1st corps reached by evening Schönberg, whence a battalion with two guns and some hussars, under Gerard (Bernadotte's aide-de-camp), was sent to the Trave, opposite Travemunde, and another detachment, under Maison, to Schlutup, both charged with the duty of attempting to intercept the Swedes, of whose embarkation at Lübeck Bernadotte had news. Soult, meanwhile, had at Roggendorf reached and inflicted some loss on Pelet's dragoons, driving his detachment to the left, away from Blucher. Proceeding to Ratzeburg, Soult's cavalry charged and captured some 300 prisoners. The bridge at that place had been broken, but was easily repaired, so that Soult stood in readiness to march next morning on Lübeck from the south, by the left bank of the Wakenitz. Murat had his headquarters at Ratzeburg, d'Hautpoult was at Holdorf, Grouchy at Meezen, and Lasalle at Einhaus, west of the Ratzeburg Lake.

The peace of the opulent city of Lübeck had first been disturbed, on the 31st October, by the arrival of 1800 Swedes from Ratzeburg, demanding the means of embarkation. Owing to diffi-

Blucher's March to Lübeck 271

culties in obtaining transport, they had not succeeded in embarking completely till the 4th November, only to find themselves detained by contrary winds in the reaches of the Trave below Lübeck.

On that day the first stragglers of the Prussian army began to arrive and encamp outside the southern gate. During the following night more cavalry appeared before the gates, bringing news of the approach of the army from Schönberg and Ratzeburg.

At midday on the 5th, Prussian troops forced their way into the city by the southern gate, and camped in the market-place before the Senate House. Presently Blucher, alighting at the Golden Angel Inn, at once betook himself to the Audience Chamber of the Rathaus, where the Senate was assembled. Addressing the senators, he said that for three weeks he had been pursued by a superior enemy, fighting every day till his troops were utterly exhausted. He sought only a few days' rest and recruitment for his men. Should he be attacked he would withdraw to fight in Holstein. He demanded the immediate supply of 80,000 loaves of bread, 40,000 pounds of beef or pork, 30,000 bottles of wine and brandy, shoes for his infantry, 50,000 ducats in cash, temporary quarters for his troops, and fodder for 5000 horses, as well as all the powder and lead available.

His demands were received with consternation and protests of the impossibility of compliance. Only quarters, food, and drink could, with difficulty, be supplied. Of ammunition there was scarce any store, and but little had been found at Ratzeburg.

Blucher thus arranged his troops for the night. Twelve battalions, with 2½ batteries, were quartered in the city. Outside the southern gate were a regiment of hussars, with some fragments of regiments behind them. A regiment of dragoons and half a horse battery were at Moisling. The rest of the 1st corps and the 1st division of the 2nd corps camped beyond Lübeck. Larisch, with the 2nd division of the 2nd corps, passed during the night, at Herrenfahre, to the left bank of the Trave, above Schlutup; Oswald's rearguard, reinforced by Yorck's and other troops, occupied a line from Herrenburg towards the Trave, with orders to fall back on Lübeck if attacked.

News had reached Blucher that a Danish force under Ewald was approaching the frontier, near Stockelsdorf, to enforce the neutrality of Denmark. A letter to the Danish general elicited the reply that he would defend the neutrality of his country equally against French and Prussians.

The city of Lübeck stands on the right bank of the Trave, at the point where that river is joined by the Wakenitz. Formerly it had been defended by a bastioned enceinte, with wet ditches filled by the waters of the Trave and the Wakenitz. In 1806 the fortifications had been partially dismantled, but there still remained the ditches and the *terre-pleins* of the bastions—quite sufficient to enable the place to be defended against an assault.

On the east side of the city there were three gates; to the north the Burgthor faced a narrow neck of land between the Trave and the Wakenitz, which latter river, after flowing north

Blucher's March to Lübeck 273

almost to the Trave, turns suddenly south to join the Trave above Lübeck, after passing through the ditches of the eastern and south-eastern fronts. The Mühlenthor, near the junction of the two streams, was protected by several ditches filled by the rivers. Between these two gates, on the east, was the Hoxterthor. To the Burgthor led the roads from Herrenburg, Schlutup, and Travemunde; the Mühlenthor and Hoxterthor were approached only from Ratzeburg. On the left bank of the Trave there was but one gate, the Holsteinthor.

Before daybreak orders were sent to Oswald to draw back towards Lübeck and take up a position at such a distance as would prevent the enemy from shelling the city. The streets were cleared of ambulances and baggage waggons, so as to leave them open for the passage of troops.

Before Müffling, carrying Blucher's orders, had reached Oswald, the rearguard had been attacked by Bernadotte, its outposts had been driven in, and the whole body fell back on the Galgenberg, to the east of the Burgthor. Here Oswald took post, with his right resting on the Wakenitz, his left occupying the wood between the roads from Lubeck to Schlutup and to Herrenfahre. Yorck's Jägers, on the flanks, were so worn out that, as Müffling reported to Blucher, they could not, with the exception of one battalion, be expected to make a good fight. Meanwhile Blucher had been personally engaged since 8 A.M. in disposing the troops in the city, himself visiting, with Scharnhorst, the most important posts. He went first to the Burgthor, where he found a small walled and palisaded semicircle in which he

S

placed 8 guns. Two more stood on the remains of the wall at the gate itself, and four were sent to the Bellevue bastion beyond the Trave, which flanked the approach to the Burgthor, at a distance of 200 paces. This bastion was also occupied by a battalion of infantry with its regimental guns, and a whole regiment held the curtain adjoining it. More infantry was sent out in front of the gate, on to the narrow neck (in one place not more than fifty paces broad) between the Trave and the Wakenitz. The guns in front of the gate were so crowded that it was difficult to serve them. The command at this gate was entrusted to the Duke of Brunswick-Oels. At the Hoxterthor Blucher posted another infantry regiment with its 4 battalion guns, supported by 2 horse artillery guns.

At the Mühlenthor were four or five weak battalions, with their own guns and a 6-pounder battery. The rest of the troops stood, partly on the intervening ramparts, partly in reserve in the open places of the city, under command of Natzmer. Altogether, in Lübeck there were nearly 17 battalions and 52 guns; the place seemed to be amply protected.

These preparations for exposing their city to all the horrors of a storm were viewed with dismay by the citizens, a deputation of whom waited on Blucher to remind him of his promise to retire if he were attacked. The old Prussian was little more troubled with scruples on such subjects than was Napoleon himself. He replied bluntly that circumstances had changed, that the enemy was nearer than he had imagined, that retreat was no longer to be thought of, that he

Blucher's March to Lübeck 275

meant to defend himself to the last man, and that the burghers had better remain quietly in their houses. The first attack of the French fell upon the Mühlenthor. Murat, leading the advance from Ratzeburg with Lasalle's brigade and Soult's light cavalry, met and charged the Pletz hussars some 2½ miles south of the gate, about 6 A.M. The Prussians, overwhelmed by superior force, were swept back to the city with a loss of some 200 men captured. Lasalle, following them, lost a few men by artillery fire from the gate. He was presently supported by the arrival of Sahuc's dragoons and the whole of the corps of Soult, whose artillery engaged in a duel with that of the Prussians at the Mühlenthor, which was supported by the guns on the embankment crossing the Wakenitz outside the Hoxterthor.

In the meantime Bernadotte had almost simultaneously come in sight of the Burgthor. Starting at 2 A.M., he reached Selmsdorf whilst it was still dark. There he and his escort were unexpectedly charged by the enemy's hussars. Bringing forward one of Drouet's battalions, he found that he had stumbled on a baggage column, with an escort of 1000 infantry and two squadrons of hussars.[1] The whole force, with some 300 waggons, surrendered. Oswald's rearguard was, at the same time, retiring before Bernadotte's advance.

At Schlutup, Bernadotte found some transports trying to get down the river. A detachment, left there under General Rouyer, compelled them to surrender, with 600 Swedish troops on

[1] This was part of the baggage which had escaped when Savary took the rest at Wismar. It was trying to reach Lübeck.

board. It is noteworthy that Bernadotte, later on, owed his selection as Crown Prince of Sweden largely to the favour gained by his politic good treatment of his Swedish prisoners taken near Lübeck.

Oswald's rearguard was gradually drawn back through the Burgthor, the cavalry first passing through the city and out at the Holstein gate. At 10.30 the Prussian outposts on the Galgenburg were driven by Drouet's skirmishers into the gardens, and a French battery, established on the Galgenburg, opened fire on the guns before the Burgthor. Under cover of its fire Bernadotte formed for attack, with Drouet on the left and Rivaud, with the remains of Dupont's division,[1] across the Schlutup road.

Werlé, with the 27th Light Infantry, moved along the wood between the two roads, to gain the Herrenfahre road; Drouet, with the 94th and 95th of the line, attacked by the Herrenburg road.

For a moment the Prussian fusiliers, holding the Church of St. Gertrude, checked the 27th Light Infantry; but, at this juncture, the fire of the Burgthor battery was disorganised by the wounding of its commander. A second stronger attack resulted in the capture of the church, and the retreat of the Prussian left towards the gate, about noon. Werlé's men now suffered severely from the flanking fire of the Bellevue bastion beyond the Trave, to which the Duke of Brunswick had betaken himself in a boat.[2] The 94th

[1] That is, what remained after detachments to Schlutup, &c.
[2] He had had to give up his horse to an aide-de-camp sent to Blucher to ask for reinforcements.

Blucher's March to Lübeck

took up the attack, turning, unperceived in the smoke, a small "tambour" which blocked the way. Nothing could check the ardour of the French, and an attempt to make another stand at the semicircular entrenchment in front of the gate failed. The guns, unable to escape, were captured, and the beaten Prussian infantry were driven through the gate, followed by the victorious 94th to the market-place in the centre of the town.

Meanwhile the Bellevue bastion, which had seriously hampered the French by its fire, and the adjoining curtain were denuded of infantry, which, with the exception of a small escort for the guns, were withdrawn, by the left bank of the Trave, to the Holstein gate. French soldiers promptly crossed in boats, and compelled the artillery to retreat also.[1]

Bernadotte was now master of the northern entrance to the city. He sent Drouet to the right to gain the Holstein gate and issue from it; Rivaud, turning leftwards, was to clear the city and take in rear the Hoxterthor and Mühlenthor, outside which latter Soult's artillery was heavily engaged.

Blucher, after seeing that Soult was unable to force the Mühlenthor, had retired to his quarters at the Golden Angel, not far from the gate. Thence he ordered detachments to Paddeluge and Moisling, by the left bank of the Trave, to prevent the French from crossing above Lübeck, and sent orders to Larisch to leave only one battalion

[1] This is Hoepfner's account (ii. 288). According to Bernadotte (Foucart, ii. 737 *n*.), the fire of the bastion continued till Drouet could get round by the bridge leading to the Holstein gate and take the bastion in rear.

in Travemunde, and, with the rest, to guard the Trave below Lübeck. The rest of the infantry was to stand behind Lübeck. In this way he hoped to prevent the French from crossing the Trave, either at, or above, or below Lübeck. He seems to have been little disturbed as to the defence of the Burgthor, which was undoubtedly a very strong position.

Presently, firing in the street outside the inn reached Blucher's ears. Rushing out to see what it meant, he found French voltigeurs leading Rivaud's column. He had just time to jump on a staff officer's horse and escape, with his son and Müffling. Scharnhorst and the staff, who were busy issuing orders, took refuge in a garret when the French entered the house.

It was about 1 P.M. when Bernadotte's troops captured the Burgthor. In the streets beyond there was a terrible scene of confusion and carnage. Dead bodies of men and horses, broken-down waggons, abandoned guns, blocked the passages in every direction. The Prussians, collecting in the squares, or barricading themselves in the houses and streets, fought with the energy of despair. Every street, every square, became a separate battlefield. Yorck and others, collecting a few Jägers, attempted in vain to stem the progress of the French. Many heroic deeds were performed. Captain Wedelstadt, wounded in defending a street, bade his men leave him where he lay whilst they continued the defence. Captain Engel, leading a few men against a French gun in the Königstrasse, was blown to pieces with almost all his men. Blucher, after his escape from the inn, placing himself at the head of a small body of cuirassiers, attempted to rescue Scharnhorst and the staff, but, beaten off by the French in the house, was forced to leave Scharnhorst to be taken.

Twice were the French forced to yield before the furious Prussians in the Königstrasse, once in front of the Senate House. Yorck, leading his Jägers, was severely wounded, and the men began to waver, when Blucher, arriving on the scene, shouted: "What! Jägers, will you abandon your wounded colonel?" and again rallied them.

All this desperate resistance by isolated bodies could do no real good in stopping the French advance. Even Blucher at last saw that further street fighting was, for himself at any rate, undesirable in the face of the tremendous odds against him, and that his proper place was now with the remains of his corps outside the Holstein gate. How was he to reach them? Drouet's guns were already firing heavily on the bridge leading across the river to the Holstein gate, and interposing between him and the bridge. Charging with his cuirassiers, he succeeded, by desperate bravery, in winning his way to and across the bridge, which, up till now, had been held by some Prussian light infantry.

Outside the city he found the Duke of Brunswick-Oels, and Natzmer. According to Hoepfner, he expressed his surprise at finding them there. Blucher's language was apt to be more forcible than polite, and it is probable that it was very plain on this occasion. The Duke could only answer that he had no idea

Blucher was still in the city; Natzmer explained that, as he was moving to reinforce the defence of the Burgthor, he had been swept back by the defeated Prussians, followed by Drouet's division. During this desperate fighting in the streets, Rivaud had forced his way to the Mühlenthor, the defenders of which now found themselves attacked by Soult and Murat in front, by Rivaud in rear. The attack in front had recommenced with vigour after a considerable lull.[1] To Legrand's division was entrusted the attack on the Mühlenthor; Leval's division was sent along the peninsula in the bend of the Wahenitz to attack the Hoxterthor, St. Hilaire's remained in reserve. Probably Soult is justified in saying that his infantry succeeded in storming the works outside the gate; but there can be little doubt that it was not till Rivaud attacked it in rear that the gate itself was taken. The fight for its possession raged furiously for some time, French and

[1] The accounts given by Bernadotte and Hoepfner on the one hand, and by Murat and Soult on the other, of the capture of the Mühlenthor, are entirely different. Both Murat and Soult allege that the gate was taken by them before the arrival of Rivaud's troops (Foucart, ii. 741 and 744). Bernadotte, whom Hoepfner confirms, asserts that it was only as Rivaud issued from the gate, after taking it, that he encountered Legrand's division. The marshal states that he arrived on the spot just in time to stop a dispute between Rivaud's and Legrand's divisions as to which of them had captured the 2000 men holding the gate (Foucart, ii. 739). On the whole, the latter account seems the more probable. No doubt Soult's troops took the works beyond the outer ditch, but after that they would have to attack, across a single bridge, a sort of fortified island, which was very difficult from their side, whilst it was, owing to a double causeway, much easier from the city side. Murat and Soult, anxious, no doubt, to have an equal share with Bernadotte in the triumph, probably exaggerated their share. "The corps commanded by Marshal Bernadotte," says Soult, "and the 4th participated equally" (Foucart, ii. 743).

Blucher's March to Lübeck 281

Prussians alike mounting to the windows and on to the roofs of the houses, in the hope of gaining a point of vantage. Overwhelmed by fire from all sides, the Prussians suffered terribly, one regiment alone losing 300 men. At last the power of resistance failed, and the defenders surrendered. At the Hoxterthor, the regiment Owstien likewise made a brave defence. It was still holding out against Leval, when the French who had captured the Mühlenthor turned the Prussian guns, as well as their own, on that regiment's right flank. Infantry occupied the houses near the gate, and opened fire from them on the Prussians. Through the now open Mühlenthor, Murat's cavalry poured into the town, making its way towards the Hoxterthor, where the Owstien regiment, after suffering great loss when formed in square, was at last compelled to surrender. By 3.30 P.M. Lübeck was in complete possession of the French; every street had been cleared of Prussian troops, though many houses were still defended.

We left Blucher, about 2 P.M., outside the Holstein gate. There he had still about eight battalions of infantry, and a great part of his cavalry, which had naturally had but little fighting on this day. The sound of the firing at the Hoxterthor and the Mühlenthor induced him to attempt a fresh advance on the city. The regiment Kunheim, facing about, moved towards the Holstein gate accompanied by Blucher; but Drouet's troops were already on the bridge, and on the walls on either side of the gate, and their fire wrought havoc in the close columns of the Prussians. The infantry, compelled to fall back behind the cavalry, marched towards Schwartau. Drouet forthwith issued in pursuit from the gate, being supported by Rivaud's division, which had completed its work in the city. The pursuit was, in some degree, checked by the Prussian dragoons.

At night the French positions were these:—

Bernadotte had his light cavalry and Rivaud's division in front of Schwartau, Drouet's in the gardens west of Lübeck, Dupont's in the city. Soult had one division on the Holstein road, the others behind the city; cavalry at Paddeluge, where it captured 4 Prussian companies and 2 guns, which it hemmed in against the Danish frontier.[1]

D'Hautpoult had taken no part in the fighting, whilst Grouchy had only assisted at the storming of the Burgthor with his artillery. In the evening, the latter general captured 4 squadrons, 1 battalion, and 4 guns, on the Hamburg road.[2] He took position for the night about Vorwerk, whence he despatched to Blucher a summons to surrender.

Whatever pity may be felt for Blucher in his forlorn situation on the night of the 6th November must be tempered by a consideration of the terrible misfortunes in which, by deciding on using their city as a fortress, he had involved the peaceful and neutral citizens of Lübeck. The state of discipline in the French army at this period has already been described. Even had French troops marched into Lübeck un-

[1] This was the detachment of Captain Witzleben retiring from Moisling.
[2] Detachment of Major Eude supporting the Moisling detachment. Grouchy speaks of a battalion (Foucart, ii. 747). The battalion was really one of hussars (Hoepfner, ii. 298).

MARSHAL SOULT
(From a lithograph in Mr. Broadley's collection)

Blucher's March to Lübeck

opposed, it might have been expected that the inhabitants would have suffered, to some extent, from their lawlessness. But under the circumstances in which Lübeck was taken, it was hardly reasonable to expect that the French soldiery would accord the unhappy city treatment other than, under the usages of war, was to be expected by a fortress taken by storm. In such conditions it is almost impossible to restrain excesses, even in a well-disciplined force which has had to fight in the very houses and streets of the conquered place. Wellington was unable to prevent the horrors which ensued after the storming of Badajoz, and similar atrocities are recorded in the case of almost every other fortress taken by assault. It seems safe to predict that such occurrences will not disgrace the warfare of the future, not because it would be possible to restrain the fury of a modern army, exasperated by a stubborn resistance successfully overcome, but because the improvement of modern artillery has rendered a recurrence of the circumstances practically impossible. The fortress of the future will be, not a town depending for its defence on an enceinte drawn close round it, but a great entrenched camp, with a large perimeter of outlying forts, lying several miles beyond the enceinte of its nucleus, defensible only by a large army. With the fall of the outlying lines, the defending army must either fight in the open or surrender.

Strasburg, as it was in 1870, could never stand more than a few hours' bombardment from modern artillery, and would be compelled to surrender without standing an assault. Strasburg, as it now is, must fall as Port Arthur did, without the besiegers ever making an assault on the portion occupied by the non-combatant population. To return to Lübeck: as soon as it had fallen into the hands of the French, scenes of pillage, rape, and murder commenced. One of the senators, waiting on Bernadotte to implore his protection for the city, was told briefly that the troops must have quarters and supplies. Those troops, as has been said, saw in the city merely a place taken by storm, to plunder which they considered their right under the usages of war. The marshals said this plainly to a deputation of the citizens. Bernadotte and the other superior officers, as Hoepfner admits, personally exerted themselves in trying to stop the pillage; but their men, exasperated by the desperate resistance in the streets and houses, were out of hand, and determined to wreak their vengeance on the inhabitants, whom they refused to distinguish from the Prussian soldiery. "A soldiery," says Jomini,[1] "inflamed by cruel scenes is not easy to restrain; the inhabitants of this flourishing city had naturally to suffer all the horrors of a town taken by assault."

Dumas, writing on the same subject, says:[2] "The combats, the carnage in the streets, in the houses, in the squares, in the churches, ceased only with the approach of night, night of horror, during which the unhappy city of Lübeck was given over to all the excesses inevitable after a storm. More than 30,000 soldiers spread through it in disorder, and in this confusion the conquered joined with the conquerors in these scenes of

[1] *Vie de Napoléon*, ii. 318.   [2] Dumas, xvi. 332.

Blucher's March to Lübeck 285

desolation. The efforts of the French officers, too long futile, gradually arrested the fury of pillage; many of them devoted themselves, at the peril of their lives, to acts of humanity which are not the least of the claims to glory of arms." Whatever may be said of the conduct of Napoleon's armies generally, the sack of Lübeck, horrible though it was, is not the worst count in the indictment against them. Blucher, on the other hand, must bear a large share of responsibility for what occurred. With his beaten army, so far inferior to his opponents in every way, he could hardly be justified in exposing even a Prussian town, ill fortified as Lübeck was, to an assault; when we consider that the city was neutral, it seems impossible to exonerate him.

He was, however, probably thinking little of Lübeck in its agony; for his own day of humiliation had arrived. As day broke on the 7th November he found himself at Ratkau with the shattered remnants of the 21,000 men whom he had commanded but ten days ago. He had lost the greater part of his remaining infantry in Lübeck, where Soult and Bernadotte calculate that they took 5000 or 6000 prisoners, besides inflicting a loss of 3000 killed and wounded. Hundreds of bodies of his gallant men were floating towards the sea in the Trave and the Wakenitz, or encumbering the streets of Lübeck. Of his artillery, he had lost 50 guns in Lübeck. During the days preceding the 6th November his strength had been reduced by death, wounds, captures, and desertions by about 5000 or 6000 men. His detachments towards Travemunde were cut off, and another force under Pelet, separated on the 5th November, was now away on the Lower Elbe. A German authority, quoted by Hoepfner, has calculated that Blucher had at Ratkau 4050 infantry and 3760 cavalry, but the estimate is probably too high.

This handful of men was hemmed in on their right by the Danish frontier, on their left by the Trave; behind them lay the sea; in front the overwhelming forces of the three French marshals were advancing at daybreak for the final attack.[1] Resistance or escape were alike hopeless, and Blucher sent out to see what terms he could get. Naturally, he was told that his army must surrender as prisoners of war. He sent back a draft capitulation, in which he recited that he surrendered to the Prince of Ponte Corvo (Bernadotte), because he was destitute of food and ammunition. To this draft Murat objected, first, that the capitulation must be to the three marshals, not to Bernadotte alone; secondly, that it was unusual to state the grounds of capitulation. Blucher held out on the second point, and, eventually, he was allowed to write at the end of the document: " I capitulate, since I have neither bread nor ammunition.—BLUCHER." At noon the remnants of his army defiled sorrowfully before the French commanders.

According to Bernadotte and Murat, there were 27 battalions and 52 squadrons, but in strength many of them must have resembled the battalions and squadrons so called which, six years later,

[1] Taking Lettow-Vorbeck's estimate of the French force at the commencement of the pursuit (47,252), and allowing for losses as well as for the worn-out men left behind by Bernadotte and Soult, there must have still been somewhere about 35,000 French troops at Lübeck.

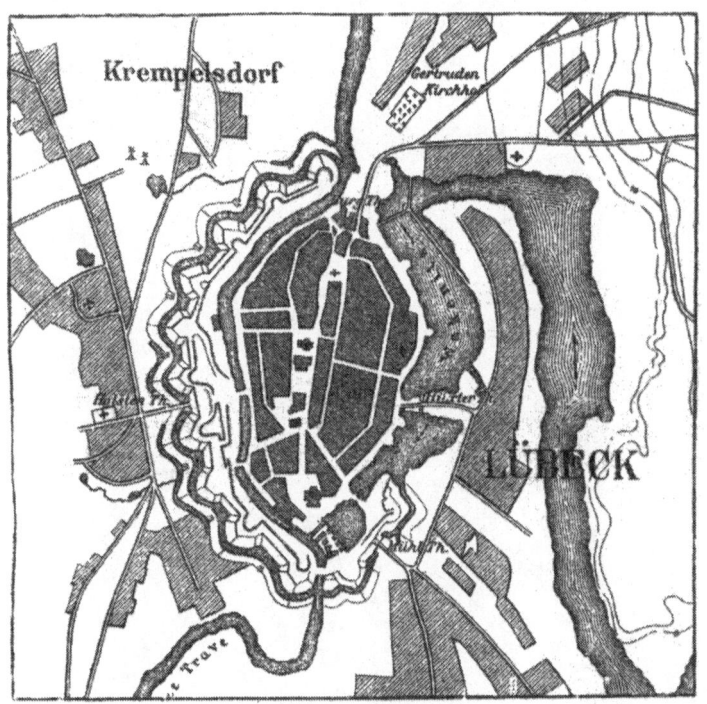

PLAN FOR STORMING OF LÜBECK

Blucher's March to Lübeck 287

returned from Russia. There certainly were not 15,000 men, as the French generals, for their own glorification, pretend; probably half that number would be an excessive estimate. The capitulation, which was to include all Blucher's detachments, was on the same terms as that of Prenzlau.[1]

On the 8th, the detachment at Travemunde surrendered to Rivaud.

Of all Blucher's army there remained but the small force under Pelet, and the troops of Colonel Osten from Hameln. These had been cut off by Soult on the 5th November. Drouet was now sent in pursuit of them towards the Lower Elbe. Pelet succeeded in getting across the Elbe, but had to surrender at Luneberg on the 10th, as he found that his detachment was included in the capitulation of Ratkau.

[1] Napoleon, according to Rapp (p. 105), at first intended to send Blucher to Dijon, but was persuaded to allow his retirement to Hamburg. He was exchanged, in the spring of 1807, against Victor, who had been captured by a Prussian party from Colberg.

CHAPTER XIV

THE FATE OF MAGDEBURG, HESSE-CASSEL, AND HAMELN

Of all the 150,000 men who, in the beginning of October, had faced Napoleon in Saxony, but a few hundreds had succeeded in reaching a place of safety behind the Oder. All the rest had been killed, wounded, taken, dispersed, or, in the case of the Saxons, disarmed and sent home, with the exception of some 25,000 who had been driven into Napoleon's "mouse-trap," Magdeburg.

The blockade of that fortress can hardly be called an interesting study, but some description of it is necessary to complete the history of the unfortunate Prussian army of 1806.

When Soult, on the 25th October, started in pursuit of Weimar towards Tangermünde, there remained for the blockade of what was then a first-class fortress, only the corps of Ney with two regiments of Klein's dragoons.[1] Altogether, Ney cannot have had more than 17,000 or 18,000 troops with which to blockade a garrison, the strength of which is stated by Hoepfner at 24,118 men, with 6563 horses and 577 guns when it surrendered. The place was more than

[1] The other three regiments had been sent back to clear the country towards Nordhausen, &c.

amply stored with ammunition, and supplies of all sorts, so that, on this score, there was never the slightest cause for anxiety.

On the other hand, the governor, General von Kleist,[1] was a veteran of seventy-three years of age, worn out by ill-health, old age, and wounds received in former campaigns. Even so early as the 23rd of October, Ney reports that the governor showed signs of a disposition to surrender so soon as a serious attack should afford him a reasonable excuse for doing so.

The commandant of the place was more or less independent of Kleist, and there was consequent friction respecting orders issued. Finally the inhabitants of the city were reluctant to incur the risks of a bombardment or a successful assault, and seriously impeded military operations.

From the very first Ney was able to report that a purely passive defence seemed to be aimed at. At the same time he much underestimated the strength of the garrison; for he was not aware how large a portion of Hohenlohe's force had, unintentionally in great part, been left behind.

On the 23rd October he had succeeded in establishing a bridge at Schönebeck, on the Elbe above Magdeburg, and by it he sent over his light cavalry to complete the very weak blockade on the right bank. His infantry and Klein's two regiments of dragoons completed the circle on the left bank. On the 30th Ney recalled two more regiments of dragoons, as the country about Nordhausen appeared now to be safe if watched

---

[1] This was, of course, not the Kleist who took so prominent a part in the events of 1813 and 1814. The latter, in 1806, was on the general staff of the Prussian army.

by a single regiment. On the 1st November the already weak French force was still further reduced by the departure of Klein, under orders to join Soult in the pursuit of Weimar. Napoleon seems to have fallen into Ney's error of underestimating the strength of the garrison; for he even asked Ney whether he could not spare one of his divisions[1] and carry out the blockade with Vandamme's division and the light cavalry only. Against this proposal Ney protested, and the Emperor abandoned the idea. His underestimate of the Magdeburg garrison had led him to overestimate Hohenlohe's strength.

The siege continued to be utterly uninteresting. Nothing occurred beyond the frequent sending by Ney of summonses to surrender, and numerous small attacks on Kleist's outposts, which compelled him to draw them close into the fortress.

On the 5th November, Napoleon approved Ney's proposal to try the effect of bombardment, and ordered him to be supplied with mortars for the purpose. On the same day Ney sent notice to the garrison of his intention to bombard. A feeble sortie on the previous night had been repulsed, and a few shells fired into the town.

[1] It is a little puzzling to follow the correspondence about Ney's divisions. Napoleon speaks of them as the 1st and 2nd, Ney calls them the 2nd and 3rd. Dupont's had been his 1st division until its transfer to Bernadotte. The 2nd division was commanded temporarily by Marcognet, till it was given to Vandamme for the siege of Magdeburg. The latter's proud and violent character had proved too much for Soult, which was the cause of his transfer to Ney. The latter could not bear with him beyond Magdeburg, so he was sent to Silesia (*cf*. Fezensac, p. 93). Napoleon once said of Vandamme that, in the event of a campaign against Satan, he would give him a high command, for he feared neither God nor the Devil.

The Fate of Magdeburg 291

On the 6th the governor received notice of the capitulation of Prenzlau through a captured officer whom Ney sent in to him. Negotiations were promptly commenced. On the afternoon of the 7th an armistice was concluded, and on the 8th, at 1 P.M., the capitulation, on the usual terms, was signed. On the 10th the French occupied the gates; on the 11th the disarmed garrison was marched off under escort as prisoners of war to Bernburg. Thus Magdeburg, with a garrison which Ney apparently underestimates at 22,000, with nearly 600 guns and vast quantities of ammunition and supplies, fell ingloriously into the hands of a besieging force much inferior to the garrison in numbers.

The defence, if such it can be called, was a disgrace to the governor, and the capitulation stands on a footing with those of Küstrin[1] (1st November) and Stettin.

When, in the beginning of October, Blucher set out to join the main army towards Erfurt, he left behind him a small force, under Generals Brusewitz and Hagken, to guard against the advance of the French from the Lower Rhine and Holland. The troops were scattered north and south of Münster and at that place itself, with some detachments in East Friesland. The Prussian authorities had recognised that the principal attack was to be expected from the south, not from this direction, as is evidenced by the small strength of the force left behind, which,

[1] It is unnecessary to deal in this volume with the capture of Küstrin, or the operations of Davout and Augereau after the occupation of Berlin, for these events belong really to the campaign in Poland, which has formed the subject of a previous volume.

including the garrisons of Hameln and Nieuburg, could not have exceeded 12,000 men. Napoleon's instructions to his brother Louis, to spread reports that he had 80,000 men, had not had the full effect hoped for in detaining a large portion of the Prussian army at a distance from the true field of operations. It will be remembered that Louis' army was to play merely the part of an army of observation, until a great victory in the chief theatre of war should render it desirable for him, in conjunction with Mortier from Mayence, to advance to the conquest of Hanover, East Friesland, and Hesse-Cassel.

The Prussian general Lecoq, who had before the outbreak of hostilities taken over the command at Münster, learned on the 2nd October that Wesel was strongly garrisoned, whilst a corps of 5000 or 6000 men stood north-east of the place, supported by a Dutch corps of about the same strength near Utrecht. His instructions were, in the event of a serious advance of the enemy from Holland or the Lower Rhine, to withdraw behind the Weser, seeking protection, as a last resource, under the guns of Hameln and Nieuburg.

Learning, on the 9th October, of the outbreak of hostilities in Saxony, both Lecoq and Hagken began to move slowly westwards. Nothing of importance, however, happened until, on the 19th, news of the disasters of the 14th warned the generals that they must fall back on the Weser. As they retreated towards Hameln, further bad news reached them, indicating the possible advent of Napoleon's army, in consequence of Hohenlohe's retreat through the Harz, and that of

The Fate of Magdeburg 293

Weimar and Blucher farther west. To Lecoq the situation seemed so desperate that he decided to hasten to Hameln, which he reached on the 23rd, occupying cantonments in the neighbourhood, and strenuously exerting himself to collect ample provisions for the defence of the place. Here he was joined by Hagken.

On the 24th, hearing that the roads to the Lower Elbe were still open, he started in that direction. On the 27th he turned back again, on the strength of a report that the enemy's cavalry was in Brunswick, but he sent Colonel Osten on, with a dragoon regiment and a battalion, to the Lower Elbe. That officer, it will be remembered, came into touch with Blucher on the 5th November, when he and Pelet were driven by Soult towards the Elbe.

Lecoq again settled down to defend himself in Hameln, the garrison of which had been increased in numbers by the arrival of some of the stragglers from the main army.

Meanwhile Napoleon, on the 17th October, wrote to his brother Louis that the time had come for changing his attitude of observation into an active advance to the occupation of the Mark, of Münster, and of Paderborn. Leaving a small garrison in Wesel, which was now safe from attack, Louis was to march with 10,000 men on Paderborn.

To Mortier, on the same date (17th), the Emperor wrote that he should now, with two Italian regiments about to reach Mayence, be able to dispose of two divisions of 5000 men each. With these he was to move on Fulda, and establish his headquarters there, thus guarding the new line of communications of Napoleon with France. For this purpose he was to keep an advance guard at Eisenach, and to communicate freely with Clarke, the French governor of Erfurt. Napoleon expected Louis to be at Paderborn, and Mortier at Fulda, about the 24th or 25th October. From those places he intended them to advance on Cassel, to make prisoner the Elector, to disarm his troops, and to annex his territory; a heavy penalty to impose on a ruler who had taken no active part in the war. Sympathy for the Elector must, however, to a great degree be modified on consideration of his conduct previous to, and during the first days of the war. His position was very different from that of Saxony. The latter state was in sympathy with Austria and the Roman Empire, by the final dissolution of which she was left with no power to which to cling. Towards Prussia she had little goodwill; her real desire was to continue neutral. Her alliance with Prussia was forced upon her, so to speak, with Prussian bayonets, when Hohenlohe reached Dresden on the 13th September. Indeed, looking to her geographical position, it was almost impossible to hope that she could remain neutral in the approaching conflict. Napoleon had wooed her as an ally, her neutrality he would scarcely have suffered to stand in the way of his strategical projects. Prussia had, equally with Napoleon, sought the Saxon alliance; but she was in a position to enforce it, which Napoleon could hardly do without precipitating events. To Prussia, therefore, fell the adherence of Saxony.

Hesse-Cassel, on the other hand, was entirely

The Fate of Magdeburg 295

in sympathy with Prussia, and, what was worse in Napoleon's eyes, with England, who had so often made use of Hessian troops. The Elector was only restrained from openly joining Prussia by his uncertainty as to the result of the war, and his conviction that, if he joined Prussia in a losing fight, Napoleon would inevitably annex his territory. He decided to play the dangerous game of sitting on the fence, sitting not evenly, but with the leg on the Prussian side almost on the ground. Napoleon had sent him a distinct warning of the dangers of his position, through the Prince Primate, to whom he wrote on the 1st October: "If the Prince of Cassel is sincere and wishes to remain really neutral, I have no intention of preventing his doing so." The Emperor went on to say that his troops should not pass through Hessian territory, that he had no ill-will against the Elector, and would not attack him willingly. It was impossible not to read between the lines the scarcely veiled threat, in case the Elector should assume a position of neutrality benevolent to Prussia and malevolent to the French. That prince, nevertheless, continued to behave towards Prussia rather as an ally than as a neutral. Prussian troops were permitted to pass through his territories, and the friendly demonstrations with which they were received were in no way condemned or discouraged by the Government. To Napoleon's warning no answer was returned, but the ambassador of Hesse-Cassel was recalled from Paris. The mobilisation of troops was actively pressed, and, so late as a few days before the decisive contest, the Elector was with the King of Prussia, almost on the point of throwing in his lot with that sovereign.

Naturally, when the crushing defeats of Jena and Auerstädt had made manifest the hopelessness of the Prussian cause, the Elector saw fit to disarm, to assume an attitude of genuine neutrality, and to endeavour to appear as if that had been his position all through.

Whether Napoleon ever intended to keep his promise of respecting Hessian neutrality may be left in doubt; he was now quite determined to wreak his vengeance on the prince who had so clearly favoured Prussia as far as was possible without actively joining her in the field. The Emperor had decided on annexation, and the dethronement of the Elector.

For this purpose Louis and Mortier received instructions to converge so as to meet on the same date at Cassel. The Elector was to be deceived with fair words until the last moment, when the two corps were ready to enter his capital. Mortier was furnished with a formal note detailing the Emperor's complaints against the court of Cassel, and announcing his intention of annexing the state, and deposing the reigning family. This was to be delivered by an aide-de-camp, only the night before the entry of the troops into Cassel. A proclamation of the annexation was also enclosed. This was on the 23rd October.

When Mortier acknowledged this despatch on the 26th he was at Brukenau, a day's march south of Fulda. His force was by no means so strong as Napoleon had expected. The two Italian regiments not having arrived, he had but

The Fate of Magdeburg

three regiments of French light infantry, in all not more than 5500 strong. On the night of the 31st October, Mortier on the south and the advance guard of Louis on the north, were each within a short march of Cassel. The former reported that no suspicions of his real intentions had been aroused, and that he was believed to be marching through Cassel to occupy Hanover. He now despatched his aide-de-camp with the Emperor's note. At 3 A.M. the Hessian ministers came with the submission of the Elector, for whom and the Hereditary Prince they asked a passport to the Emperor's headquarters. This being refused, the two princes left Cassel and succeeded, after narrowly escaping some French troops, in getting away towards the north. Next morning, Cassel was occupied without resistance by Mortier, who was joined there by Louis's troops. The Hessian troops there were disarmed and disbanded. A few days later Hanau was occupied peaceably, and the rest of the Hessian troops were disarmed.

The corps of Louis and Mortier were now available for the conquest of Hanover. For the moment Mortier was placed under the nominal command of Louis, who was required to give him a corps of about 12,000 men, with which to occupy Hanover and Hamburg. Louis, on the plea of ill-health, was allowed, on the 9th November, to retire to his kingdom, leaving Mortier in command.

French troops began to appear before Hameln on the 7th November; on the 10th part of Mortier's corps arrived. The place had, since its surrender by the French in March 1806, been placed in a good state of defence; its works were strong; it was amply provisioned, and Lecoq occupied it with about 10,000 men.

When Mortier proceeded to Hanover and Hamburg he left but 6000 men, under Dumonçeau, to blockade the fortress with its garrison nearly twice as strong.

It seems unnecessary to go into any detail of this blockade, which was of very little interest.

About this time, Napoleon had concluded with Luchesini, the envoy of the King of Prussia, an armistice, on terms very hard towards the latter, amongst which was a provision for the surrender of the remaining Prussian fortresses. Napoleon, pretending to believe in the immediate ratification of this agreement (which was, as a matter of fact, refused by the King), despatched Savary to Hameln to see what he could effect by means of diplomacy. Savary, arriving before Hameln on the 19th November, immediately entered into negotiations with Lecoq and the other Prussian generals. After pointing out to them the hopelessness of their position, with no Prussian force to come to their assistance within 250 miles, he clinched the matter by explaining the agreement with Luchesini. Lecoq decided to surrender next day. That he must eventually surrender was certain, but he was equally certainly wrong not to hold out to the last, thereby detaining a substantial portion of Napoleon's army, every man of which was required for the prosecution of the campaign in Poland, Silesia, and Pomerania. When the terms of the capitulation, which were similar to those of Prenzlau, became known to the Prussian troops, they broke into open mutiny;

MARSHAL NEY
(*From an engraving in Mr. Broadley's collection*)

The Fate of Magdeburg 299

discipline was at an end; the wine-shops were broken open; crowds of drunken troops paraded the streets, robbing, and even firing upon one another and the inhabitants. Even the officers broke out, demanding orders for their pay on the treasuries of the provinces occupied by the French, and for the soldiers permission to retire to their homes, instead of being treated as prisoners of war.

Savary took strong measures to enforce the capitulation. His cavalry entered Hameln, driving the Prussian troops through the place on to the plain outside, where they were surrounded and disarmed.

Leaving Dumonçeau at Hameln, Savary went on to the little fortress of Nieuburg, before which also a blockading force had been left. The fortress surrendered on the 25th November. Mortier occupied Hanover on the 12th November without opposition. Plassenberg, a small fort near Hof, which had been blockaded by a few Bavarians, surrendered on the 25th November, without a shot being fired.

CHAPTER XV

CONCLUDING REMARKS ON THE SECOND PERIOD OF THE WAR

HERE we conclude the history of the campaign of 1806; for the conquest of Silesia and the campaign of 1806–7 in Poland have already been fully described in the author's previous work.

Napoleon's advance against the Saxo-Prussian army began on the 8th October. Precisely one month later, there surrendered, at Magdeburg, the last remaining organised body of that army. His bulletin of the 16th November, summarising the results of the campaign, puts the strength of the Saxo-Prussian army, including the corps of Weimar and Würtemberg, at 145,000 men. All of these had, he says, been either killed, wounded, or taken prisoner: "The King, the Queen, General Kalkreuth, and 10 or 12 officers are all that have escaped." Unlike most of Napoleon's bulletins, this one contained scarcely a word of exaggeration. The results were magnificent, and had been attained with comparatively little loss to the French army, which, by constant reinforcement, had been kept up almost to its original strength. It was about to advance on the Vistula in two great bodies of about 80,000 each. The stores of clothing, food, ammunition,

Concluding Remarks 301

guns,[1] and military requisites of every sort which had been taken were enormous. The horses, taken in great numbers from the Prussian and Saxon cavalry and artillery, served to provide Napoleon with a better class of remounts than he could draw from France, and were at once pressed into his service.

The course of the war after the 14th October was of an entirely different character from that of the first week. At the two great battles the main army had been broken in pieces. There remained but two corps which had not suffered defeat, those of Würtemberg and of Weimar. The former was reduced to the condition of the armies of Hohenlohe and Brunswick by Bernadotte, on the 17th October, at Halle. Weimar's escaped defeat and demoralisation for some time longer, and was able to show, by its rearguard action at the crossing of the Elbe, and still more on the 1st November at Waren, the immense difference between troops which had hitherto suffered no defeat, and those which had been broken and dispirited by constant misfortune.

The defeat of the army at Jena and Auerstädt was by far the most complete that Napoleon ever inflicted on an enemy. It afforded him his best opportunity for a relentless pursuit, an opportunity which he utilised to the fullest extent. For the first two or three days after the great battles, we find him in doubt as to the

---

[1] Hoepfner (ii. 383) gives the Prussian loss, independently of that of the Saxons, as 275 field guns, 236 battalion guns, 12 train columns, and 3 pontoon trains. This does not include the garrison guns of Magdeburg, Stettin, and the other fortresses.

directions taken by the defeated army; consequently, his corps were somewhat widely scattered, searching for the enemy, with orders to attack him wherever found. The *corps d'armée*, as constituted by Napoleon, was designed to be a self-contained force of all arms, capable of independent action—a small army which, in an emergency, could shift for itself and rely upon being able to avoid annihilation if properly handled.[1] In the confusion and panic known to prevail in the Prussian army during the first few days after its crushing defeat, there was no risk of any body of troops being brought together which could endanger the existence of the weakest of the French corps. As the first effects of the disasters wore off, it might be less safe to expose isolated corps; though, as a matter of fact, there was probably no day, after the 14th October, on which the risk would have been considerable. Still, Napoleon never allowed victory, however complete, to relax his habitual caution. Accordingly, we find him again, as he acquired knowledge of the true direction of the enemy's principal forces, combining his corps into bodies which must, undoubtedly, be able to oppose an overwhelming superiority of numbers to any portion of the Prussian army they were likely to encounter. We find him working with his usual system of two wings, with a centre so placed as to be able to assist either. His right wing, at the passage of the Elbe, comprised the

---

[1] "A *corps d'armée* of 25,000 to 30,000 men can be isolated; well led, it can fight, or avoid a battle and manœuvre according to circumstances, without incurring misfortune, because it cannot be forced into an engagement and, anyhow, it ought to make a long fight" (Napoleon to Eugène, 7th June 1809).

Concluding Remarks 303

corps of Lannes, Augereau, Davout, the Guard, and a great part of the cavalry reserve; his left consisted of Soult, Ney, and Murat. Between these two, designed to support either, but especially the left, was Bernadotte.

When Napoleon had definite information of Hohenlohe's departure from Magdeburg, a similar order is preserved. Murat indeed passed to the right wing for the advance on Berlin, which, designed as it was to head off Hohenlohe and cut him from the Oder, required a strong force of cavalry.

At the same time, the left wing was kept strong in cavalry, for it had to discover and dispose of the corps of Weimar, the sole undefeated Prussian corps, contact with which had been lost by Murat after Muhlhausen. It is clear that Murat's failure to follow up this corps caused the Emperor some anxiety. He had already lost a column of prisoners from Erfurt; it was possible Weimar might turn back, when he found himself unpursued, to carry out enterprises against the new line of communications direct from Mayence to Erfurt. Therefore three regiments of dragoons were sent back to guard against such eventualities.

When, at last, Soult discovered Weimar's direction and marched against him, his corps was somewhat widely separated from the rest of the army, though, when Weimar had passed the Elbe, there was little risk, owing to his being the last organised force to be dealt with between the Elbe and the Weser.

In leaving Ney's corps alone to blockade Magdeburg there was a risk, which the Emperor ran owing to false information. He believed the force which had left Magdeburg with Hohenlohe to be stronger, and the garrison of Magdeburg to be weaker, than they really were. Had he known that there were in the fortress many more troops than Ney had outside it, there can be little doubt that he would not have trusted to a display of incompetence such as was actually exhibited by Kleist. Ney reported that the garrison was only about 8000 strong, less than one-third of what it actually was.

The extreme caution of the Emperor is well illustrated by his instructions to Soult to fortify an island above Magdeburg, so as to serve as a place of refuge for the blockading force if necessary, and to provide one more bridge by which the Emperor could retreat in the event of disaster. By this bridge Soult was to cross. The Emperor did not contemplate his passage at Tangermünde until, the marshal being on the spot, it was thought better to leave him a free hand. Arrived at Potsdam, the Emperor's first care was the acquisition of definite information as to the movements of Hohenlohe. Hence Savary's first deputation on reconnoitring duty, and the movement of Lannes on and beyond Spandau. Had not that place surrendered as promptly as it did, it would, doubtless, have been masked by a small force, which would have amply sufficed.

Turning now to Hohenlohe's movements after leaving Magdeburg, we find him censured by Hoepfner for the following faults:—

(1) He delayed his march from Burg, thereby losing invaluable time on decisive days.

(2) He wrongly separated, and kept on his

left where it was useless, the mass of his cavalry. Its proper place was, with Schimmelpfennig, in front, opposing a serious resistance to Murat's movement on Templin.

(3) He kept his best troops as rearguard. The real danger of attack was not in the rear, but on the right flank.

(4) Acting on the advice of Massenbach, he kept bearing too much to his left, thus making unnecessary circuits.[1]

Delay also resulted from the system of quartering the troops in villages each day, instead of bivouacking. This was done in consequence of the scarcity of clothing, of the means of cooking, &c.

As it was, Hohenlohe very nearly succeeded in escaping. He got a large portion of his force through Prenzlau before Murat. Had he but gained a very few hours between Magdeburg and Prenzlau, he must have succeeded in reaching Stettin in safety. He failed, too, to keep his army sufficiently concentrated. At Prenzlau, he was deprived not only of the services of Blucher, who had been left behind to keep off an attack of which there was little danger, but also of those of Hagen's brigade and a large force of cavalry. Even so, he was largely superior to Murat, and should never have surrendered as he did. His decision to do so

[1] Hoepfner, ii. 318. The direction suggested by Hoepfner is Rathenow to Friesack, 14 miles; Friesack to Fehrbellin, 13 miles; Fehrbellin to Lindow, 16 miles; Lindow to Zehdenick, 13 miles. This route as far as Zehdenick was a good day's march shorter than the one he actually followed. He lost more time after the action of Zehdenick. There seems, therefore, little doubt that, had he followed Hoepfner's route, he could have reached Prenzlau a day sooner than he did. That was ample to save him.

was due to the fatal influence acquired over him by the self-satisfied, but incompetent, Massenbach.

For the surrender of Stettin, a fortified place with a large garrison, to a handful of light cavalry, what possible excuse can be made?

After Prenzlau, Blucher's and Winning's position was almost hopeless as regards eventual escape. Marches were delayed and the troops worn out by the same causes as had acted in Hohenlohe's case. It is not probable that, with Murat marching up the Peene, they could have succeeded in reaching Rostock as Winning proposed. Had they got there, the chances were against their being able to embark; if they did embark, what certainty was there that they would not, like the Swedes at Travemunde, be detained by contrary winds, only to be compelled to surrender to the fire of the French artillery?

By his march on the Elbe, Blucher could not hope to escape eventually, but he did hope to draw a large portion of the French army back after him to the west, and, possibly, by joining Lecoq, to be able to inflict serious damage on Napoleon's communications. There were possibilities, too, from a march on Magdeburg by the left bank of the Elbe. The Emperor himself feared Blucher might get across, for he writes to Mortier on the 7th November, "Try to cut off the column of Blucher which was at Criwitz on the 3rd."

Blucher appears to have abandoned his project of passing the Elbe at Boitzenburg when it was still feasible. False information led him to believe that Soult had already got between him

Concluding Remarks 307

and Boitzenburg, when the road was really open. At that moment Wobeser had been separated from him, and must be abandoned to his fate, if the march on Boitzenburg was to continue. The separation of Wobeser and Usedom was, as Hoepfner points out, due to the position in which they were cantoned on the 3rd November, with the lake of Schwerin behind them, rendering it necessary for them to move along it to reach the passage at Fahre. Had Blucher succeeded in getting across the Elbe, drawing Murat, Bernadotte, and Soult after him, he might well have caused such delay in the advance on Poland as would have prevented the French from passing the Vistula, or wintering beyond it.

His decision to march on Lübeck could only result in his capture; for, even if the gates had been held on the 6th November, as they might well have been, the immense superiority of the French forces would have enabled them to turn the position the next day by the Upper Trave. For Blucher to have fought on the 7th at Ratkau would have been mere waste of life. He might perhaps have done as Bourbaki did in 1871, crossing the Danish frontier and submitting to be interned. He probably felt that there was little chance of Napoleon's respecting the neutrality of Denmark under such circumstances. Possibly the Emperor would have welcomed an excuse for subjugating the Danes and seizing their fleet, several months before it was annexed by England.

With the capture of Blucher, of Magdeburg, and of Hameln, and the crushing of such small forces as the Elector of Hesse-Cassel might have used against him, the Emperor was left absolutely free to move on the Vistula, with no apprehensions for his communications in North Germany, except from the English, Swedes, and Austria. Against the two first he was able to insure their safety by means of Mortier's corps and the Dutch troops. Austria was always a cause of some anxiety to him up till the following June; but the likelihood of her running the risk of interference, after her experiences of 1805, was immensely diminished by the complete destruction of the Prussian army. The few thousand men forming the wreckage of that army, after the conquest of Silesia by Jerome and Vandamme, were reduced to the position of auxiliaries of the Russian army in the Polish campaign.

When the Tsar Alexander I., after the battle of Friedland in June 1807, was constrained to ask for terms, Prussia was abandoned to the mercy of Napoleon. With her fell the whole of Northern Germany. For six years Frederick William of Prussia became the vassal of the French Empire. Reduced by the terms of the Treaty of Tilsit to half her former size, there were many occasions during the period 1807-1813 when it hung in the balance whether the Emperor would leave Prussia to exist as a nominally independent state or not. With Frederick William himself it is difficult to feel much sympathy. He was at the best but a poor creature, one who could never make up his mind to act boldly and independently. His policy before his great disaster at Jena was characterised by weakness and duplicity. He was driven into war in October 1806 by the influence of the war party, at the head of which was his beautiful and noble but unfortunate wife, Queen Luise. It was too late then, for he had missed his great opportunity for intervention just a year before.

For the Prussian and North German people a very different feeling must be entertained. For six years they were ground under the iron heel of the conqueror. They suffered insults, indignities, and injuries, for which, as a people, they were in no way responsible. Their Sovereign, haunted by the dread of what he considered the worst of evils, the political power of his people, was out of touch with them, and thought little of their woes in comparison with his own. When he went to war in 1806, he did so with an army purely professional; his soldiers were ill-treated and unwilling. His officers were recruited solely from the aristocracy, and they looked upon their men as mere *chair à poudre*, worthy of no consideration or care. In such circumstances, there was no possibility of expansion of the military forces of the kingdom, and, once the regular army was defeated, there was nothing else to fall back upon. There was no *landwehr*, still less any *landsturm*. There was no possibility of a national uprising such as Napoleon afterwards had to meet in Spain. It took six years of strenuous exertion by the German patriots, Stein, Scharnhorst, Blucher, Gneisenau, Jahn, Yorck, and the rest, before there was any national organisation for the recovery of the liberty which had been banished by Napoleon. But for his ill-treatment of the German people, no such organisation would, perhaps, have come into existence, for it was certainly never encouraged by the King of Prussia, who dreaded popular movements almost as much as he feared Napoleon. He only consented, as a last resource, to utilise the weapon prepared for him by men whom, as a rule, he regarded as demagogues and revolutionaries.

The story of the German struggle for liberty may be read in the fascinating pages of Poultney Bigelow. It is the history of a splendid national movement which ended, sixty years later, in the great German Empire of to-day. But, as one reads it, it is impossible to avoid the reflection that all the efforts of the years 1806–14 might have been unnecessary had Prussia, in the first years of the nineteenth century, kept herself abreast of the times, instead of blindly confiding in the fancied security of her army and a military system which had stood still for a quarter of a century. Never was there so terrible an example of the consequences of military unreadiness as was afforded by Prussia in 1806, except, perhaps, that of France herself in 1870.

Is not the lesson one which may be taken to heart, pondered over, and acted on by the nation which has so far been content to "muddle through"? War is not what it was a hundred years ago. Soldiers cannot be made in a month, as Kellerman boasted that they could be in 1807. Military training and service, as a preventive of a possible disaster such as befell Prussia in 1806, should surely be considered a privilege, not merely a duty, of every Englishman to whom

Concluding Remarks 311

the freedom and the prosperity of his country is dear. That was the view of the downtrodden Germans who, in 1814, marched to Paris. It had been impressed on them in the bitter school of adversity. We Englishmen have this terrible example of 1806 before our eyes. Is it not a sufficient warning to induce us, by proper preparation, to guard against the bare possibility of our case becoming a similar lesson for future generations?

INDEX

ALTENZAUM, action of, 233
Anklam, Bila capitulates at, 254
Ansbach, 2, 5, 7
Army (French), its excellence, 18; pillage by, 19, 222; organisation, 25, 26; distribution, 46, 47, 57, 74; strength, 46, 47, 74; system of supply, 20, 83; relative value, 71, 167 *n.*
—— (Prussian), want of progress, 43, 44; strength, 46; incomplete mobilisation, 46, 65; commissariat, 20
—— (Saxon), strength, 46
—— (Rhenish Confederation), strength, 10, 46. See also "artillery," "cavalry," "corps d'armée," "councils of war," "divisions," "infantry," "staff," "troops' positions at different dates," "command," "discipline," "marches"
Artillery (French), 23, 24
—— (Prussian), 23, 24
Auerstädt, battle of, 149–164; Prussian positions overnight, 149–150; Davout at Koesen, 150; strength of armies, 150; battlefield described, 151; battle till 9 A.M., 153; Blucher's cavalry, 154; Gudin takes Hassenhausen, 155; battle from 9 to 10 A.M., 157; Schmettau's attack, 157; Prussian right, 160; defeat after 10 A.M., 159; defeat of Gudin's peril, 159; battle Friant's movements, 157, 158;

of Kalkreuth, 162; general retreat, 163; losses, 163
Augereau, Marshal, 79, 102; exposed beyond Saale, 109, 169; at Jena, 131, 137, 138
Augsburg, 10
August, Prince, at Prenzlau, 242, 246
Austria, 2–5, 9–11, 12, 52, 59

BAIREUTH, 5, 53, 75
Bamberg, 16, 53
Base of operations, Napoleon's choice, 48–52
Basel, treaty of, 1
Bavaria, 5, 9, 11
Bavarian divisions, 73, 74; at Dresden, 213
Berg, Grand Duchy of, 5, 7
Bernadotte, Marshal, 74, 76, 79; at Schleiz, 84, 86; conduct at Jena, 171–174; at Halle, 204–211; at passage of Elbe, 221; joins Soult, 261; at Waren, 261; at Criwitz, 266; at Lübeck, 275, &c.; at Ratkau, 286
Berthier, Marshal, 5, 7; position as chief of staff, 33; his personal staff, 34; his assistants, 34
Bila I., surrender at Anklam, 254
Bila II. at Schleiz, 85; surrender at Anklam, 254
Blucher at Auerstädt, 154, 156; at Nordhausen, 200; crosses Elbe, 231; joins Hohenlohe, 236; march to Lübeck, 256–270; at Lübeck, 271–282; capitulation at Ratkau, 286

313

Index

Boguslawski, 84, 87, 144
Boitzenburg, combat of, 241
Boldekow, capitulation at, 255
Bonaparte, Jerome, 90; at Dresden, 213 *n*.
—— Joseph, King of Naples, 9
—— Louis, King of Holland, 9, 47; Napoleon's instructions to, 55–58; at Cassel, 297; resigns command, 297
Bonnal, General H., cited, 128 *n*., 134 *n*., 169 *n*. 2
Brunswick, Duke of, age and position in command, 29; activity, 42, 43; leader of peace party, 68; orders concentration at Hochdorf, 88; at Auerstädt, 149, &c.; death, 159
Brunswick-Oels, Duke of, 274, 276, 279
Burke (or Bourke), 154

CAMBACÉRÈS, Napoleon's instructions to, 60
Capitulation of Erfurt, 195; Spandau, 237; Prenzlau, 248–250; Stettin, 252; Pasewalk, 252; Anklam, 254; Wolgast, 254; Boldekow, 255; Ratkau, 286; Magdeburg, 291; Küstrin, 291; Hameln, 298; Nieuburg, 299; Plassenburg, 299
Cavalry (French), 24; as "eyes of army," 24; Napoleon's orders as to, 81, 82, 83; at Jena and Auerstädt, 179
—— (Prussian), 24; at Jena and Auerstädt, 160, 179; Hohenlohe's waste of, 304–305
—— (Saxon), 25; at Jena, 179; during retreat, 187
Civilians on French staff, 35
Clausewitz on Prince Louis, 93; on strategical situation, 116
Command, French and Prussian systems, 27, 28; Prussian confusion, 29, 30

Commanders (French), ages of, 42; old officers weeded out, 41
—— (Prussian), character of, 41; ages, 42; defence of, 42, 43
Communications, lines of, Napoleon's at commencement, 54; lateral, 76; change of, 212, 227
Corps d'armée formed by Napoleon, 26; functions of, 302
Councils of war, 28, 29, 65
Criwitz, action at, 266

DALBERG, Prince Primate, 10, 16 *n*.
Daru, Intendant-General, 32, 35
Davout, Marshal, 74, 86; at Auerstädt, 149–164, 178; and Bernadotte, 171–174; passes Elbe, 220; at Berlin, 228
De Billy killed at Auerstädt, 160
De Fezensac, cited, 19, 21
De Ségur, 13 *n*., 145, 148, 183, 230
Desjardins at Jena, 135, 137, 143
Discipline in French army, 19, 222; in Prussian, 44
Divisions constituted, 26; size of, 27
D'Oubril, 8, 15
Dresden, 52, 78; occupied, 213
Drouet at Schleiz, 85; at Halle, 209; at Lübeck, 275–277, 282
Dumas (Matthieu), cited, 284
Dumonçeau, 299
Dupont, 101, 206, 207, 262, 276, 282
Duroc, 32
Dutch, 9; army, 57

ELBE, passages of, by Davout, 220; by Bernadotte, 221; by Lannes, 221; by Blucher, 231; by Weimar, 233; by Soult, 256
England, 5–9, 57, 191
Erfurt, capitulation of, 195

Eugène Beauharnais, Napoleon's instructions to, 59, 60

FORCHHEIM, 54, 55, 73, 78
Fox, C. J., on Prussia, 8, 9
Franconian Forest, passage of, 73–83; strength of French columns in, 74
Frederick William I., King of Prussia, 2, 4, 68; character, 29; at Auerstädt, 159; during retreat, 186; leaves Magdeburg, 218; passes Elbe, 225 *n*.
Frederick the Great, 2, 20, 21, 24, 25, 43, 62, 229
French coasts, defence of, 60–62
Front, Prussian extension of, 66–68
—— Napoleon's change of, 104, 108

GEUSAU, Prussian Quartermaster-General, 36
Goeschwitz, action of, 108
Goltz, Baron von der, cited, 43, 44, 45, 52 *n*., 137, 250
Greussen, action of, 199
Grouchy at Zehdenick, 239; at Prenzlau, 246

HAGEN surrenders at Pasewalk, 252
Halle, action of, 24, 204–211
Hameln, 5; blockade, 297; capitulation, 298
Hanover, 5–8, 13, 14; invasion of, 297
Hardenberg, 8
Hartzfeldt, Prince, 230
Harz Mountains, pursuit of Prussians through, 215, &c.
Haugwitz, his policy, 1; and Napoleon, 2–7, 15
Henry, Prince of Prussia, at Auerstädt, 159, 162
Hesse-Cassel, 11, 16, 58; annexation, 293–297
Hesse-Darmstadt, 10, 46

Heudelet at Jena, 143
Hinrichs at Halle, 206
Hoepfner (historian), 22, 41, 65, 150, 163, 275 *n*., 304
Hoepfner (artillery column) surrenders at Boldekow, 255
Hohenlohe, Prince, 29, 42, 43, 66, 67, 70, 88; ordered to concentrate, 104; on eve of Jena, 117–118, 124–125; at Jena, 132, 138; retreat through Harz, 215, &c.; at Magdeburg, 218, 226; march from Magdeburg to Prenzlau, 234–243; at Prenzlau, 243–257
Holland, defence of, 57
Holtzendorf at Jena, 125, 133, 134
Hugues, Captain, at Prenzlau, 244, 245, 250

ILM (river), Prussian march behind, 117
Infantry (French) compared with Prussian, 21; tactics, 21, 22; marching powers, 21
—— (Prussian) compared with French, 21; tactics, 21, 22; musket, 22
—— (Saxon) at Saalfeld, 96; surrender at Jena, 144
Initiative of subordinates, Napoleon's suppression of, 33, 36, 41, 102
Intelligence, defective, of Prussians, 63, 67, 69; of Napoleon, 77, 87, 88; Napoleon's false deductions from, 89, 105
Italy, 59, 60

JENA, description of, 113, 114; panic at, 111
—— battle of, eve of, 118–120; French artillery delayed, 119; Hohenlohe's camps, 124; Hohenlohe at Dornburg, 125; description of plateau, 121–124; French position in night, 125; French strength avail-

able, 126, 175, 176; Prussian strength, 127; Napoleon's orders, 127–129; his address to troops, 129; Tauenzien's combat, 130–133; Holtzendorf's attack, 133, 134; Ney's arrival, 135; struggle at Isserstadt and Vierzehnheiligen, 136–140; rout of Prussian centre and left, 140, 141; Ruchel's effort, 142, 143; capture of Saxons and Boguslawski, 143–145; fight at Webicht, 146; losses, 147

Jomini, quoted, 284

KALKREUTH, 29, 42, 43; at Auerstädt, 162, 163; at Weissensee, 197; at Greussen, 199; at Nordhausen, 199; separates from Hohenlohe, 217; crosses Elbe, 225

Klein allows Prussians to pass at Weissensee, 197, 198; dragoons sent to guard communications, 214

Kleist, 42, 43, 289, 290, 291

Königshofen, 54, 78

Kraft zu Hohenlohe-Ingelfingen, Prince, cited, 13, 38, 39, 66, 71, 77, 81, 99, 108, 167 n.

Kronach, 78

Küstrin capitulates, 291

LAFOREST, 14

Lannes, Marshal, 76, 78, 79; at Saalfeld, 92–95, 98, 102; at Goeschwitz, 108; peril on 12th–13th October, 109, 169; eve of Jena, 114, 118; at Jena, 127, 130, 133, 134; at Prenzlau, 244–251

Larisch at Erfurt, 193

Lasalle, 82; lets Prussians pass at Weissensee, 197, 198; at Zehdenick, 239; at Prenzlau, 244, 245; at Stettin, 252

Lauderdale, Lord, 9

Lecoq, campaign in Hanover, 292, 293, 297–299

Lessons of campaign, 45, 310

Lindau, 10

Losses at Schleiz, 86; at Saalfeld, 98, 99; at Jena, 147; at Erfurt, 195; at Halle, 210; at Prenzlau, 252; at Lübeck, 285, 286; total of Prussians, 288

Louis Ferdinand, Prince of Prussia, 6, 42, 68; at Saalfeld, 92–97; character, 93; death, 97; conduct at Saalfeld, 99–101

Lübeck, Blucher reaches, 271; his preparations for defence, 272, 273; description, 272; storming of, 273–282; sack of, 283–285; losses at, 285, 286

Luchesini, 13, 298

Luise, Queen of Prussia, 2, 6, 93, 147, 225 n., 300

MAGDEBURG, King leaves, 218; Hohenlohe reaches, 218; Murat summons to surrender, 218; Hohenlohe leaves, 226; blockade of, 225, 288–290; capitulation, 291

Mannheim, 54

Marches, length of French, 21

Marmont, Marshal, 60

Marshals, Napoleon's estimate of, 27

Massena, Marshal, 20, 27

Massenbach, 29, 30, 37–39, 43, 66, 67, 88, 117, 139, 245, 247, 250, 251

Mayence, 51, 53, 54

Milhaud at Boitzenburg, 241; at Pasewalk, 252

Mobilisation, incompleteness of Prussian and Saxon, 46, 65; Prussian orders for, 63, 65

Mollendorf, Marshal, 42; at Erfurt, 194

Montesquiou captured, 112

Mortier, Marshal, 56; in Cassel and Hanover, 293–298

Müffling, 43, 69, 273

Index 317

Murat, Marshal, Grand Duke of Berg, 5, 7; intelligence gathered by, 24; Napoleon's instructions to, 82; at Schleiz, 85; at Jena, 140, 144, 145; at Weimar, 148; at Erfurt, 193; at Boitzenburg, 241; at Prenzlau, 244-248; joins Bernadotte, 268; at Lübeck, 275 *et seqq.*; at Ratkau, 286

NATZMER at Lübeck, 279
Neufchatel, Berthier's Principality, 5, 7
Ney, Marshal, at Jena, 128, 135; at Magdeburg, 222, 289, 290
Nieuburg, capitulation, 299
Nordhausen, action of, 199
North German Confederation, 11, 12, 17

OPERATIONS, plan of, Napoleon's, 48-63; Prussian, 65-67
Orange, Prince of, at Auerstädt, 159, 162
Orders, system of issue, 27, 28

PASEWALK, capitulation at, 252
Pelet at Saalfeld, 92, 94, 98
Phull, 4, 29, 37, 43
Plassenberg, capitulation of, 299
Potsdam, convention of, 2, 3; Napoleon at, 228-229
Prenzlau described, 243; action of, 244-248; Hohenlohe capitulates at, 248-250; criticisms, 250, 251
Presburg, Peace of, 9, 52
Prisoners, rescue of, 196
Proclamations, decrees, &c., Napoleon to his army, 80; address at Jena, 129; fixing war indemnities, 191; annexing Prussia west of Elbe, 227; deposing Elector of Hesse-Cassel, 296
Prussia, policy of neutrality, 1; convention of Potsdam, 2, 3; ultimatum of 1805, 2; attitude after Austerlitz, 4; negotiations with Napoleon, 4-16; resolves on war, 12, 63; duplicity, 1, 16, 44; ultimatum of 1806, 16, 17, 72, 112, 125; her failure to progress, 44; causes of defeat, 44-46; parties, 68
Pursuit, cause of delay after Jena, 181-184

RAIDS, Napoleon's provision against Prussian, 56, 57; against English on French coast, 60-62
Rapp, 148, 174, 230
Reille at Saalfeld, 97; at Jena, 115
Retreat, line of, on Danube, 55; Lannes on Bamberg, 79; by Magdeburg, 227; Napoleon's caution in regard to, 54, 227
Rhine, Confederation of the, constitution of, 10; armed strength, 10 *n.*; and Saxony, 11
Rivaud, 202, 206, 207, 208, 276, 277, 278, 280, 282
Roads in Franconian Forest, 51, 76; in Thuringian Forest, 49, 50
Roman Empire, dissolution of, 10, 11
Rosbach, battle of, Napoleon on its field, 215
Ruchel, 68, 70; at Jena, 139, 142, 143; found by Soult, 197; reaches Tangermünde, 225 *n.*
Russia, 3-8, 12

SAALBURG, skirmish at, 83
Saalfeld, action of, field described, 91, 92; Lannes at Grafenthal, 92; Prince Louis' force, 92, 93; his character, 93; posting of his force, 93, 94; Lannes' advance, 94; early action, 95; Lannes moves to left, 95; Prince Louis' attack and repulse, 96;

Reille captures Sandberg, 97; death of Louis, 97; French pursuit, 98; losses, 98, 99; effects of action, 99; criticism of Louis' action, 99–101; of Lannes', 102
St. Hilaire at Jena, 131; at Lübeck, 280
Savary, 174; deputed to reconnoitre, 260 *n.*; at Waren, 261; captures Usedom and baggage, 268 *n.*; at Hameln, 298, 299
Saxony, her difficult position, 11, 12; Napoleon's use of, 15; his conciliation of, 189, 190; Dresden occupied, 191, 213; peace, 192
Scharnhorst, 43; taken at Lübeck, 278, 279
Schimmelpfennig in Hohenlohe's retreat to Prenzlau, 237–239
Schleiz, action of, 84–86
Schmettau at Auerstädt, 157–159
Seidlitz, 24
Sénarmont, 23
Soult, Marshal, and discipline, 19, 222; Napoleon's instructions to, 73; in first advance, 73–78, 89; at Jena, 131; pursues Weimar, 231–233; crosses Elbe, 256; joins Bernadotte, 261; at Lübeck, 275, &c.
Spandau, capitulation, 237
Spies, French, 24
Staff (French), account of, 30–36; Berthier's position in, 33; suppression of initiative, 33; defects, 36, 40; system of work, 32; assistant to Major-General, 34; aides-de-camp, 35; staff of corps, 36
—— (Prussian), described, 36–38; position of Massenbach and Phull, 37; duties, 37; defects, 38; attempted remedy, 38; compared with Napoleon's, 39, 40

Stettin, capitulation of, 252, 253
Strategy and tactics discussed, plans of campaign, 48–71; Napoleon's choice of base, 48–51; "je n'ai jamais eu un plan d'opérations," 52; objective, 52, 53; communications thrown back, 54, 55; line of retreat on Danube, 55; Napoleon's principle of concentration on single object, 55; his position compared with Frederick's, 62; Prussia's position, 63; her strategical problem, 63; attempted solution, 64, 65; Hohenlohe's and Massenbach's schemes, 66; final plan, 66; criticisms, 67; orders on realising Napoleon's plan, 69, 70; why Dresden was aimed at, 78; cavalry at commencement, 81, 82; action of Saalfeld, 99–101; crossing of French columns, 106, 108, 109; Clausewitz on strategical position, 116; strategy and tactics of first period, 165–180; pursuit after Jena, 181–184; Halle, 210, 211; Prenzlau, 250; strategy and tactics, second period, 300–311
Suchet at Saalfeld, 95, 99; at Jena, 115, 132–134, 137
Sweden and Swedes, 8, 57, 269, 270, 275, 276

TALLEYRAND, 3, 4
Tangermünde, Soult passes Elbe at, 256
Tauenzien, 83; at Schleiz, 84–86; eve of Jena, 115; at Jena, 130–132, 142; in retreat, 187, 197
Telegraph (semaphore), 16
Theatre of war and battlefields, descriptions of, 48–50, 75, 76, 91, 92, 113, 114, 121, 122, 151–153, 204, 234, 243, 272, 273

Index 319

Thuringian Forest, 49–51
—— States, 12
Treskow at Halle, 209
Troops, positions on various dates: French army before war, 46, 47; at end of September, 68, 69; 8th October, 73, 74; both sides, evening 8th October, 84; 9th October, 86, 87; 10th October, 103; 11th October, 107; 11 A.M. at Jena, 134; night of 14th, 184; 18th, 214; 19th, 217; 22nd, 224; 24th, 228; 30th, 258; 1st November, 264
Tyrolese, 9

USEDOM captured by Savary, 268 *n.*

VIENNA, convention of, 4, 6, 7

WAR indemnities, Napoleon's assessment of, 191 *n.*
Waren, action of, 261
Wartensleben at Auerstädt, 159, 160
Wedel at Jena, 133, 136

Weimar, Duke of, 42; detached to south, 70; march to Erfurt, 187–189, 195; march to Elbe, 231–233; suspended from command, 233
—— town, supper party at, 147
Wesel, 7, 17, 56, 57
William, Prince of Prussia, at Auerstädt, 160
Winning, 87, 104, 107, 233, 258
Wittenberg, Davout crosses Elbe at, 220
Wolgast, capitulation at, 254
Würtemberg, State, 10, 11
—— Duke Eugene of, 70; at Halle, 204–211
Wurzburg, 54, 55, 78

YARMOUTH, Lord, 9
Yorck, General, at Altenzaum, 233; at Waren, 261; at Lübeck, 279
—— Count (historian), 19 *n.*, 41, 54 *n.*, 58 *n.*, 77 *n.*, 247 *n.*

ZEHDENICK, action of, 239
Zeschwitz I. at Jena, 143–145
Zeschwitz II. at Jena, 145

Map for Operations 9th to 20th Octr 1806.

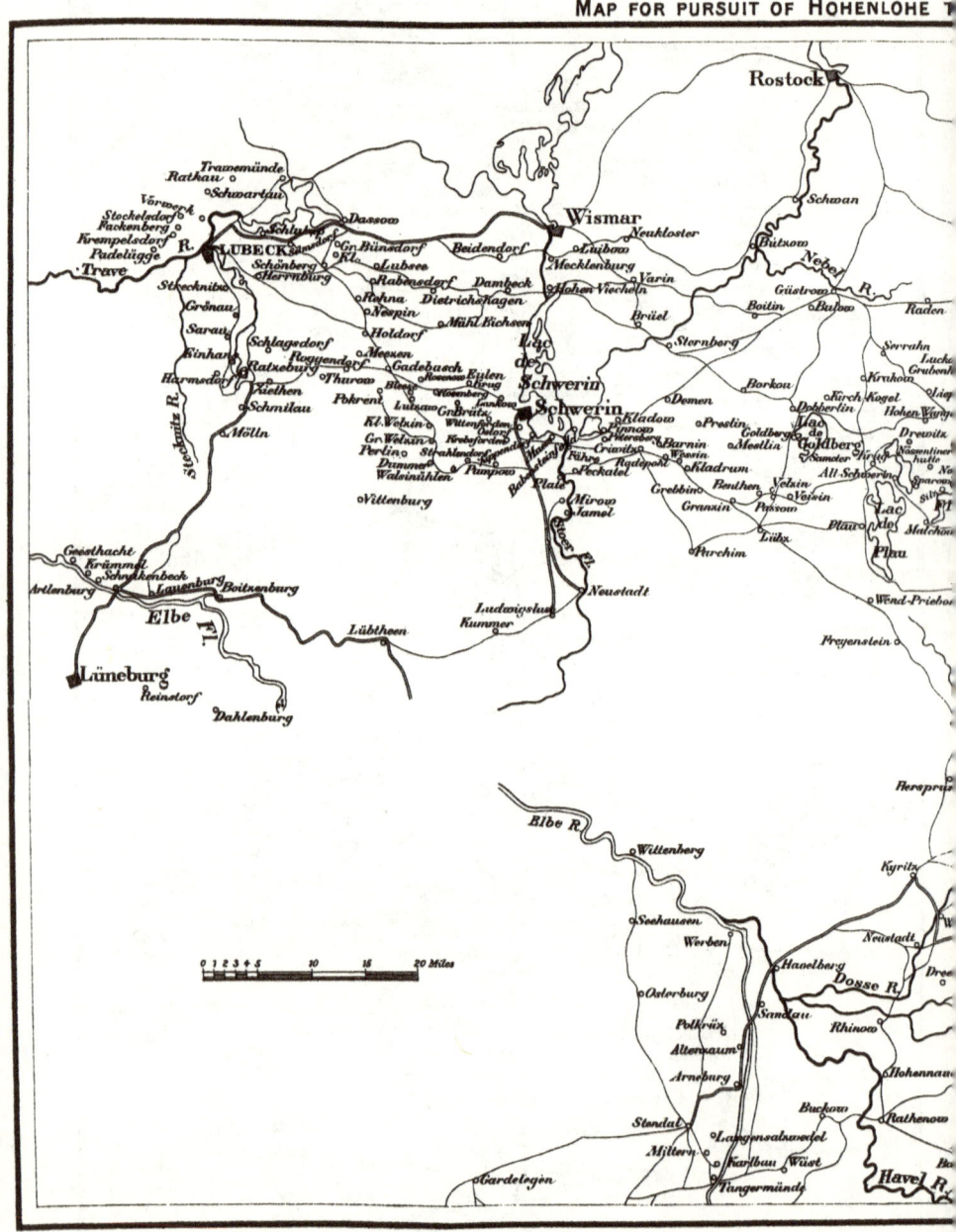

RENZLAU, AND BLUCHER TO LÜBECK

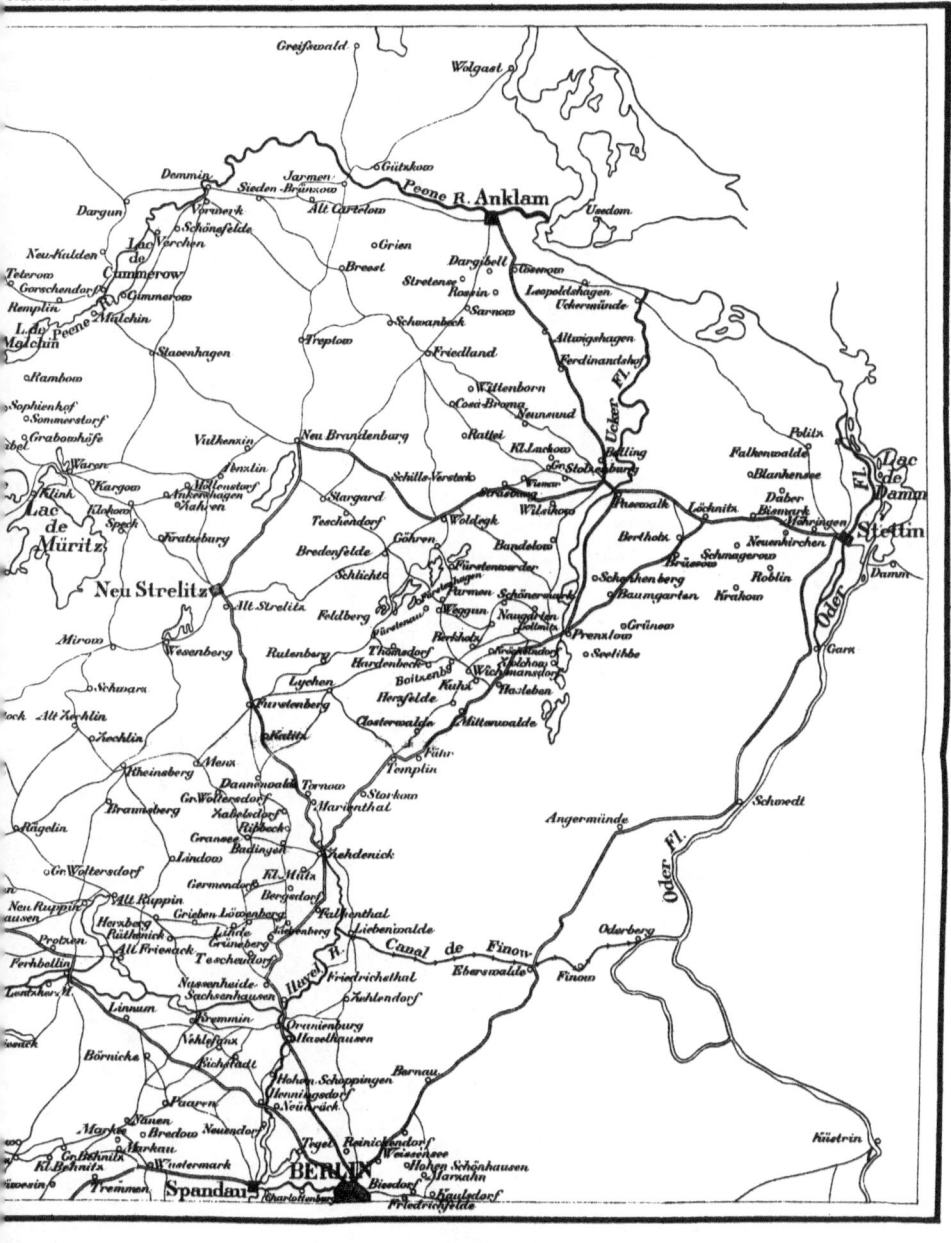

www.ingramcontent.com/pod-product-compliance
Lightning Source LLC
Chambersburg PA
CBHW031249230426
43670CB00005B/99